the village VOICE Film Guide

the village VOICE Film Guide

50 Years of Movies from Classics to Cult Hits

EDITED BY DENNIS LIM

John Wiley & Sons, Inc.

This book is printed on acid-free paper. ♾

Published by John Wiley & Sons, Inc., Hoboken, New Jersey
Published simultaneously in Canada

Design and composition by Navta Associates, Inc.

Library of Congress Cataloging-in-Publication Data:

The Village Voice film guide : 50 years of movies from classics to cult hits / edited by Dennis Lim.

p. cm.
Includes bibliographical references and index.
ISBN-13 978-0-471-78781-5 (pbk. : alk. paper)
ISBN-10 0-471-78781-7 (pbk. : alk. paper)
1. Motion pictures—Catalogs. I. Lim, Dennis, 1973– II. Village Voice (Greenwich Village, New York, N.Y.)
PN1998.V47 2007
791.43'75—dc22

2006022006

Printed in the United States of America

10 9 8 7 6 5 4 3 2

CONTENTS

ACKNOWLEDGMENTS

Thanks to Joshua Land, the assistant editor on this project, who helped select, track down, and edit the reviews; Tom Miller and James Fitzgerald for their support and enthusiasm; Ben Kenigsberg, who proofread the manuscript; and an army of *Voice* film interns, led by Jaime Mastromonica and most of all the tireless James Crawford. Thanks also to all the critics who participated in this collection.

ACKNOWLEDGMENTS

[illegible]

Introduction

By Dennis Lim

For five decades, the *Village Voice*'s movie reviews have been uniquely attuned to New York City's film culture. Written by and for cinephiles, the paper's film section has filled the void left by the timidity and the complacency of mainstream movie reviewing. The *Voice*'s film pages recontextualized Hollywood and explored the avant-garde—no other mass publication has produced a body of criticism as politically engaged and historically grounded, as dedicated to seeking out the new, the marginal, and the underseen.

This guide constructs a canon of great films from the *Voice*'s archive of movie reviews. Given the tastes and the sensibilities of the paper's critics, this is an idiosyncratic selection, one that defies conventional wisdom and abides by the tradition of advocacy that has long informed film criticism at the *Voice*. It was, after all, a *Voice* staffer, Andrew Sarris, who essentially originated the idea of canon formation as criticism, in his seminal volume *The American Cinema*.

Our Top 150 films are not without a few usual suspects. Masters like Alfred Hitchcock and Orson Welles are duly acknowledged. That said, you'll find a Welles film that's a fixture on other all-time-great lists (*Citizen Kane*) but also a Welles film that turns up on almost none of them (*F for Fake*). Obviously, there are house favorites: Jean-Luc Godard, Robert Bresson, Luis Buñuel, David Cronenberg, and Wong Kar-wai all have at least three entries each.

There are also omissions. Films released before the *Voice* began publication in 1955 are naturally underrepresented (although thanks to the section's diligent coverage of the repertory circuit, we were able to include a good number of older movies, including silents). Given this book's mandate, we mostly restricted ourselves to positive reviews. As such, some films are missing because of what now seem like critical blind spots—John Cassavetes's 1970s work, for instance, was not favorably reviewed in the *Voice* (though the controversy over *Shadows*, a film that the paper's first film editor, Jonas Mekas, championed, then disowned after Cassavetes recut it, is documented here in full). Other exclusions can be blamed on the vagaries of theatrical distribution. Some world-cinema greats (Raul Ruiz, Edward Yang) and entire national cinemas (notably Brazil's) have enjoyed only limited exposure in U.S. art houses.

If a film was covered several times over the years, we often included various pieces to reflect evolving critical perspectives (or sometimes different opinions from the same writer—see Sarris on *2001: A Space Odyssey*). Many of these reviews were edited for space and some topical references were removed, but we've tried to preserve the character of the original pieces.

Any list of favorites unavoidably reflects the period in which it was compiled. One of the goals of this book was to shake off the cobwebs of the Eurocentric art-film orthodoxy—hence the absence of some mustier standbys. My personal tastes were certainly a factor, as were those of the *Voice*'s current film-reviewing team, many of whom I canvassed. Above all, though, the book was guided by the particular passions of the three singular critics who, more than anyone else, defined the identity of the *Voice* film section and established its legacy: Mekas, Sarris, and J. Hoberman.

A History of Film Criticism at the *Village Voice*

By J. Hoberman

Not exactly trekking to the one-room schoolhouse six miles across the tundra but a schlep nonetheless for the Teenage Me to find the one newsstand in Flushing (and later, Binghamton, New York) that carried the *Village Voice*. The paper ran many interesting things, to be sure, but (for the TM) the must-reads were Jonas Mekas's "Movie Journal" and Andrew Sarris's "Films in Focus."

How fortunate, for a young cineaste, to grow up in central Queens in the mid-1960s with high schools so overcrowded the Board of Ed instituted triple sessions and a senior like the TM finished classes by noon and had the rest of the day to take the number 7 train to the city and go to the movies. How unbelievably lucky to have revival dumps like the Bleecker Street, the New Yorker, and the Thalia—not to mention the 42nd Street grind houses and the Museum of Modern Art. And how utterly essential were the *Village Voice* listings and the excitements of Messrs. Mekas and Sarris.

"The French call adolescence the 'age of film-going,'" I would write in that same *Village Voice* some twenty years later. "And it may be that the movies you discover then set your taste forever." It will be years before the collected writings of Mekas and Sarris are enshrined between the Library of America's glossy black covers—although, in his native Lithuania, the former is a celebrated poet. Mekas's *Movie Journal: The Rise of a New American Cinema* and Sarris's *The American Cinema: Directors and Directions, 1929–1968* are classic books, but writing is the least of it. Between them, back in the day, these guys knew everything that was happening, movie-wise, in New York. The TM expected no less. I didn't buy the *Voice* (which, for many years, maintained economic parity with two other local necessities, a subway token and a slice of pizza) to confirm my taste. I wanted an education—and the *Voice* movie pages provided that.

An impoverished poet, 16mm film diarist, and little magazine editor, Mekas was not as interested in reviewing movies as in remaking cinema. (Also, film criticism: in its firsthand account of the underground film scene, "Movie Journal" was a blog *avant la lettre*.) He didn't just report on underground movies, he was a tireless advocate who organized distribution co-ops, film series, and cinematheques. "It is not my business to tell you what it's about. My business is to get excited about it, to bring it to your attention. I am a raving maniac of the cinema."

Mekas left the *Voice*, along with another avant-garde proto-blogger, Jill Johnston, in the paper's first great "normalization," following its 1974 purchase by *New York* magazine mogul Clay Felker. There has never been another Mekas. (Closest was the erstwhile actor/performance artist/filmmaker Amy Taubin, who wrote for the *Voice* from the mid-1980s through 2001, mixing polemical reviews with advocacy reportage.) But traces of his mania remain.

While Mekas was totally committed to the new, Andrew Sarris was the first regular movie reviewer who consistently and programmatically put current movies in their film-historical context. As Mekas illuminated the underground, Sarris explicated the past—specifically, the Hollywood past—with his so-called auteur theory. He didn't review movies, he wrote the ongoing sagas of heroic directors. (His first *Voice* review hailed *Psycho* as a great avant-garde film.) Giants still bestrode the earth, not just Hitchcock but John Ford and Howard Hawks. (If it weren't for Sarris, who of us would have ventured to 42nd Street to see *El Dorado* in 1967—not the TM, that's for sure.)

Mekas was an inspired propagandist; Sarris was a gifted pedagogue. In some respects, his greatest role was guiding readers through the history of American cinema, still in heavy rotation on New York's independent TV stations. I vividly remember Sarris—who for a time broadcast "Films in Focus" over listener-sponsored WBAI—simply going through the week's TV listings, pointing out the 3 A.M. must-sees.

(During the late 1970s and into the 1980s, this function would be performed at the *Voice* by Sarris's devoted acolyte Tom Allen.)

Although Sarris frequently (and hilariously) quarreled with Mekas over the significance of avant-garde film, his interests were not restricted to Hollywood. He was one of Robert Bresson's early champions. His 1970 review of *Au Hasard Balthazar* is a landmark, and his 1974 review of *The Merchant of Four Seasons* was, without doubt, the most crucial review R. W. Fassbinder would receive in this country.

In short, both Mekas and Sarris were devoted to making film culture—not surprisingly, the name of Mekas's magazine—and because of them, the *Voice* was as well. Molly Haskell, who joined them around 1970, was the first regular movie reviewer in America to write from an explicitly feminist point of view, creating a precedent that exists at the *Voice* to this day. (The ideological analysis of mainstream movies became a house specialty after Ronald Reagan was elected president.)

From time to time, the *Voice*'s notorious fractiousness carried over into movieland, with the staff contributing its (mostly negative) opinions of some current sensation. As a youngster, I participated in one such pile-on in response to Bob Dylan's *Renaldo and Clara*; Sarris was understandably incensed when the staff took issue with his praise for *Manhattan*. Those amateur hours notwithstanding, the paper published an impressive number of distinguished or promising film writers. (In addition to those already mentioned, these include Michael Atkinson, Georgia Brown, Stuart Byron, Katherine Dieckmann, Terry Curtis Fox, Tad Gallagher, Dennis Lim, William Paul, B. Ruby Rich, Jonathan Rosenbaum, P. Adams Sitney, Elliott Stein, and Jessica Winter. Other erstwhile *Voice* film writers—Manohla Dargis, David Edelstein, and Carrie Rickey, as well as former film editor Lisa Kennedy—have gone on to high-profile careers as daily critics. And Oliver Stone, who contributed a review of *Breathless*, enjoyed another sort of fame.)

If movie reviews are understood as a form of journalism, *Voice* critics broke a number of stories. Obscure underground filmmakers (Stan Brakhage, Michael Snow) were championed, along with "difficult" directors from Senegal or Iran. Once unknown and ignored genre flicks like *Night of the Living Dead*, *Halloween*, and *The Evil Dead* received partisan reviews. The *Voice* was the first paper to review "midnight" movies like *El Topo* and *Pink Flamingos* (the latter by Jack Smith, no less). The first review I was assigned, in late 1977, was David Lynch's *Eraserhead*, then playing to audiences of four and five at the Cinema Village. And where else could the ex-TM have reviewed Todd Haynes when he was working in Super-8 or Wong Kar-wai before his movies played above Canal Street?

Not only did the *Voice* give Chantal Akerman's *Jeanne Dielman* double coverage when the movie had its U.S. opening at Film Forum, but it made that event its cover story—a tribute to the passionate advocacy of film editor Karen Durbin. (I remember that Karen also fought successfully to find double jump space for me to review Claude Lanzmann's *Shoah*—and, as used to happen with some regularity in those days, I needed the extra room to take issue with another critic's notice.)

It was precisely because the *Voice* was so site specific, so committed to film culture as it was being made and experienced in New York City, that its coverage engaged not only the Teenage Me but cineastes all over the country and even the world. There's been an erosion of space and an imposition of format, but I'd like to believe that this readership is still there and that the commitment remains. These reviews are a testament to those readers and that faith.

Adapted from an essay published in the Voice's *fiftieth anniversary issue, October 26, 2005.*

L'Age d'Or (1930)

Dir. Luis Buñuel; Scr. Luis Buñuel and Salvador Dalí
60 min.

Luis Buñuel began his movie career with the most notorious opening sequence in movie history. *Un Chien Andalou*, which Buñuel and his then pal Salvador Dalí first sprang on the world in late 1929, begins with the apparent close-up of a razor slicing open the eyeball of an impassively seated actress.

Buñuel and Dalí were young punks hoping to impress Paris's ruling surrealist clique. With *Un Chien Andalou*, they succeeded beyond their wildest fantasies. What to do for an encore? The pair was commissioned to write a script by a wealthy nobleman. As with *Un Chien Andalou*, Dalí provided Buñuel with a number of fantastic images and outrageous notions; once more, Buñuel directed and edited the movie himself. But this time he raised the stakes by making *L'Age d'Or* (The Golden Age) at once more banal and more shocking than *Un Chien Andalou*—privileging politics over poetics (much to Dalí's dismay).

From a surrealist perspective, the movie couldn't have been better. *L'Age d'Or* sparked a riot and was banned by the Paris police. The aristocrat producer was threatened with excommunication, and although a print was smuggled to Britain, the camera negative was locked behind seven seals for nearly sixty years. Why? A collage of modes, *L'Age d'Or* begins as a documentary, shifts to an entropic costume drama, turns blatantly allegorical, pretends to be a travelogue of imperial Rome, drops in at a snooty garden party, and winds up cribbing the conclusion of the Marquis de Sade's *120 Days of Sodom*. Ten minutes into the action, *L'Age d'Or* declares its subject: a pompous nationalist religious ceremony is disrupted by the noisy lovemaking of a passionate couple who are forcibly separated and will spend much of the movie trying to get back together.

Although Buñuel would write that *L'Age d'Or* was about "the impossible force that thrusts two people together [and] the impossibility of their ever becoming one," he scarcely idealizes the lovers, who, having been introduced rolling in the mud, are no less self-absorbed than their fellow bourgeois. Together at the garden party, they resume their lovemaking with thrilling ineptitude—biting each other's hands, falling off the lawn furniture. When the man is called away to take a telephone call from the minister of the interior (a transmission from his unconscious?), the woman consoles herself by fellating the toe of a marble statue.

L'Age d'Or climaxes with murder rather than sexual release (inviting Jesus Christ to the orgy). Despite this and several instances of blatant scatology, however, the movie refuses to be as visceral as *Un Chien Andalou*. Thanks to his mastery of montage, Buñuel naturalizes Dalí's images into a duplicitous rhythm of normality and outrage. The film suggests instances of sex and violence far more extreme than any actually represented, while contriving effronteries so offhanded you can't believe you've actually seen them. [J. Hoberman, 1/28/04]

Once upon a time, there was a little film that sundered virtually every classic Old World taboo, against sexual lust, fetishism, sadism, coprophilia, blasphemy, antinationalism, anticlericalism, you name it. In those youthful, passionate, surrealist days of yore—1930—the film's affront was such that right-wing groups protested and mobilized their newspaper readers to physically decimate the theater in which it played (slashing Dalí and Ernst paintings hanging in the lobby as they went); two days later, police shut the movie down for good. Four years later, beset by a sudden Catholicism, the family of the vicomte who financed the film officially withdrew it from circulation. Beginning famously with an educational documentary about scorpions and climaxing with the revelation of a beardless, Sadean orgy–exhausted Christ, Buñuel's devilish gob-in-the-eye can now reclaim its rightful throne as subversive culture's seminal anthem film. [Michael Atkinson, 12/8/04]

The Age of Innocence (1993)

Dir. Martin Scorsese; Scr. Jay Cocks and Martin Scorsese
139 min.

Well, Scorsese's *The Age of Innocence* finally meets its public. A woman friend calls the film a male weepie. A male who wept says it's Marty's *Leopard,* his most Italian film yet. A fan who's seen it twice, and is poised to return, views the film as a Rorschach and predicts vast disagreements over who's worth weeping for. If you don't know Edith Wharton's 1920 novel, the inward-leaning figures on screen—reticent, opaque, suffering in such decorous, decorated silences—may be hard to *place,* much less surrender your heart to. If you do know the book, they're still difficult.

The film is sumptuous, layered, meticulously controlled, stringent, and enigmatic; it shifts under the gaze. It's not, like *GoodFellas,* a gripper, and it isn't meant to be. Once more, Scorsese has swung to another pole, fastidiously groping in a fastidious world. It's easy to show passion. But to show passion's silences?

Scorsese and his collaborator Jay Cocks are almost religiously respectful of Wharton's novel. Like an archaeologist, Scorsese goes to every length in re-creating the 1870s—to get the second and the third of a thirteen-course dinner precisely, to re-create paintings mentioned in the novel and imagine unmentioned paintings. There's an awesome collection of period paraphernalia here.

The movie's strategy is to impress us with the vast sensuous layer over the hidden one. Wharton's story concerns people who live in a "hieroglyphic world." Paying so much attention to detail, to codes of correctness, they're almost wholly distracted from their inner lives.

The story is simple. Just as Newland Archer (Daniel Day-Lewis) and May Welland (Winona Ryder) announce their engagement, an older cousin of May's, the Countess Ellen Olenska (Michelle Pfeiffer), retreats from Europe, a whiff of scandal following. According to rumors, she's seeking a divorce from a caddish husband. Immediately, however, the countess beckons Archer enticingly. Come on over. Call on me. Tomorrow at five, then?

It's not clear whether Wharton or Scorsese mean the countess to be an aggressor, a tease, but, given Archer and May's announcement, she is. Her demeanor is careless, blunt, her manners as frizzy as her hair. She's a version of *Cape Fear*'s Max Cady, come to shake up the cozy, if fetid, nest.

The heroes of *Taxi Driver* and *The Last Temptation of Christ* conceive it their mission to lift up a fallen woman. Here again, the male's protective instinct—along with the sexual—is aroused. He resents how she's snubbed by the local powers. Her tastes and irreverence seem fresh to him. Archer has pretensions to broader, more cosmopolitan sensibilities. He starts viewing the eternally virginal May—always associated with white—less as a blank slate (on which he intended to write) and more as an empty vessel.

Newland Archer is the novel's point of view. But is he reliable? The two women are seen entirely through his eyes. Exchanging one ideal (chastity, innocence) for another, he interprets May and Ellen through his own emotional needs—reducing, typing, and destroying. Deceived or not, Archer suffers. So does the countess. The lover's vocation (renunciation) is like a priest's. Inside, Archer creates a little private chapel, a "sanctuary," says the novel, a shrine. At the end, middle-aged and gray, he's virtually absent, preferring fantasy to reality.

This is why I love how Scorsese, inadvertently or not, rescues May from Archer's—and Wharton's—disdain. Or perhaps Ryder is simply electrifying; every time she's on screen, she's riveting. (Perhaps Scorsese is tipping his hand by inserting himself as her bridal photographer. Father of two daughters, he can't resist capturing the wedding.) May is always turning, surprised, smiling like a radiant sunbeam at the camera—that is, at the increasingly insentient Archer. Her studied speech patterns—meant to show how much a creature of artifice she is—are filled with nuance. She's wily and clever and, more often than not, right about Archer. She's fighting for her life and their children. The movie makes me feel a great pity for wives.

What I find most moving (perversely maybe) aren't the agonizingly chaste love scenes between Archer and the countess but the painful domestic awkwardnesses between him and May. How gingerly they treat each other—carefulness somehow masking genuine care. Bound by decorum, they can easily avoid intimacy for a whole lifetime. His longing for the countess comes to seem like another way to evade what's nearby.

Despite Wharton's effective polemics, her main characters in *The Age of Innocence* remain shadowy and insubstantial. Since Scorsese seems increasingly to have trouble creating people we care deeply about, this elegy of manners may be a doubly distanced project. Both times I've seen it, the movie left me slightly stunned, but by what I'm still not sure. Desire for desire?

What do you say about a reviewer who can't make up her mind? This is such a beautiful, difficult movie, it's almost surreal. It makes me wonder if I saw what I think I saw or if I've just invented everything. [Georgia Brown, 9/21/93]

Most of the films I have a passion for seemed a bit off-putting at first—puzzling, disturbing, unresolved. At first sight, I could tell that *The Age of Innocence* was skillfully made and deeply respectful of Edith Wharton's novel. I cried at the end, although I wasn't sure if my tears were inspired by the picture or by my memory of the book. I cared, but I wasn't sure how much or what about. This ambivalence made me want to see it again, and then again. I mean, if a film just hands itself over to you, why bother to pursue it?

The Age of Innocence doesn't offer much in the way of first-time rushes. A friend remarked that the love scenes between Daniel Day-Lewis and Michelle Pfeiffer are so awkward, it seems as if neither of them had ever kissed anyone before. No, I said, after the second viewing, it's because they're caught between fantasizing and doing it.

The third time, though, I flashed on a scene from another film—the sequence in *Vertigo* where Scotty (Jimmy Stewart) awaits the ultimate transformation of Judy into Madeleine (Kim Novak). Here Hitchcock shifts from anticipation to disappointment back to anticipation and then to release. And I found in *The Age of Innocence*, just as I always do in *Vertigo*, my nervous system miming the churning sensations of dread and desire that are supposedly tearing up the character on the screen though he's hardly moving a muscle. I am flooded with that old familiar feeling—the anguish of being in love, an anguish that—do I need to say it?—seems pitiful, irritating, ridiculous when one is not in its thrall. *Vertigo* and *The Age of Innocence* are films for the vaguely reformed romantic. For those who find it safer to look at such feelings from a distance. The safest sex is in the movies.

To be precise, there isn't any sex in *The Age of Innocence* (unless you count fulfilling one's marital duty as sex, which Scorsese, following the path of Edith Wharton, is loath to show on-screen). There's only an endless yearning, a lifetime of unfilled desire. It's a film about repression in which the repressed never returns. The gap between desire and action can't be bridged, as it is in *Raging Bull* or *Mean Streets*, with violence. Scorsese says that what moved him in Wharton's novel was "the emotion of Newland's relationship to Ellen and his not being able to fulfill it as he would like to . . . the things you miss in life or the things you *think* you miss."

If you understand that this is a film cast in the negative, that it's not about the decor and the costumes, the funereal profusion of food and flowers, but rather the unseen and the unspoken, that which doesn't happen on the screen and could never happen, then it's sad in a way that films seldom are. The implication is, one can survive passion only by renouncing it. From the opening slo-mo image of the flower unfurling, sensuality is posed as overwhelming—a threat, a disruption, you could be sucked into that sweetness, you could die. Better to keep it at a distance. Make it into art. A moviegoing affair. A fetishistic object.

What I'm talking about is the way a film about obsession mirrors the viewing experience of a person obsessed with film. Such a film must present a rich lode of material for interpretation and yet set in motion desires so contradictory that they can't be fulfilled. What's relevant to criticism is the interpretive part. The object choice is purely personal (which, it goes without saying, is also political, cultural, etc.). The smartest film theorist I ever knew got great pleasure confessing that he had watched *The Exorcist* more than a hundred times. [Amy Taubin, 11/9/93]

Ali: Fear Eats the Soul (1974)

Dir./Scr. Rainer Werner Fassbinder
94 min.

Rainer Werner Fassbinder's work has always been characterized by a dichotomy between the plot conventions of melodrama and an extremely stylized mise-en-scène. His claustrophobic camera style forces his actors to move in space as if part of a series of still lifes. If *The Merchant of Four Seasons* leans more toward stylization, *Ali: Fear Eats the Soul* relies more on melodrama as a means of attacking German bourgeois values. A black Moroccan "Gastarbeiter," Ali, meets an elderly German cleaning woman, Emmi, in a pub frequented by emigrant laborers. Although she is at least twenty years older than he is, they end up sleeping together. Not really sexual, their attraction is based on a need for human warmth and companionship. They move invisibly on the edge of middle-class society, his color and her age having isolated them physically and emotionally.

Ironically, their relationship only increases their isolation from society. Emmi's children kick in her television in shame, while the cleaning women at the office ostracize her as a "nigger-whore." Ali's Moroccan friends, on the other hand, ridicule him for marrying "a grandmother." The first part of the film ends with the couple going on a trip, hoping "everything will be better when we get back."

Paying homage to the Hollywood melodramas of another German director, Douglas Sirk, Fassbinder in fact uses Sirk's *All That Heaven Allows* as a source for *Ali*. In the original, a New England town is turned upside down when a respectable widow (Jane Wyman) has an affair

Ali: Fear Eats the Soul, 1974; written and directed by Rainer Werner Fassbinder

with a young gardener (Rock Hudson). Just as Sirk veiled his critique of America's shallow and artificial existence during the Eisenhower years in the genre conventions of the women's picture, so Fassbinder uses melodramatic devices to crystallize his critical vision. Through these conventions, he is able to execute a major plot reversal.

When Ali and Emmi return, they are inexplicably greeted by the same neighbors who had shown them nothing but contempt earlier. To be sure, selfish motives are involved: a neighbor asks Ali to move some furniture, while the local shopkeeper wants Emmi's business again because "she was a good customer." Even Emmi's children (Fassbinder plays the son-in-law) begin to accept her life with Ali. Without external forces holding them together, internal pressures inevitably begin to affect their relationship. Fassbinder's patently artificial plot is used to expose the deeper psychological effects of social repression.

Emmi, once again accepted by her German friends, hopes Ali will conform to her image of respectable society. Her subconscious cultural chauvinism is clearly shown when she reluctantly joins her fellow workers in giving a new Turkish worker the cold shoulder. In another scene, Emmi proudly puts on display Ali's strong muscles for her lady friends, not realizing how dehumanizing her action appears. The old ladies even snicker about the size of other muscles not presented in public.

Still suffering from cultural displacement, Ali attempts to cure his depression by getting drunk with his Moroccan friends. Not unlike Hans in *Merchant of Four Seasons*, he is unable to verbalize his emotions, a situation only made worse by his broken German. Again, Fassbinder's inherent mistrust of language becomes apparent. Language is used by society's ruling power structure to control (*Effi Briest*), to isolate individuals (*Ali*), and to denounce (*Merchant*). Even the German title, *Angst essen Seele auf* ("Fear Eat Soul"), is taken from Ali's awkward use of language.

Under emotional strain, Ali collapses with a bleeding ulcer. As in many Sirk films, Fassbinder uses physical disease as a correlative for psychic and social illnesses. The doctors tell Emmi that ulcers are extremely common among transient laborers, with the only permanent cure being a one-way ticket to another country.

Although their future remains unresolved, the consistent claustrophobia of Fassbinder's compositions indicates the bleakness of their situation. Often Fassbinder presents the action through doors, thus decreasing the size of the frame, or in stairwells and hallways, limiting the compositional space. His exterior shots—if used at all—are characterized by the same sense of claustrophobia; one need only remember the 360-degree subjective pan shot in the courtyard near the beginning of *Merchant*. The actors, Brigitte Mira and El Hedi Ben Salem, move about inside Fassbinder's cramped compositional space almost paralyzed by their social inhibitions. The stylization of the acting and the portraitlike placement of actors (in shots often held a few seconds after the action has ceased) tend to reinforce the tension born from repressed passions.

The most striking example of this conflict between stylization and melodrama occurs when Ali collapses in the Moroccan pub while dancing with Emmi. The scene is an almost exact replay of their first encounter, only this time she is retrieving him after he has been unfaithful. Their movements take on a ritualistic quality, framed by silent onlookers aware of the unspoken emotions charging the atmosphere.

The miracle of Fassbinder's direction is that his characters remain thoroughly human. His anguish over the fate of Emmi and Ali is expressed without inhibitions. According to Fassbinder, it was his contact with Sirk that gave him the courage to choose such openly emotional subject matter. The result is one of the most original films to appear this year. [Jan-Christopher Horak, 10/3/74]

Andrei Rublev (1969)

Dir. Andrei Tarkovsky; Scr. Andrei Konchalovsky and Andrei Tarkovsky
205 min.

When *Andrei Rublev* first materialized on the international scene in the late 1960s, it was an apparent anomaly—a pre-Soviet theater of cruelty charged with resurgent Slavic mysticism. Today, Andrei Tarkovsky's second feature seems to prophesy the impending storm.

Its greatness as moviemaking immediately evident, *Andrei Rublev* was also the most historically audacious Soviet production since Eisenstein's

Ivan the Terrible. Tarkovsky's epic—and largely invented—biography of Russia's greatest icon painter, Andrei Rublev (circa 1360–1430), was a superproduction gone ideologically berserk. Violent, even gory, for a Soviet film, *Andrei Rublev* was set against the carnage of the Tatar invasions and took the form of a chronologically discontinuous pageant. Its pale-eyed, otherworldly hero wanders across a landscape of forlorn splendor—observing suffering peasants, hallucinating the scriptures, working for brutal nobles until, having killed a man in the sack of Vladimir, he takes a vow of silence and gives up painting.

The first (and perhaps the only) film produced under the Soviets to treat the artist as a world-historic figure and the rival religion of Christianity as an axiom of Russia's historical identity, *Andrei Rublev* is set in the chaotic period that saw the beginning of that national resurgence of which Rublev's paintings would become the cultural symbol.

Andrei Rublev is itself more an icon than a movie about an icon painter. At once humble and cosmic, Tarkovsky called *Rublev* a "film of the earth." Shot in widescreen and sharply defined black and white,

Andrei Rublev, 1969; directed by Andrei Tarkovsky; written by Andrei Konchalovsky and Andrei Tarkovsky

the movie is supremely tactile—the four elements appearing as mist, mud, guttering candles, and snow. Although this is a portrait of an artist in which no one lifts a brush, it's difficult to think of another film that attaches greater significance to the artist's role. It's as though Rublev's presence justifies an entire world.

Tarkovsky works with the entire frame throughout, most impressively in long shot. Undirectable creatures animate his compositions—a cat bounds across a corpse-strewn church, wild geese flutter over a ravaged city. The birchwoods are alive with water snakes and crawling ants, the forest floor yields a decomposing swan. The soundtrack is filled with birdcalls and wordless singing; there's always a fire's crackle or a tolling bell in the background. The film provides an entire world—or rather the sense that as predicted by Bazin's "Myth of Total Cinema," the world itself is trying to force its way through the screen.

Like Bazin, Tarkovsky privileges mise-en-scène over montage, but although his complicated tracking shots suggest those of his Hungarian contemporary Miklós Janscó, his interest is not in choreography. A 360-degree pan around a primitive stable conveys the wonder of creation. Such long, sinuous takes are like expressionist brush strokes; the result is a kind of narrative impasto. From a close-up recording the micro impact of a horse's hooves on the surface of a turbid river, Tarkovsky's camera swivels to reveal a Tatar regiment sweeping across a barren hill. Other times, the camera hovers like an angel over the suffering terrain. The film's brilliant, never-explained prologue has some medieval Daedalus braving an angry crowd to storm the heavens. Having climbed a church tower, he takes flight in a primitive hot-air balloon—a sudden exhilarating panorama before he crashes to earth.

In the forty-minute final sequence that brings *Rublev* full circle, the teenage son of a master bell maker successfully supervises the casting of a huge silver bell. The casting of the bell, everyone's will concentrated on a single aesthetic object, is a synecdoche for the film. Rublev wanders through the rainy panorama, ceding the foreground to the skinny kid, giggling with hysterical confidence as he directs a landscape of workers. It is the magnitude of the bluff that restores Rublev to the human community. After the job is done, the monk comforting the sobbing boy hears his confession: "My father never told me—he took his secret to the grave."

On one hand, *Rublev* is founded on the conflict between austere Christianity and sensual paganism—whether Slavic or Tatar. On the other, it puts the artist in the context of state patronage and repression. (Tarkovsky originally planned to call the movie *The Passion According to Andrei*—like his namesake and creator, Rublev is a nail biter.) When Rublev stumbles upon the midsummer mysteries of Saint John's Eve—an alien rite, delicate and strange with naked peasants carrying torches through the mist—the monk himself is captured and tied to a cross. One wonderful touch: Andrei inadvertently backs into a smoldering fire and has the hem of his robe set, momentarily, aflame.

For Tarkovsky, Rublev's story is "the story of a 'taught,' or imposed concept, which burns up in the atmosphere of living reality to arise again from the ashes as a fresh and newly-discovered truth." In a brief coda, the movie explodes into color with abstract close-ups of actual icons—cracked and charred by "living reality." [J. Hoberman, 2/25/92]

Aparajito (1957)

See THE APU TRILOGY.

The Apu Trilogy (1955–1959)

Pather Panchali (1955)

Dir. Satyajit Ray; Scr. Bibhutibhushan Bandyopadhyay and Satyajit Ray
115 min.

Aparajito (1957)

Dir. Satyajit Ray; Scr. Bibhutibhushan Bandyopadhyay and Satyajit Ray
110 min.

The World of Apu (1959)

Dir. Satyajit Ray; Scr. Bibhutibhushan Bandyopadhyay and Satyajit Ray
117 min.

We have seen Satyajit Ray's *Pather Panchali*, *Aparajito*, and *The World of Apu*, one by one, as they came. Now the new Carnegie Hall Cinema has put all three parts together in a marathon show. Wow! It's like reading all of *David Copperfield* in one day.

I have sat through two marathons before. My first one was Pagnol's *Marius*, *Fanny*, *César*, ten years ago, in my first cinema fever. I was drunk with it for a long time in my Brooklyn factories, drunk with Provence. I revisited it again recently, at the New Yorker Theatre, and found big holes in it; the wind was blowing through. My second marathon was Donskoi's "Maxim Gorki" trilogy. I never had a chance to recheck this one; it still looms in my memory—huge, rich, a mountain. Ray's trilogy, however, may be the greatest of them all.

Since the arrival of the Nouvelle Vague, the attention of our more adventurous film critics has turned toward the truth of cinema: style, how the scene is lit, how the camera moves, how the people move, what means of expression are used by the director, and in what personal way. Applying all this to Ray, there is nothing much to say about him: his stylistic means are simple and few. He is as plain as Hemingway. No embellishments. Just compare Ray to Chabrol, for instance, whose camera is turning and twisting, making knots around its own neck. Ray is as plain as day. A few slight pans, a slight movement there, a high angle, a moving-in close-up—that's all. The best moments of the trilogy are achieved through utmost simplicity. The style never takes the lead over the content. A snake moving lazily across an empty yard and into the house is enough to imply the complete abandonment of a house.

Ray fails only when he exchanges his insight into life for the truth of cinema, which he does often in the second and third parts. *Panchali* is still the purest of all three. Its episodes are not connected with one another, its action is not explained. *Panchali* is a necklace of episodes, each one pure, beautiful, and true, and together they all build an aesthetic and emotional unity.

The difference between the first part and the latter two can be best seen in the treatment of death, one of Ray's recurrent themes. In the first part, the old granny dies simply and by herself, without an emphasis of camera or sound. Nevertheless, we feel her death like few others we have ever felt. The deaths in the other two parts seem mere necessities of plot; they come with big cinematic bangs, with flocks of black birds and dramatic music. But they never say as much about death as that first one did.

Scene after scene, Ray has packed into this huge work his observations, his memories, the visual texture of the ancient and modern India going through an eternal circle of birth, suffering, disease, death. I was born and grew up many thousand miles from all these places—but it seemed to me, as I sat there, through the five hours, that I recognized all those people, that he was telling my own story. Wasn't that me, listening with my ear on the telephone pole to the mysterious singing of the wires, with the smell of the summer flowers in the air? Wasn't that me, running across the fields with a black rain cloud hanging over the sky? Wasn't that me, rushing back to school, stealing days from my mother; wasn't that my mother who was waiting and waiting for a never-coming letter? Wasn't that me, somewhere in Brooklyn—was it on Thompson or Howard Street?—who through an open door watched the workers around a huge table of bracelets, with the smell of the copper in my nostrils? Wasn't that me who watched the water flies dancing on the water-edge?

It was all there, it was all in Ray's movie, as if he were reading into my memory, my heart, my life, your life. . . . Oh, it made me sentimental again, damn it to hell. [Jonas Mekas, 8/3/61]

L'Argent (1983)

Dir./Scr: Robert Bresson

85 min.

Robert Bresson's *L'Argent* justifies all by itself the twenty-one-year existence of the New York Film Festival. It is not a particularly "easy" film for a general audience; in this, it is quintessentially Bressonian. Most hard-core Bressonians profess to prefer it to *The Devil, Probably* (1977). I see the two as very closely related. After one viewing, I am struck most strongly by its more despairing tone. The somewhat ironic hypothesis of the devil in *The Devil, Probably* has been developed in *L'Argent* into a logical and sociological certainty. Freed of the constraints of love and justice, evil emerges completely triumphant. Yet most viewers will respond to *L'Argent* more favorably than they might have toward the still unreleased *The Devil, Probably*. Why? Largely, I think, because of a fortunate misunderstanding. The plot of *L'Argent*, adapted very freely from a Tolstoy story on the consequences of counterfeiting, lends itself to a class-conscious righteousness about the corruption of a proletarian protagonist by the irresponsible bourgeoisie.

Indeed, to hear the story synopsized is to visualize the late Henry Fonda in one of his surly, justice-seeking ex-con characterizations in such 1930s melodramas as *You Only Live Once* and *Let Us Live* on the way to his epochal Tom Joad in *The Grapes of Wrath*. As Bresson's working-class victim, Yvon Targe, Christian Patey is, if anything, the antithesis of Fonda's facade of snarlingly outraged innocence. Patey suffers his injustices proudly, stoically, and inexpressively, to the point that his demeanor is virtually indistinguishable from those of the more privileged people responsible for his plight. "I will not grovel," Yvon declares to his more practical wife when she suggests that he "explain" his predicament to a boss who has fired him after he has been falsely accused of passing counterfeit money. The calmness with which Patey reads this line invests it with a fearful gravity and portentousness. The fires of hell quickly consume the flimsy social fabric that has kept everyone in an uneasy moral equilibrium until that very fateful moment in *L'Argent*: a schoolboy with inadequate pocket money is absentmindedly turned down by his preoccupied parents when he requests an additional sum to pay a personal debt. A chum shows him how to pass a fake bank note, the storekeeper in turn passes the note on to our oil-supplying protagonist, and so on and so forth, to prison and, eventually, to mass murder, and, ultimately, if not entirely convincingly, to a cryptic ceremony of confessional redemption and grace.

Aside from the familiar gambit of having all the action rigorously repressed to form a monolithic bloc of what Bresson regards as "being," the film disconcerts us also with its thoroughly incongruous sensuousness. The frequent recourse to metonymy and ellipsis (particularly in the gory murder scenes) is also characteristically Bressonian. Time and again, he lingers on the inanimate fixtures within a frame long after its human figures have departed. Time and again, he breaks the smooth flow of images in order to emphasize the jarring autonomy of each individual image.

Why, then, was I more moved by *The Devil, Probably*? Possibly because I felt that in its suicidal ending was a more hopeful irony at work in Bresson's art. Life was still something to cling to all the way to the last syllable of the most banal utterance. In *L'Argent* I sense an unconditional surrender to despair and disgust. I would not say that the film is lacking even the slightest gesture of hope. Bresson has described his protagonist's climatic expiration as "a routing of the forces of evil." What I do question is Bresson's continuing commitment to finding Grace in Other People. Yvon in *L'Argent* stands on the edge of the abyss, in that there is no other human being in whom he can see his own moral reflection. No other Bresson character, not even any of his suicides, has ever been left quite so abjectly alone. That a filmmaker can lift us to these levels of contemplation and speculation is proof enough of his greatness. [Andrew Sarris, 10/4/83]

L'Atalante (1934)

Dir. Jean Vigo; Scr. Jean Guinée, Jean Vigo, and Albert Riéra

89 min.

L'Atalante may be the greatest film ever made. Mutilated by its backers before its disastrous 1934 opening as *Le Chaland Qui Passé*, Jean Vigo's masterpiece (or, if you prefer, his *other* masterpiece) has never been shown in its intended form; purists are complaining that this restoration based on a long-lost print isn't definitive either.

The movie's simple story—fledgling marriage tested by life on a river barge—wasn't Vigo's own. After the commercial disaster of his autobiographical *Zéro de Conduit*, *L'Atalante*'s scenario was foisted on him by a producer, and initially, Vigo resisted the idea; in the end, he revised the script drastically and reimagined it wholly. The result is an enchanted film with the obsessive narrative purity of a fairy tale and grounded, like fairy tales, in the mundane. Call it a poetic or a psychological documentary. Here's a partial list of its subject matter: the worm at the heart of love; women's order-threatening ambitions and men's attendant confusions; the great modern conflict between a consumer society and the spirit's mounting hungers.

L'Atalante opens with two incredibly graceful, hypnotic episodes. In the first, a bride and a groom leave the village church and, followed by a grim wedding party, march through the town, around haystacks, across fields, and down to the river where the groom's barge waits. He (Jean Dasté) seems buoyant, she (the marvelous Dita Parlo) looks alternately pensive and tormented. From remarks of the wedding guests, we gather that she's committing a minor crime by marrying outside the local crop of males and that she's leaving the village for the first time. At the water's edge, they're met by the crew: the clownish "Père Jules" (Michel Simon) and an eager, awkward boy (Louis Lefèvre). In a wonderfully droll low-angle shot, Juliette, in her wedding dress, swings onto the barge by hanging over a boom.

The next sequence, the wedding night, is just as lovely but more ominous. It involves the stray cats collected by Père Jules: one cat attacks the bride and another the groom, Jean, bloodying his face. Still in her wedding dress, Juliette has broken away from Jean and—in an indelible, melancholy image—makes her way along the length of the barge in the dusk. (Vigo's gifted cinematographer was Boris Kaufmann.) On the bank, an old woman, witnessing the sight, crosses herself. Only when Juliette spots the blood on Jean's face does she suddenly laugh and turn passionate. The episode marks the first time she leaves him, and the first time he retrieves her.

Often women have married (or moved into "relationships") to escape former confinements, then found themselves pacing new cages and needing to go further—to individuate, as the jargon goes. Like provincials before and after her, Juliette hears the siren song of Paris: "Paris calling" on the wireless, the lines "Paris, Paris, O infamous and marvelous city" sung by Père Jules. (A haunting score by Maurice Jaubert is another of the movie's marvels.) The barge arrives in the Saint Martin canal locks, but Juliette doesn't get out into the infamous city. The more Jean senses her discontent, the more he forbids her. He has trouble seeing her—there's the fog, his own work, sexual jealousy. Juliette's advice: when under water, don't close your eyes.

At first, it may look as if the Père Jules episodes were conceived merely as comic relief. Then it becomes clear that he's a crucial player (and that Simon's ebullient, vaguely sinister performance may top even his contemporaneous 1932 Boudu). Down inside Jules's messy, cat-littered cabin, Juliette uncovers bizarre treasures—like the pickled hands of his old friend. The famous shot of Simon sticking a cigarette into his belly button—the mouth on a tattooed face—turns up here as Jules performs for Juliette. She domesticates him—washes his things, combs his hair, even gets him to model a skirt. He intuits her wildness and responds in kind—pretending to choke her, casually slicing his hand with a stiletto. Jean catches them together and starts smashing the old man's things.

Jules's junk is personal and primitive ("an old museum," he says), but Juliette is tempted next—literally charmed—by the chic trash of a flirty street peddler (Gilles Margaritis). This time she sneaks off the barge for a quick solo visit to Paris, but finding her missing, irate Jean embarks without her. What happens next is truncated, but it's clear that after being robbed, maybe molested, Juliette fends for herself; the ending isn't a defeat but a coming into her desire. The famous, sexy double dream—hers and Jean's superimposed—tells us so.

My discussion is truncated, too. What I've meant to suggest is that every image and line in *L'Atalante* counts. If Vigo had grown into ripeness like his contemporaries Renoir and Buñuel, he might have been greatest of all. Instead, like Keats, he flamed early. Completed while he was twenty-nine and on his deathbed, *L'Atalante* is one of those precious works singed by a genius's final fever. [Georgia Brown, 10/23/90]

Au Hasard Balthazar (1966)

Dir./Scr. Robert Bresson

95 min.

Robert Bresson's Balthazar is a donkey born, like all beings, to suffer and die needlessly and mysteriously. Hence, the Russian roulettish "au hasard" in both the title and the arbitrary fragmentation of the framing. It is not that we see everything from Balthazar's point of view as if from some blessed vision of a doomsday donkey, but rather that we see past the meager milestones of Balthazar's existence to the fitful spasms of human vanity and presumption, the pathetic charades of good and evil, choice and necessity, tenderness and cruelty, order and chaos, joy and sorrow. To the spectacle Bresson has built around his beast of burden, Balthazar does not so much bear witness as breathe and bray from one dimension of time (the physical) to another (the spiritual). Balthazar is born among children and dies among a flock of sheep, partaking in the beginning of the illusion of innocence and in the end of the symbolism of innocence. And if we weep at the fate of Balthazar, it is not through a misplaced sentimentality for the fate of a creature unmindful of its ultimate destiny, but through a displaced response to the heightened awareness Balthazar has inspired in us.

Au Hasard Balthazar is the seventh of nine films Robert Bresson has directed in twenty-seven years of a cultishly maximal and commercially marginal career. In their total context, Bresson's works are obsessively, often oppressively, religious and not merely in their subjects but also in their style, which is another way of saying that Bresson practices what he preaches. The recently concluded Bresson retrospective at the Museum of Modern Art traced the evolution of his style from the dramatic dialectics of Jean Giradoux (*Angels of Sin*) and Jean Cocteau (*Les Dames du Bois de Boulogne*) into the voluptuous passivity and impassivity of his more controlled works. Bresson virtually abandoned histrionic expression after *Angels of Sin* and *Les Dames du Bois de Boulogne*, relying instead on one-shot nonprofessionals with meaningfully blank faces. But even in *Angels* and *Dames*, there are curious intimations of a tension between theatrical gestures and the Bressonian inevitability and implacability that engulf them.

By the time of *Balthazar*, Bresson has abandoned dramatic spectacles altogether. A passion for precision now so dominates his work that the extraordinary unity of his method and his meaning becomes almost boring. A recurring Bressonian mannerism is the shot of a place held long after the people have departed. The world—Bresson implies, indeed demonstrates—will be here long after we have gone. We must learn to accept the visual depopulation of this world as a token of our own imminent departure. A gang of curiously contemporary hooligans, wholly evil and malicious, spread an oil slick on the road and wait for a car to skid off the embankment. We wait with the mischief-makers,

Au Hasard Balthazar, 1966; written and directed by Robert Bresson

share their boredom and impatience, and then hear the sound of a crash without being visually released by the spectacle of destruction. We remain chained to the agents of evil on their terms, not ours, and Bresson will not deliver us to our own evil fantasies. This, then, is the key to his austerity, the rationale of his antidrama. He never bandages a moral wound if he can let it fester instead and if, in letting it fester, he can cause a spiritual delirium in his characters.

But let us not overlook the extraordinary sensuality of *Au Hasard Balthazar*. As a donkey conveyed Mary to her Immaculate Conception, so did it also figure in mythology as the symbolic evocation of sensuality. For Bresson, it is sufficient for Balthazar to oppose his ancient significations to the cruel modernity of machinery and thus be tortured with the same vile eroticism employed to seduce his mistress. The carnal humiliation of the character played by Anne Wiazemsky unfolds with the same rhythm of metaphysical anticlimax characteristic of all the other episodes of the film. Only Balthazar's sublime self-absorption can provide any lasting perspective on Bresson's fragmented human dramas.

I cannot in all candor consider myself the most devoted Bressonian.

And yet, all in all, no film I have ever seen has come so close to convulsing my entire being as has *Au Hasard Balthazar*. I'm not sure what kind of movie it is, and indeed it may be more pleasingly vulgar than I suggest, but it stands by itself on one of the loftiest pinnacles of artistically realized emotional experiences. [Andrew Sarris, 2/19/70]

Before I say anything else: go and see *Au Hasard Balthazar* at the New Yorker Theatre. Bresson's film is the most articulate voice of cinema that you can see and hear in New York this week. All the blabbering of all the movie writers fades away, and all the movies that are playing in New York evaporate before *Au Hasard Balthazar*. We go to the movies, we discuss movies, and everything is fine. And then, suddenly, a movie like this one comes, and the whole perspective of cinema—the standard and the quality, as language, as art, and as articulation—shifts, and all the cinema that made us so happy on a day-by-day basis disappears into nothing. The seriousness, the substance, the bone, and the blood of life and art is reestablished again, for a brief moment, for one week, at the New Yorker. [Jonas Mekas, 2/26/70]

To cut to the chase, Robert Bresson's heartbreaking and magnificent *Au Hasard Balthazar*—the story of a donkey's life and death in rural France—is the supreme masterpiece by one of the greatest of twentieth-century filmmakers. Bringing together all of Bresson's highly developed ideas about acting, sound, and editing, as well as grace, redemption, and human nature, *Balthazar* is understated and majestic, sensuous and ascetic, ridiculous and sublime. It would be a masterpiece for its soundtrack alone. Before the credits are over, solemn Schubert is interrupted by a prolonged hee-haw. *Balthazar*, Bresson once explained, was inspired by a passage in *The Idiot* where Prince Myshkin tells three giggling girls of the happiness he experienced upon hearing the sound of a donkey's bray in a foreign marketplace, and the movie's premise is suitably "idiotic."

Three children baptize a baby donkey and thereby give him a soul. This innocence lasts about five minutes: a brief montage has Balthazar hitched, shoed, and sentenced to a lifetime of labor. Marie, the girl who names him, grows up somber and slack-jawed, regarding the world with a kindred steady gaze. (As noted by Jean-Luc Godard, who later married the actress, Anne Wiazemsky, Marie, too, is a donkey.) Barefoot in her shift, she makes a garland for Balthazar and nuzzles him—then hides as the town punk, Gerard, and his friends jealously beat the animal.

Marie's schoolteacher father is a man whose pride leads him to make one mistake after another; Marie (Nastasya to Balthazar's Myshkin) helplessly gives herself to her family's tormentors. Meanwhile, Balthazar is sold and resold; he's saved by a drunken vagabond named Arnold; he briefly joins the circus (a truly magical interlude) and falls into the hands of the town miser (novelist Pierre Klossowski), who emerges from the midst of a teenage bacchanal in an example of Bresson's unfailingly brilliant method of introducing characters. In the end, Balthazar reverts to Marie's father—who has lost everything and is about to lose even more.

For years, *Au Hasard Balthazar* could only be seen in New York in a beautiful but unsubtitled print. With a year of high school French, I understood somewhat less of the dialogue than the donkey, but seeing alone was sufficient to convince me that Bresson was the greatest narrative filmmaker since D. W. Griffith. No one has ever made better use of close-ups, more precisely delineated off-screen space, or so flawlessly established a dramatic rhythm. *Balthazar* is predicated on an astonishing tension between formal rigor and, as embodied by its protagonist, the random quality of life. At the same time, it recognizes the thingness of things—as in the stunning sequence wherein mystery tramp Arnold bids farewell to a stone marker and a power line, then slips from Balthazar's back, dead.

Oblique as it is, Bresson's narrative hints at an immense story involving betrayal, theft, even murder. But its real concern is the state of being. Crowned with flowers, spooked by firecrackers, struck without cause, Balthazar bears patient witness to all manner of enigmatic human behavior. (Even more than Myshkin, he is a spectator.) This expressionless donkey is the most eloquent of creatures—he is pure existence, and his death, in the movie's transfixing final sequence, conveys the sorrow that all existence shares. [J. Hoberman, 10/15/2003]

L'Avventura (1960)

Dir. Michelangelo Antonioni; Scr. Michelangelo Antonioni, Elio Bartolini, and Tonino Guerra

145 min.

So far this year it has been all *Breathless*, but now it is time for another blast of trumpets. The sixth feature film of Italian director Michelangelo Antonioni, *L'Avventura*, will probably be even more controversial than its French predecessor, which has been conveniently misunderstood as a problem tract on old age, childhood, juvenile delinquency, miscegenation, nuclear warfare, or what have you.

With *L'Avventura*, the issue cannot be muddled. The plot, such as it is, will infuriate audiences who still demand plotted cinema and potted climaxes. A group of bored Italian socialites disembark from their yacht on a deserted island. After wandering about a while, they discover that one of their number, a perverse girl named Anna, is missing. Up to that time, Anna (Lea Massari) had been the protagonist. Not only does she never reappear, the mystery of her disappearance is never solved. Anna's fiancé (Gabriele Ferzetti) and her best friend (Monica Vitti) continue the search from one town to another, ultimately betraying the object of their search by becoming lovers. The film ends on a note of further betrayal and weary acceptance with the two lovers facing a blank wall and a distant island, both literally and symbolically.

The film is almost over before we learn that the hero is an architect who has sacrificed his ambitions for the lucrative position of a middleman in the building industry. The other characterizations are sketched in much the same apparently incidental manner. A graduate of Screenwriting 1 and 2 might dismiss this method as casualness or even carelessness, but every shot and bit of business in *L'Avventura* represent calculation of the highest order. The characteristic Antonioni image consists of two or more characters within the frame not looking at each other. They may be separated by space, mood, interest, but the point comes across, and the imposing cinematic theme of communication is brilliantly demonstrated.

If Antonioni's characters are unable to communicate with those who should be closest to them, they are also unable to avoid the intrusion of strangers. When Monica Vitti is contemplating suicide, a passerby looks up at her and jars her sense of solitude without relieving her of her loneliness. Is this not typical of modern society where crowds supersede communities?

For Antonioni, there is no solution to the moral problem created by the failure of contemporary behavior to meet the hypocritical standards of ancient codes. The architect observes that his predecessors built for the centuries, while he would be building for decades or less. Love, fidelity, and mourning are similarly abbreviated in the hectic chronology of our time, even though social customs still insist on concealing a shameful change of heart.

Antonioni stated in a recent interview that eroticism was the disease of our age, and the eroticism in *L'Avventura* is presented with this clinical awareness. The four sexual encounters in the film are so graphically complete in their sensual essence that it becomes quite clear that Antonioni is demonstrating the inadequacy of sexual encounters as a means of moral communication. The erotic disease subordinates the person to the process, and one's specific identity is lost. It is no accident that a copy of F. Scott Fitzgerald's *Tender is the Night* is found with the missing girl's possessions. Fitzgerald's stylistic device of replacing protagonists, Nicole for Rosemary, is repeated in *L'Avventura* with a vengeance. Later in the film, when Anna's blond friend adorns herself with a dark wig, we are confronted with a breathtaking Pirandellian moment of confused identities. For the hero, there is really little difference between his missing fiancée and her successor. There is much more to this modern Odyssey for an alert audience. The travels of the characters are paralleled by the meaningfully shifting backgrounds of geography, architecture, and painting. This intellectual muscle should appeal to anyone who seeks something more from the cinema than the finger exercises of conventional films. [Andrew Sarris, 3/23/61]

Bad Lieutenant (1992)

Dir. Abel Ferrara; Scr. Abel Ferrara and Zoë Lund
96 min.

As a season in hell or a stake through the heart, *Dracula* pales next to *Bad Lieutenant*. Plumbing the depths of spiritual degradation, scuzzmeister Abel Ferrara elevates himself to a new plane.

A startling portrayal of sin and salvation in godless New York, as well as a vehicle for Harvey Keitel's lacerating portrayal of a lapsed-Catholic junkie cop, *Bad Lieutenant* opens with Chris "Mad Dog" Russo on WFAN, defending the New York Mets against a succession of irate callers. The Mets are down 0–3 to the Dodgers in the National League playoffs—something Ferrara, with his unerring sense of local color, immediately correlates to the precarious state of his antihero's soul.

Bad Lieutenant is a movie of fantastic conviction, much of it derived from Keitel's uninhibited performance. The nameless lieutenant's cases are an abstract succession of corpses left in bloody cars—the scene of the crime typically swarming with bored cops talking baseball and placing bets. When not "working," the lieutenant is out scoring crack, confiscating drugs, or shaking down suspects. The money goes to shoot smack with a thin, mannered druggy played by Zoë Lund, the star of Ferrara's *Ms. 45* and coauthor of *Bad Lieutenant*'s script, or to hire an S and M lesbian sex circus. (The latter scene, with the tearful cop slugging Stoli from the bottle and heedlessly letting his bathrobe fall full-frontally open, is the first of Keitel's several weeping and moaning tours de force.)

As sordid as the material is, the movie isn't oppressive. Ferrara frames the action with a wide-angle lens and often allows it to evolve over relatively long takes. The performances are behavioral; the mode analytic. (Nor is it devoid of a certain horrific humor. Doubling his bets against the Mets each time he loses until he's ultimately a hopeless hundred grand in the hole, the lieutenant shoots out his car radio when the Dodgers blow another game, puts the siren on, and drives through Times Square traffic screaming, "You fucking piece of shit.") Indeed, unlike Ferrara's expressionistic gangster opus *King of New York*, *Bad Lieutenant* is made with a powerful restraint that allows for such eruptions of hysteria or hallucination.

The most explicit sex scene—the Keitel character harassing two teenagers from New Jersey—is all the more remarkable for being the most distanced representation of fellatio since Andy Warhol's *Blow Job*. Similarly, the movie's most lurid, highly edited sequence—the graphic gang rape of a nun in church—is juxtaposed with the soft violence of a child watching TV, cartoon mice marching off to a cartoon war. Although cynical about the violated nun ("the church is a racket"), the lieutenant puts himself on the case in the hopes of securing the fifty-thousand-dollar reward the diocese has offered. That the nun refuses to cooperate, having forgiven her attackers, is the epiphany that ultimately splits the cop's skull like a migraine.

Bad Lieutenant has obvious affinities to the splatterific masculinist cinema of the Scorsese/Schrader *Taxi Driver* and James Toback's *Fingers*, but it's less flashy and more tragic. There's a carefully crafted argument going on—albeit not in words. The fallen world has never been more totally evoked. The decision to stage the nightclub scene at the desanctified church Limelight, the strategic use of the ethereal "Pledging My Love" by Russian-roulette suicide Johnny Ace, the visualization of Jesus as a bloody hunk, the resurrection of the New York Mets to effect a miracle, are all of a piece.

According to *Variety*, Ferrara is currently planning a movie that portrays the last days of Pier Paolo Pasolini, and as in Pasolini's swan song, *Salo*, the thrills here don't come cheap. Neither does the lieutenant's redemption. *Bad Lieutenant* is not for the timid, but it's a movie whose considerable formal intelligence is infused with an agonized sense of spiritual emptiness and even transcendence. [J. Hoberman, 11/17/92]

Barry Lyndon (1975)

Dir./Scr. Stanley Kubrick
184 min.

Barry Lyndon is the loveliest of Stanley Kubrick's films. Indeed, it's the one Kubrick movie that could even invite that adjective (or epithet).

Adapted from William Thackeray's obscure first novel, *Barry Lyndon* is the saddest of swashbucklers and the most melancholy of bodice-rippers. Kubrick visualizes the late eighteenth century as a death-haunted realm of perpetual summer. The verdant landscapes recall Constable and Watteau, but the idyll is haunted by inane military pageants; the architecture is majestic, but the grand empty spaces are inhabited by the narcissistic zombie likes of Ryan O'Neal and Marisa Berenson, mouthing elaborate formalities over delicately heaving bosoms.

As reconceived by Kubrick, Thackeray's novel—itself a period piece, tracking the rise and fall of a fortune-seeking scoundrel—is a solemn picaresque. The action unfolds over twenty-five years, moving from Barry's native Ireland to England to Germany, then making a stately about-face to England and ending back in Ireland. Where the novel's originality lay in its unreliable first-person, Kubrick eliminated the hero's voice—a not inappropriate strategy for a movie so fixated on human solitude—to make the omniscient narrator the warmest presence. Muting the novel's satire while fashioning a three-hour movie from fewer than half its episodes, Kubrick was less concerned with Barry's dubious character than with his world—and ultimately his condition.

Framed by duels and filled with betrayals, *Barry Lyndon* establishes its hero's sense of grievance with scenes of British soldiers parading in the Irish fields and a smirking British captain making off with Barry's flirtatious cousin. The young man seeks vengeance, gets packed off to Dublin, is waylaid on the road, and finds himself left with no choice but to enlist himself in the king's army. Shock cut to the Seven Years War. (Although *Barry Lyndon* is only incidentally a combat film, the battle scenes are among Kubrick's most futile. The brightly uniformed soldiers are simply mowed down as they march straight into enemy fire.) Barry deserts the British and is drafted by Prussians. He is recruited by the local secret police to spy on a gentleman gambler but, upon discovering that this rouged and bewigged French chevalier is an Irishman like himself, joins the charade.

Back in 1976, *Barry Lyndon*'s most problematic aspect was its blatant stunt casting—the equivalent today of using Leonardo DiCaprio and Kate Moss to anchor something like *The Charterhouse of Parma*. Still young and beautiful, O'Neal starts out as a ridiculously po-faced dullard and eventually "matures" into a stern-looking dolt. But *Barry Lyndon* is a movie that encourages the long view, and seen from the perspective of a quarter-century, the actor appears as a blank stand-in for himself, just a good-looking chess piece for Kubrick to maneuver around the board.

Full of professional self-regard, this emotional cipher comes into his own as a swaggering cardsharp working the candlelit courts of Saxony. There he meets and courts the married Lady Lyndon (supermodel Berenson, then declared by *Elle* "the most beautiful girl in the world"). Berenson speaks as little as possible. She's a presence even more decorative and less expressive than O'Neal—who, in character as Thackeray's shallow, social-climbing opportunist, told a reporter he found her "overbred" and "vacuous." Her elegantly long, grave face provides a suitably foolish substitute for the imitation of inner life.

Barry Lyndon breaks for intermission with Lady Lyndon's apoplectic husband suffering a fatal stroke; it resumes with her wedding to Barry and his usurping the late Lord Lyndon's title. Where the movie's first half offered a welter of absurd adventures, the second charts the overreaching hustler's slow decline from the pinnacle of success—brought down by the emptiness of his achievements, the constraints of his wife's position, and the lethal drawing-room manners of the English ruling classes. The mode presages *The Shining*'s domestic apocalypse; the most violent scene has Barry busting up his wife's harpsichord recital to tackle and thrash his insolent stepson.

Protocol thus broken, *Barry Lyndon* wends toward a gloomy conclusion, with Kubrick shamelessly milking the death of a child and brilliantly staging the last of the movie's three duels. (Based on a single sentence in Kubrick's screenplay, this remarkable scene takes nearly ten minutes.) With a final dance of death, Kubrick closes the parentheses. Summer ends, and so does the movie.

Barry Lyndon was in production for over two years, and to a large degree, the reception it received in December 1975 anticipated that accorded the unfinished *Eyes Wide Shut*. The ever perverse Kubrick had adapted an unknown literary classic, stocked it with celebrity stars, and worked in well-publicized secrecy over an extended period of time under security so tight, his studio barely knew what he was doing. Heralded by a worshipful *Time* cover story, the movie received notices ranging from the ecstatic to the brutally dismissive.

Unlike *Eyes Wide Shut*, however, *Barry Lyndon* could be considered Kubrick's masterpiece. At the very least, this cerebral action film represents the height of his craft. Working for the last time outside the studio, the director shot entirely on location in England and Ireland, with a second-unit crew dispatched to East Germany. Kubrick undertook massive period research, even using actual period clothing, and the movie is a triumph of production design. The audio design is scarcely less busy, underscoring voice-over narration with all manner of exaggerated sound effects and near-constant baroque music. (According to the composer Leonard Rosenman, Kubrick was initially interested in obtaining the theme from *The Godfather*—which sheds another light on this profoundly eccentric filmmaker and his most eccentric project.)

Kubrick's admirers were enchanted that after three highly unusual science-fiction films, the director decided to land a time machine on Planet Europe. (More than one compared *Barry Lyndon*'s settings to the eighteenth-century room the astronaut inhabits in the last third of *2001*.) Appropriately, Kubrick availed himself of sci-fi technology to evoke the past. He made extensive and graceful use of the then largely abused zoom, while thanks to a customized lens developed for NASA satellite photography, cinematographer John Alcott shot much of the movie under impossibly low levels of illumination—many scenes were lit entirely by candles. Others found *Barry Lyndon* too detached and overdetermined. In this, however, it was truer to its source than its detractors knew. Anne Thackeray introduced the republication of her father's novel with the observation that it was "scarcely a book to like, but one to admire and to wonder at for its consummate power and mastery."

So too this deeply forlorn movie. *Barry Lyndon* was born anomalous. In 1976, Harold Rosenberg damned it with faint praise, suggesting that the movies might make their "maximum contribution to culture" by following Kubrick's lead in "recycling unread literature." Of course, after a decade of adaptations from Jane Austen, Henry James, and Thomas Hardy, Kubrick's oddest project seems twenty years ahead of its time. *Barry Lyndon* is the movie Miramax would most want to release, albeit polished by Tom Stoppard and cut by ninety minutes. [J. Hoberman, 4/19/00]

The Battle of Algiers (1965)

Dir. Gillo Pontecorvo; Scr. Gillo Pontecorvo and Franco Solinas
117 min.

Last week, the New York Film Festival opened its fifth season with *The Battle of Algiers*, that neorealistic film about the wretched of the earth, which has taken prizes at all the festivals where the nonwretched gather.

From the beginning, it was obvious that a number of parallels could be drawn between the French position in Algeria and our own policies both abroad and at home, between the rebels in the Casbah and our own nationalist leaders in our own "Arab quarters." And, as the film rolled on, the audience drew every one of them. Waves of applause broke out at scenes of terrorism against the French colonials, at individual acts of murder. At times, there were cheers. "Saigon next!" a man shouted as the Algerians blew up a crowded café in the French quarter. "What do you people want?" a French officer asked on screen. The audience laughed in understanding and waited for the next bomb blast.

If it was the intention of the program committee to épater the bourgeoisie with its choice of an opening film, then it entirely misread the temper of the bourgeoisie. It doesn't épater, these days. It just has fun. Has there ever before been such a time when the oppressors themselves sit and applaud their own symbolic murder? It was all so much like a leftist policy meeting, years ago, at the beginning of the civil rights movement, when a famous actress, trailing clouds of perfume and gin, batted her false eyelashes and asked in a husky voice, "Oh, dear—is it to the barricades again?"

In an age of decadence, a particular pleasure is the playing of games. And the name of the game our left-wing bourgeoisie is playing these days is Revolution. The New Politics Conference nonsense, the suggestions of gun-running to guerrilla leaders in the ghettos, the general air of mea culpa are all based on one essential subterranean premise: the revolution may come tomorrow, but tomorrow never comes.

Who, after all, would consider giving guns to those who have told him he is to be the victim? Only one who is convinced those guns will never be used. What a patronizing left we have become. Marie Antoinette and her milkmaids in the fields.

In *The Battle of Algiers* the captured leader of the rebels says, "You cannot defeat History!" There was applause. But, as the audience well knew, history is only those events that have occurred. A failed rebellion is not a revolution, and an uprising that has never taken place is nothing. [Margot Hentoff, 9/28/67]

Gillo Pontecorvo's *The Battle of Algiers* is an Italian Marxist reconstruction of a certain segment of the Algerian War. Indeed, a foreword proudly proclaims the fact that not one scrap of newsreel footage was used in the film. Curious that after seventy years of conflict between realism and stylization in the cinema, a film should boast of its complete fakery. Goodbye, Robert Flaherty. Hello, Cecil B. DeMille. By its very nature, the film is stirring rather than moving. The violence is never sentimentalized, but Pontecorvo juggles his point of view quite shamelessly.

For most of the film, we see everything from the point of view of the doomed Algerian revolutionaries. Then suddenly we see the Arab demonstrations entirely from the point of view of the befuddled French colonialists. No mention is made of De Gaulle's return to power, and the viewer is left with the feeling that the Arab masses erupted miraculously without leadership in a spontaneous surge for freedom and dignity. The final mob scenes are undeniable as coups de cinema, particularly on the sound track, but Pontecorvo can hardly be blamed for the masochistic tendencies of some Americans. The French government will not allow *The Battle of Algiers* to be shown in France, and Italian Marxists know better than to make films in Italy attacking the sinister power and influence of the Vatican. French filmmakers know better than to reconstruct the agonies of the Algerian War, and European communists are too well-mannered to make jokes about the Red Guards. That leaves Vietnam as the one subject on which the intellectuals of the world can unite. [Andrew Sarris, 10/5/67]

This past August, as both Iraqi and "coalition" cadavers piled up in post-"Victory" insurgency fighting, the Pentagon's Special Operations and Low-Intensity Conflict office sent out an e-mail advertising a private screening of Gillo Pontecorvo's 1965 *The Battle of Algiers.* "How to win a battle against terrorism and lose the war of ideas," the flyer opined: "Children shoot soldiers at point blank range. Women plant bombs in cafés. Soon the entire Arab population builds to a mad fervor. Sound familiar? The French have a plan. It succeeds tactically, but fails strategically. To understand why, come to a rare showing of this film."

We don't know who attended or what impact upon Pentagon-think this legendary handmade-bomb of a movie might've had. Former national security adviser Zbigniew Brzezinski, for one, remembered it without being reacquainted—at an October 28 D.C. conference called "New American Strategies for Security and Peace," he told the crowd of feds, politicos, and op-ed people, "[I]f you want to understand what is happening right now in Iraq, I suggest a movie that was quite well-known to a number of people some years ago. . . . It's called *The Battle of Algiers*. It is a movie that deals with . . . [a] resistance which used urban violence, bombs, assassinations, and turned Algiers into a continuing battle that eventually wore down the French." Obviously, this fierce piece of agitprop has seen its moment arrive for a second time. Is it tragic irony, or merely the evolutionary nature of realpolitik, that such a passionate, righteous revolutionary document is now most famous as an ostensible training film for neocon strategists?

Who cares? The movie arrives bristling with its own indefatigable legitimacy. Empathize with your enemy, as Robert McNamara says in *The Fog of War*, but the harsh reality of Pontecorvo's film serves only to strip down imperialist rationales to their Napoleonic birthday suits. Did the Pentagonians even notice that the film, an Algerian project produced by one of the nation's liberation leaders, sides squarely with the oppressed, bomb-planting Arabs? Has any movie ever made a more concise and reasonable argument for the "low-intensity," low-resource warfare referred to by powerful nations as terrorism? Famously, a reporter in the film asks an Algerian rebel how moral it is to use women's shopping baskets to hide bombs, to which the apprehended man answers, we do not have planes with which to rain munitions on civilians' homes (which is implicitly, then and now, the far more moral action). If you'll give us your planes, he says, we'll hand over our baskets.

Sound familiar? If any movie squeezes you into the shoes of grassroots combatants fighting a monstrous colonialist power for the right to their own neighborhoods, this is it. There are no subplots or comedy relief. A prototype of news-footage realism, the film makes shrewd use of handheld sloppiness, misjudged focus, overexposure, and you-are-there camera upset; the payoff is the scent of authentic panic.

We follow both sides of the combat—the uprising Casbah natives and the merciless, if disconcerted, French army—from 1954's initiation of the rebellion to the official French victory, in 1957, over the National Liberation Front. It was a Pyrrhic victory, as the harrowing, riot-mad coda makes clear—the terrorist organization may have been rooted out, but the Algerian people still resisted occupation. Hard-edged he may be, but Pontecorvo cannot be called unromantic. Starting with the grifter-turned-assassin-turned-movement leader Ali La Pointe (Brahim Haggiag), the actors playing the Arab seditionists were all chosen for their soulful beauty. (Not, it's safe to say, for their chops; nearly all of their dialogue is post-dubbed, another factor in the movie's on-the-fly affect.) Lizard-eyed ramrod Colonel Mathieu (Jean Martin, the only pro actor in the cast) is sympathetic insofar as he affects admiration for his antagonists (including coproducer Saadi Yacef, who essentially plays his FLN-leader self after writing the book on which the film was based) as civilian neighborhoods are obliterated into rubble, and a barbed-wire wall with armed checkpoints (!) is erected between Algiers's Muslim and French quarters. French government officials complained that the film's politics were anything but "fair and balanced," and they weren't wrong—it's a revolt anthem, mature enough to document violative extremes on the Algerian side but never surrendering its moral rectitude. [Michael Atkinson, 1/7/04]

Beau Travail (1999)

Dir. Claire Denis; Scr. Claire Denis and Jean-Pol Fargeau

90 min.

Claire Denis is a sensational filmmaker—with all that implies. Her *Beau Travail* is a movie so tactile in its cinematography, inventive in its camera placement, and sensuous in its editing that the purposefully oblique and languid narrative is all but eclipsed.

"I've found an idea for a novel," a Godard character once announced. "Not to write the life of a man, but only life, life itself. What there is between people, space . . . sound and colors." His words might serve as Denis's manifesto. Her transposition of Herman Melville's novella *Billy Budd* to a French Foreign Legion post on the Horn of Africa is a mosaic of pulverized shards. Every cut is a small, gorgeously explosive shock.

Denis's main principle is kinesthetic immersion. A former French colonial who spent part of her childhood in Djibouti, she introduces her material with a pan along a crumbling wall mural, accompanied by the legionnaire anthem; this is followed by close-ups of the soldiers dancing with their sultry African dream girls—a vision of sexual glory accentuated by the flashing Christmas lights that constitute the minimalist disco decor—and then by images of the shirtless recruits exercising in the heat of the day to excerpts from Benjamin Britten's *Billy Budd* oratorio.

The filmmaker's style is naturally hieroglyphic. There is little dialogue, and although *Beau Travail* feels present-tense, it is actually an extended first-person flashback. Denis puts her version of the Melville tale of the "handsome sailor" martyred by an evil superior in the villain's mouth. The movie is narrated by the ex-sergeant Galoup (Denis Lavant), after he has been expelled from the Legion for his mistreatment of the popular and gung-ho recruit Sentain (Grégoire Colin). Short and bandy-legged, with odd aquatic features and a face like a Tom Waits song, Lavant's Galoup is a figure of pathos. The Legion, if not the legionnaire, he loved is lost to him.

Time drifts, memories flicker. *Beau Travail* is the recollection of elemental pleasure. The recruits drill under the sun or scramble around the empty fort, when they are not skin diving or performing tai chi. The heat, the disco, the golden beaches, and the turquoise sea suggest a weird sort of Club Med. Apparently crucial to their basic training is the ability to iron a perfect uniform crease. Forestier (Michel Subor), the commanding officer, is fond of chewing the local narcotic, qat. "If it wasn't for fornication and blood, we wouldn't be here," he tells someone.

Sentain rescues a downed helicopter pilot, and Forestier takes a liking to him, further feeding Galoup's jealousy. The sergeant orchestrates a situation to destroy Sentain, bringing the recruits to a barren strip of the coast for some character-building convict work, digging a purposeless road or doing their exercises at high noon. (The locals impassively watch these peculiar antics, modernistic hug-fests that might have been choreographed by Martha Graham.) The movie turns wildly homoerotic. Egged on by Galoup, and Britten's incantatory music, these legionnaires are exalted in their minds. Finally, but without overt cause, Galoup and Sentain stage a one-on-one bare-chested face-off, circling each other on a rocky coast with Britten's oratorio soaring.

In its hypnotic ritual, *Beau Travail* suggests a John Ford cavalry Western interpreted by Marguerite Duras—Galoup always has time to scribble his obsessions in a diary. As in *Billy Budd*, the sergeant suckers the enlisted man into the fatal mistake of slugging him. (Typically, the filmmaker handles this crucial incident in four quick shots.) But, unlike Melville, Denis has no particular interest in Christian allegory. She distills Melville's story to its existential essence. A final visit to the disco finds Galoup flailing out against the prison of self, dancing alone to the Europop rhythm of the night. [J. Hoberman, 3/29/00]

Before Sunset (2004)

Dir. Richard Linklater; Scr. Richard Linklater, Julie Delpy, and Ethan Hawke
77 min.

A modest movie and a near impossible feat, Richard Linklater's sweet, smart, and deeply romantic *Before Sunset* reunites Jesse (Ethan Hawke) and Celine (Julie Delpy), the endearingly prolix protagonists of his 1995 *Before Sunrise*, nine years later in Celine's hometown, Paris.

Illustrating the infinite possibility of its title, *Before Sunrise* chronicled the chance meeting and twelve-hour adventure of these soul mates—Jesse the sensitive, callow American slacker and Celine the venturesome, pretentious French student—to conclude with the open-ended likelihood that they would never meet again. *Before Sunset* revisits this particular alternate universe, and with stars Hawke and Delpy working on the script, it's boldly self-reflexive. The movie opens with Jesse, no longer goateed and now a successful author, winding up his European book tour with a reading at the Left Bank institution Shakespeare & Co. from his version of *Before Sunrise*. He's scheduled to fly home to the United States in a few hours when Celine materializes—their first meeting since they promised (and failed) to keep a rendezvous six months after their brief encounter.

They talk, of course. But the extraordinary thing is not just the quality of their conversation but the way Linklater stages it—a series of long, flashback-punctuated tracking shots in which the camera simultaneously draws the couple through the streets of Paris and back into their respective pasts. Initial ickiness is swept away by the distinctive narrative rhythms. Hyperconscious of the fleeting time, Celine and Jesse rapidly walk and talk, literally catching up with each other, then sit for a dozen minutes at a café to reestablish the respective fictions of their lives and annotate their earlier meeting. Back on foot, in a dappled bower under light so natural it can't be ignored, they reveal more about their personal entanglements.

Linklater's characters are the most loquacious in American cinema—nearly a match for those of Eric Rohmer. But the raps in *Before Sunset* go beyond the monologues that characterize *Slacker* or *Waking Life* (or even *School of Rock*). Celine and Jesse are alone together; as in *Before Sunrise*, they tumble for each other in a tumble of words. Their dialogue—on the nature of coincidence and memory, getting older and being in the moment, intimations of mortality and the possibility of personal change—is both the subject of the movie and a commentary on it. For now, these stars personify the passage of time. (So does the movie, which takes eighty minutes to tell an eighty-minute story in which the clock is always running.)

None of this would work without the uncanny naturalism of the rapport the actors re-create from the earlier film. Neither Delpy nor Hawke had ever been more appealing than in *Before Sunrise*. His ardency brought out an unexpected warmth in her, while her intelligence inspired a genuine wit in him. They made a great team—the Astaire-Rogers of undergraduate philosophizing—and it's understandable why Linklater gave their digitalized forms a scene in *Waking Life*. Even more than *Eternal Sunshine of the Spotless Mind*, *Before Sunset* dramatizes the effect of love—and no less than that other paradigm of the new romanticism, *Lost in Translation*, *Before Sunset* acknowledges love's evanescence. Brilliantly, Linklater stages the regret scene on one of the tourist boats that work the Seine—there's no reversing the river's flow.

Before Sunset provides two dramas. The first involves Celine and Jesse and, full of surprises that make perfect sense in retrospect, is best appreciated with a spotless mind. The second drama is Linklater's personal tightrope act. Can the filmmaker balance his two stars, their unresolved situation, and his own stringent aesthetic without slipping into sentimentality? I'd say he carries it off—even if this extraordinarily likable movie is two minutes too long to fulfill the melancholy perfection of its title. In every other way, however, *Before Sunset* is all one could wish for in a sequel—it enriches, glosses, and completes the original. [J. Hoberman, 6/30/04]

Belle de Jour (1967)

Dir. Luis Buñuel; Scr. Luis Buñuel and Jean-Claude Carrière
101 min.

The beauty of *Belle de Jour* is the beauty of artistic vigor and intelligence. Given what Luis Buñuel is at sixty-seven and what he has done in forty years and twenty-seven projects and what and whom he had to work with and for, *Belle de Jour* reverberates with the cruel logic of formal necessity. From the opening shot of an open carriage approaching the camera at an oblique ground-level angle to the closing shot of an open carriage passing the camera at an oblique overhead angle, the film progresses inexorably upward, an ascent of assent, from the reverie of suppressed desires to the revelation of fulfilled fantasies. But whose desire and whose fantasies? Buñuel's? His heroine's? Actually, a bit of both.

Severine Serizy, happily married to a handsome young surgeon, goes to work in a house of ill repute, actually less a house than an intimate apartment. The money involved is less the motivation than the pretext for her action. Pierre, her husband, provides for her material needs handsomely, but his respectfully temporizing caresses fail to satisfy her psychic need for brutal degradation, a need awakened by a malodorous molester when she was a child of eight. To preserve a facade of marital respectability, Severine works at her obsessive profession only afternoons from two to five, her matinee schedule causing her to be christened Belle de Jour.

The most striking variation between Joseph Kessel's novel and Buñuel's film is in the latter's elaborately structured dream apparatus. Kessel's Severine never dreams the concrete images of Buñuel's surreal reveries of feminine masochism. There are no floggings in the book as there are in the film, no binding of hands with ropes, no sealing of mouths, no splattering with mud. Kessel's Severine never really dreams at all; she merely recollects the past and anticipates the future. Except for the bells that signal the movement of the horse-drawn carriage, Buñuel uses no music whatsoever. No Simon and Garfunkel, no Donovan, not even the realistically based music of radios and record players. There is no radio or television in the modern world of *Belle de Jour*, but there is a Diner's Club credit card. Buñuel has stripped modernity of its specificity. Thus we are not bothered so much that the horse-drawn carriage is not as likely to figure in the reveries of Severine's (or Catherine Deneuve's) as in the memories of Buñuel's.

Buñuel wants us to understand Severine by contemplating the nature of her obsession. Instead of indulging in Kessel's sentimental psychology by staring into Deneuve's eyes, Buñuel fragments Deneuve's body into its erotic constituents. His shots of feet, hands, legs, shoes, stockings, undergarments, etc., are the shots not only of a fetishist, but of a cubist, a director concerned simultaneously with the parts and their effect on the whole. Buñuel's graceful camera movements convey Deneuve to her sensual destiny through her black patent leather shoes, and to her final reverie through her ringed fingers feeling their way along the furniture with the tactile tenderness of a mystical sensuality—Severine's, Deneuve's, or Buñuel's, it makes little difference.

It is Buñuel himself who is the most devoted patron of chez Madame Anais and the most pathetic admirer of Catharine Deneuve's Severine–Belle de Jour. Never before has Buñuel's view of the spectacle seemed so obliquely Ophülsian in its shy gaze from behind curtains, windows, and even peepholes. Buñuel's love of Severine is greater than Kessel's simply because Buñuel sees Belle de Jour as Severine's liberator. The sensuality of *Belle de Jour* is not metaphorical like Genet's in *The Balcony* or Albee's in *Everything in the Garden*. Even the most radical writers treat prostitution as a symptom of a social malaise and not as a concrete manifestation of a universal impulse. Buñuel reminds us once again in *Belle de Jour* that he is one of the few men of the left not afflicted by Puritanism and bourgeois notions of chastity and fidelity.

The ending of *Belle de Jour* is tantalizingly open. Some critics have suggested that Severine has been cured of her masochistic obsession by becoming Belle de Jour. Hence, the empty carriage at the end. She will no longer take that trip. One French critic has argued that the entire film is a dream, but the big problem with such an argument is Buñuel's visually explicit brand of surrealism. We are such Puritans that we talk of surrealism almost exclusively in the solemn terms of social defiance. Humor is only a means to an end, but not an end in itself. No, never? Well, hardly ever. And in Buñuel's case, laughter serves to disinfect libertinism of its satanic aura. If we can laugh at the prissiness of perversion and the fastidiousness of fetishism not with smug superiority, but with carnal complicity, we become too implicated to remain indifferent.

The entire film turns in upon itself by ending with the question with which it began: "Severine, what are you thinking of?" At the end, she is still dreaming, and who is to say that the dream is any less real or vivid than the reality it accompanies? Certainly not Buñuel's probing but compassionate camera. There are several possible interpretations of Buñuel's ending, but the formal symmetry of the film makes the debate academic. Buñuel is ultimately ambiguous so as not to moralize about his subject. He wishes neither to punish Severine nor reward her. He prefers to contemplate the grace with which she accepts her fate, and Buñuel is nothing if not fatalistic. His fatalism undercuts the suspense of narrative to the extent that there is no intellectual pressure for a resolved ending. [Andrew Sarris, 5/2/68, 5/9/68]

The Bicycle Thief (1948)

Dir. Vittorio De Sica; Scr. Vittorio De Sica and Cesare Zavattini
93 min.

The most influential movement in film history consisted of about twenty movies produced between 1944 and 1952. Italian neorealism was the original new wave. The inspiration for Jean-Luc Godard and John Cassavetes, Satyajit Ray and Ousmane Sembene, André Bazin and cinema verité, neorealism was understood as a double renaissance—both the medium's post–World War II rebirth and a means for representing human experience outside the conventions of the Hollywood entertainment film.

Roberto Rossellini's *Open City* came first. This dramatization of Italian partisans was planned under Nazi occupation and went into production only weeks after Rome's liberation in May 1944. Rossellini shot mainly on the street, using whatever 35mm short ends he could scrounge. Such pragmatism matched the film's urgent quality—many early viewers thought they were watching a newsreel. After an American GI purchased the rights for thirteen thousand dollars, *Open City* opened in February 1946 in New York and ran for two years; its reception at the first Cannes Film Festival, in May 1946, was scarcely less enthusiastic.

Open City created the neorealist paradigm—location shoots using available light, long takes, and few close-ups; postsynchronized vernacular dialogue; working-class protagonists played by nonactors (especially children); and open-ended narratives. But it was *The Bicycle Thief* (1948), directed by the Fascist-era matinee idol Vittorio De Sica from a script by veteran screenwriter Cesare Zavattini, that parlayed that paradigm into the most universally praised movie produced anywhere on planet Earth during the first decade after World War II.

The Bicycle Thief was the latest manifestation of a recurring impulse—the desire to wrest a narrative movie from the flux of daily life. Zavattini had expressed the desire to make a film that would do no more than follow a man through the city for ninety minutes, and, in some ways, *The Bicycle Thief* is that film. Bazin, who would be neorealism's key celebrant, praised *The Bicycle Thief*'s premise as "truly insignificant . . . A workman spends a whole day looking in vain in the streets of Rome for the bicycle someone has stolen from him."

If *The Bicycle Thief* understood neorealism as a style, Bazin appreciated it as "pure cinema. . . . No more actors, no more story, no more sets . . . the perfect aesthetic illusion of reality." In fact, De Sica created a neorealist superspectacle. Six writers worked on the script; at one point, the project was even pitched to Hollywood producer David O. Selznick, who proposed Cary Grant to play Ricci, the unemployed protagonist given a job putting up posters. De Sica countered by requesting Henry Fonda, a star with a marked resemblance to the eventual lead, steelworker Lamberto Maggiorani.

Although the three leads were all nonactors, *The Bicycle Thief*'s modest $133,000 budget was far larger than those of previous neorealist films, including De Sica's own *Shoeshine*. De Sica used many more locations and extras—forty market vendors hired for a single scene—and even effects (fire hoses employed to simulate rain-soaked streets). The production was deliberate. The crowds were rehearsed and the camera moves choreographed. Editing took two months.

Scarcely a story found in the street, *The Bicycle Thief* is an allegory at once timeless and topical. (Among other things, it reflects the battle for the lucrative Italian movie market. The first poster the luckless Ricci puts up is for the Rita Hayworth vehicle *Gilda*. There were fifty-four movies made in Italy in 1948 and ten times as many imported from the United States.) Italian unemployment was at 22 percent, but Ricci, who has not worked in two years, is also a version of the urban everyman. As a type, he had inhabited the movies since the dawn of the twentieth century.

Ricci is a member of the crowd, a walker in the city. He's one step up the social ladder from Chaplin's Little Tramp, in that he has a wife and a child. Throughout, De Sica's mise-en-scène emphasizes the urban mass (waiting for jobs and streetcars) and its mass-produced objects—the piles of pawned linens, the rows of bicycles. Translated correctly from the Italian, the title should really be the more provocatively totalizing *Bicycle Thieves*.

The city is alternately empty and teeming. Although shot in an authentic environment, *The Bicycle Thief* is no less stylized in its way than the other European masterpiece of 1948, Jean Cocteau's *Orpheus*. There are few establishing shots. Unlike Rossellini's, De Sica's Rome is a baffling, decentered labyrinth. The stolen bicycle is swallowed up by the city itself. People disappear to reappear within the urban flux.

Where the optimistic *Open City* celebrated a potential alliance between communists and Catholics, *The Bicycle Thief* parodies both party and church as unable to help the humiliated Ricci. Indeed, the hero's experience of these institutions, as well as of the police, borders on the Kafkaesque. There is no justice. Ricci's life is ruled by a catch-22: he needs a bicycle to get the job that will enable him to buy a bicycle. Not for nothing is the bicycle brand-named Fides ("Faith") or the innocent vision of Ricci's seven-year-old son Bruno (one of the greatest kids in the history of cinema, played by Enzo Staiola) increasingly privileged.

Although not a comedy, *The Bicycle Thief* was inevitably compared to Chaplin in its content, its structure, its pathos, and its universality. (The mournful music and circular narrative predict the post-neorealist mannerism of Federico Fellini.) *The Bicycle Thief* looks back at the nickelodeon and forward to the European art film. De Sica's masterpiece was not so much part of a new wave as the crest of an old one—the epitome of movies as a popular modernism. [J. Hoberman, 9/30/98]

The Birds (1963)

Dir. Alfred Hitchcock; Scr. Evan Hunter
119 min.

Drawing from the relatively invisible literary talents of Daphne Du Maurier and Evan Hunter, Alfred Hitchcock has fashioned a major work of cinematic art, and *cinematic* is the operative term here, not *literary* or *sociological*. There is one sequence in *The Birds* where the heroine is in an outboard motor boat churning across the bay, while the hero's car is racing around the shore road to intercept her on the other side. This race is seen entirely from the girl's point of view. Suddenly, near shore, the camera picks up a seagull swooping down on our heroine. For just a second, the point of view is shifted, and we are permitted to see the bird before its victim does. The director has apparently broken an aesthetic rule for the sake of a shock effect—gull pecks girl. Yet this momentary incursion of the objective on the subjective is remarkably consistent with the meaning of the film.

The theme, after all, is complacency, as the director has stated. When we first meet each of the major characters, their infinite capacity for self-absorption is emphasized. Tippi Hedren's bored socialite is addicted to elaborately time-consuming practical jokes. Rod Taylor's self-righteous lawyer flaunts his arrogant sensuality. Suzanne Pleshette, his ex-fiancée, wallows in self-pity, and Jessica Tandy, his possessive mother, cringes from her fear of loneliness. With such complex, unsympathetic characters to contend with, the audience quite naturally begins to identify with the point of view of the birds, actually the inhuman point of view. As in *Psycho*, Hitchcock succeeds in implicating his audience to such an extent that the much-criticized, apparently anticlimactic ending finds the audience more bloodthirsty than the birds. Although three people are killed and many others assaulted by man's fine feathered friends, critics and spectators have demanded more gore and more victims.

In *Psycho*, there is a moment after Tony Perkins has run Janet Leigh's car into a swamp when the car stops sinking. One could almost hear the audience holding its breath until the car resumed its descent below. At that first intake of breath, the audience became implicated in the fantasy of the perfect crime. In *The Birds*, the audience is similarly implicated, but this time in the fantasy of annihilation. The point Hitchcock seems to be making is that morality is not a function of sympathy but a rigorous test of principles. If we can become even momentarily indifferent to the fate of a promiscuous blonde (Janet Leigh in *Psycho*) or a spoiled playgirl (Tippi Hedren in *The Birds*), we have clearly failed the test.

As symbols of evil and disorder, Hitchcock's winged bipeds lend themselves to many possible interpretations—Freudian, Thomistic, Existential, among others—but imaginative spectators can draw their own analogies. What is beyond speculation is the strikingly visual potential of the subject. One penultimate shot of a row of blackbirds perched magisterially above the fearfully departing humans is worth a thousand words on man's unworthiness. Hitchcock's dark humor is as impressive as ever on both human and ornithological planes. There is something indescribably funny in the familiar gesture of a man winding up to throw a rock at some crows before being deterred by his prudent girlfriend. Her "let sleeping birds perch" philosophy explodes its grotesque context into half-fragmented memories of human presumption.

Yet in the midst of all the human guilt, the idea of innocence survives. When the survivors of the bird attacks venture past thousands of

The Birds, 1963; directed by Alfred Hitchcock; written by Evan Hunter

their erstwhile enemies, now ominously passive, the hero's eleven-year-old sister asks him to return to the house for her caged love birds. "They did no harm," she insists. The audience fears and anticipates the worst, but nothing happens. The caged love birds do not arouse the free hordes of the species. Instead, these two guiltless creatures seem to clear the path to the car as if the rediscovery of innocence were yet the only hope of the world.

The Birds finds Hitchcock at the summit of his artistic powers. His is the only contemporary style that unites the divergent classical traditions of Murnau (camera movement) and Eisenstein (montage). If formal excellence is still a valid criterion for film criticism, and there are those who will argue that it is not, then *The Birds* is probably the picture of the year. [Andrew Sarris, 4/4/63]

However familiar, lionized, and patronized as a genre goof, Alfred Hitchcock's *The Birds* remains the overdiscussed filmmaker's strangest, most consciously surrealist film—indeed, it is the most deeply irrational film ever made by a Hollywood studio. The nature-gone-berserk scenario, now a pop-cult reflex, is still remarkable for having no reasonable foundation, so the extraordinarily evocative set pieces—the bird-covered jungle gym, the attack on the phone booth, the torrent of birds pouring in through the fireplace, the final world-of-perched-birds apocalypse—suggest less an exercise in terror/suspense than a nervous, dreamy dose of Hollywood Dada. Hitchcock has always been greater for his moments of madness and passion than for his lauded machine-like ingenuity, and whether you saw it in 1963, on TV since, or see it now, *The Birds* feels, for all of its contrivance, like a primal howl of dread. Moreover, Hitch's infamous tricks—the discombobulating process shots, the lurking soundtrack, the editing flourishes (like the three still shots of Tippi Hedren's alarmed kisser as she watches the gas station explode)—aren't effective narrative tools; they're creepy, stylized visions of a reality jacked into a disoriented panic. Along with *Vertigo*, *The Birds* may be mainstream American film's most fascinating psychotic episode. [Michael Atkinson, 8/25/98]

Blow-Up (1966)

Dir. Michelangelo Antonioni; Scr. Michelangelo Antonioni and Tonino Guerra
111 min.

Michelangelo Antonioni's *Blow-Up* is the movie of the year. It provides more thrills, chills, and fancy frissons than any other movie this year.

Blow-Up is never dramatically effective in terms of any meaningful confrontations of character. The dialogue is self-consciously spare and elliptical in a sub-Pinteresque style. Fortunately, the twenty-four-hour duration of the plot makes it possible for Antonioni to disguise most of the film as a day in the life of a mod photographer in swinging London town. What conflict there is in *Blow-Up* is captured in the clash between vernal greens on one plane and venal blues, reds, yellows, pinks, and purples on another. The natural world is arrayed against the artificial scene; conscience is deployed against convention.

Blow-Up abounds with what Truffaut calls "privileged moments," intervals of beautiful imagery while nothing seems to be happening to develop the drama or enhance the narrative. Very early in the film, the camera confronts the photographer's long black convertible head-on at a crossroads. Suddenly, the entire screen is blotted out by a blue bus streaking across from right to left, followed quickly by a yellow truck. That sudden splash of blue and yellow defines Antonioni's mood and milieu better than any set of speeches ever could. Wherever Antonioni's camera goes, doors, fences, poles, even buildings seem to have been freshly painted for the sake of chromatic contrast or consistency. Part of Antonioni's ambivalence toward his subject is reflected in the conflicting temptations of documentary and decoration. After painting the trees in *Red Desert* a petrified gray, Antonioni feels no compunctions about painting a phone booth in *Blow-Up* a firehouse red. If reality is not expressive enough, a paintbrush will take up the slack.

The ultimate beauty of *Blow-Up* is derived from the artistic self-revelation of the director. *Blow-Up* is a statement of the artist not on life, but on art itself and the consuming passion of an artist's life. As David Hemmings moves gracefully through offbeat sites in London, his body writhing to meet the challenges of every new subject, we feel that Antonioni himself is intoxicated by the sensuous surfaces of the world he wishes to satirize. Curiously, he is more satisfying when he succumbs to the sensuousness than when he stands outside it. The unsuccessful sequences—the rock 'n' roll session, the marijuana party, the alienation conversations—suffer from the remoteness of cold chronicles recorded by an outsider. Antonioni is more successful when he forgets his ennui long enough to photograph a magnificent mod fashion spectacle, which transcends the grotesquely artificial creatures that lend themselves to the illusion. Even more spectacular is the teeny bopper sandwich orgy that digresses from the main plot.

The fact that Antonioni can be entertaining even when he is not enlightening makes the eruption of his plot all the more stunning. It starts simmering in the midst of apparent aimlessness. The photographer-protagonist drifts into a park, passes by a tennis court, photographs pigeons, then stalks a pair of lovers up a hill. Here Hemmings becomes a weakened voyeur as he scurries behind fences and trees with his telescopic lens. This is raw, spontaneous Life in an ominously leafy setting. Vanessa Redgrave, she of the incredibly distracting long legs and elongated spinal column extended vertically through an ugly blue-plaid mini-suit, runs up to Hemmings to plead for the pictures, but everything in the movie has been so fragmented up to this point that we accept her trivial invasion-of-privacy argument at face value. Hemmings refuses to return the negatives and later tricks her into accepting bogus negatives while he "blows-up" the real ones. What seemed like a tryst in the park is magnified into a murder. Death, which has hovered over Antonioni's films from the beginning of his career, makes its grand entrance in a photographer's studio through the eyes of a camera, which sees truth whereas the eyes of a photographer see only reality. This is the paradox of Antonioni's vision of art: the further away we draw from reality, the closer we get to the truth.

From the moment of his artistic triumph, the protagonist becomes morally impotent. He has discovered truth but is unable to pass judgment or secure justice. Antonioni has come out in the open with a definitive description of his sensibility, half Mod, half Marxist. Unlike Fellini, however, Antonioni has converted his own confession into a genuine movie that objectifies his obsessions without whining or self-pity. As befits the classical tradition of movie-making, *Blow-Up* can be enjoyed by moviegoers who have never heard of Antonioni. [Andrew Sarris, 12/29/66]

Blue Velvet (1986)

Dir./Scr. David Lynch
120 min.

Blue Velvet is a film of ecstatic creepiness—a stunning vindication for writer-director David Lynch. This is the first time since his midnight classic *Eraserhead* that Lynch has vented the full force of his sensibility, and the result is astonishing.

Continually unpredictable, *Blue Velvet* is generically a teen coming-of-age film crossed with a noir. But Lynch is weirdest precisely when attempting to be most normal. (He attacks the material with the sublime discordance of Charles Ives singing "Rally Round the Flag.") *Blue Velvet* could be described as *Archie and Veronica in the Twilight Zone* or John Hughes meets Buñuel or *The Hardy Boys on Mars*, but no single phrase captures the film's boldly alien perspective, its tenderness and disgust.

Ostensibly set in the present, *Blue Velvet* suggests the 1950s the way

Eraserhead evoked some entropic, postnuclear future. The film celebrates and ruthlessly defamiliarizes a comfortable, picture-postcard facade of malt shoppes, football fields, and rec-room basements—not to mention Roy Orbison and film narrative itself. For Lynch, the veil of appearances is precisely that; he effortlessly attains the downbeat visionary quality Francis Coppola was groping for in the overwrought *Rumble Fish*.

In one sense, *Blue Velvet* is the continuous subversion of apple-pie normalcy (call it "Blue Velveeta"). In another, it represents a terrifying collapse of authority that, as if through a trapdoor, plunges Lynch's college-age protagonist Jeffrey (Kyle MacLachlan, a kind of air-brushed doppelgänger for Lynch himself) into a murky vortex of sex, death, and mutilation, where corruption of the body and corruption of the body politic are part of the same mindless cosmic drama.

Lynch is basically a non-narrative filmmaker, and even when *Blue Velvet*'s plot becomes apparent, you still can't help wonder what the "normal" version of the script might be. From the opening evocation of idyllic Lumberton (the town that *knows* how much wood a woodchuck chucks), the film is instantly and insistently bizarre. To the accompaniment of the lachrymose Bobby Vinton title ballad, the camera caresses an incandescent white picket fence fronted by glowing red roses—a kind of kryptonite Kodachrome effect that dissolves into graciously slo-mo calendar images of friendly firemen and solicitous crossing guards. For all these guardians of public safety, however, the surface of Lumberton seems as gaudy and fragile as an Easter egg, and surely enough, it's immediately shattered by a ridiculous catastrophe. Watering his lawn, Jeffrey's father is stung by a bee and collapses. For Lynch, this is like a message from beyond—he uses an escalating series of mega-close-ups to literally rub your nose in the terrifying profusion of life.

Did I say nose? Returning home across a vacant lot after visiting his grotesquely hospitalized father, Jeffrey discovers a severed, slightly moldering, ant-covered human ear. Like a good Lumberton lad, he gingerly puts it in a paper bag and brings it to the police station. "Yes, that's a human ear all right," Detective Williams (George Dickerson) assures him with the impersonal solicitude of an airline captain or a hologram. With his haunting juxtaposition, brazen non sequiturs, and eroticized derangement of the ordinary, Lynch has affinities to classic surrealism. But Lynch's surrealism seems more intuitive than programmatic. For him, the normal is a defense against the irrational rather than vice versa.

The story behind the ear becomes Jeffrey's obsession, leading him—with the ambivalent help of Sandy (Laura Dern), Detective Williams's engagingly gawky daughter—to explore the Deep River apartments, a musty dive out of *Eraserhead*, where the lushly carnal, bewigged Dorothy (Isabella Rossellini), a nightclub chanteuse at once Madonna and whore, makes her enigmatic home. The film features a dual sexual initiation that's all the more powerful for being only partially expressed. *Blue Velvet* is a film about what goes on behind closed doors.

Jeffrey's baptism in the Deep River is best experienced without too much prior knowledge. Suffice it to say that *Blue Velvet* is ornately framed by the euphemistic "facts of life" (birds, bees, flowers), while the heart of the film is a twenty-minute sex scene replete with voyeurism, rape, sadomasochism, implied castration, all manner of verbal and physical abuse, elaborate fetishism, and a ritualized kinkiness for which there is no name. It's a sequence Alfred Hitchcock might have given a year off his life to direct—appalling, erotic, appallingly funny, and tragic.

Given the surprises of *Blue Velvet*'s story, I'm inclined to write around the film's action and celebrate its texture—the hilariously stilted education-film dialogue (people will be quoting it for years), the transcendently seedy compositions, the dank aroma of skid-row porn that even the sunniest sequences exude, Dorothy's definitively lugubrious rendition of the title ballad. While *Eraserhead* had a dreamlike flow, *Blue Velvet* is hallucinated and hyperreal. The colors are oversaturated, the motion blandly discontinuous. There's a schizophrenic vividness that's underscored by the film's microcosmic backdrop and absolute representation of moral qualities. "I'm *not* crazy. I know the difference between right and wrong," Dorothy assures Jeffrey pathetically, as if by rote.

Blue Velvet is a triumph of overall geekiness—a fat man in shades walking a tiny dog, the deadpan Dick-and-Jane detective who wears his gun and badge in the house, the references to Jehovah's witnesses, strategic uses of the world's loudest flushing toilet. As the demiurge of raunchy, lower-class sexual menace, Dennis Hopper is a virtual

Harkonnen on Main Street—a violent, volatile hothead, periodically dosing himself with ether to further addle his turbulent, fuck-obsessed stream of consciousness.

There hasn't been an American studio film so rich, so formally controlled, so imaginatively cast and wonderfully acted, and so charged with its maker's psychosexual energy since *Raging Bull*. But *Blue Velvet*'s unflinching blend of raw pathology and Kabuki sweetness is pretty much sui generis. One doesn't know what to make of it, which may be as disconcerting for some as it is exciting for others. In some respects, it is as exhausting as it is exhilarating—movies have become so depleted, one scarcely expects to be confronted with this much *stuff*. The more you see it, the more you get. [J. Hoberman, 9/23/86]

The last real earthquake to hit cinema was David Lynch's *Blue Velvet*—I'm sure directors throughout the film world felt the earth move beneath their feet and couldn't sleep the night of their first encounter with it back in 1986—and screens trembled again and again with diminishing aftershocks spread out over the next decade as these picture makers attempted to mount their own exhilarating psychic cataclysms. But no one could quite match the traumatizing combination of horrific, comedic, aural, and subliminal effects Lynch rumbled out in this masterpiece—not even Lynch himself in the fun-filled years that followed before he recombined with himself to invent *The Straight Story* and *Mulholland Drive*. Lynch was born in 1946, part of that first litter of boomers sired by the paranoia of unmedicated war vets jittering and fisting their way through the sudden proliferation of film noir product. In spite of Lynch presenting his tale in the comforting saturated Kodachromes his generation associates with the "innocence" of their childhood years, there is much of what noir does best in *Blue Velvet*: Kyle MacLachlan's Jeffrey Beaumont slips past the safety rails and hops right into a raging maelstrom of guilt and evil as blithely as any noir protagonist ever did; and Dennis Hopper's Frank Booth is just the necessary incarnation of nightmare that Steve Cochrane's Eddie Roman was in Arthur Ripley's *The Chase* (1946), the most surrealism-propelled crime film ever to sleepwalk out of the Dark City. But perhaps it is Isabella Rossellini's femme fatale Dorothy Vallens that is *Blue Velvet*'s greatest gift to posterity. Director and neophyte actress collaborated to retool the old genre's often-stock figure, to deglamorize and humiliate the supermodel, to knead her pulpy nakedness into a bruise-colored odalisque of inseminated sensualities and untrusting ferocity. There is something sharply porno-entomological, something of the implacable godless terror with which insects mate and devour, and something terrifyingly true in the bearing of this bravely performed character. Nuns at Rossellini's old high school in Rome held a series of special masses for her redemption after the release of this film—still a hilarious, red-hot poker to the brain after twenty years. [Guy Maddin, 3/1/06]

Breathless (1960)

Dir. Jean-Luc Godard; Scr. Jean-Luc Godard
87 min.

Nine years ago, I fell in love with *Breathless*. Time has aged her since, but poems of chaos, having little structure, are gloriously free from decay. They die young, but as the novelist Parvulesco (Jean-Pierre Melville) of the film says when asked his ambition in life: "Devenir immortel . . . et puis mourir." *À Bout de Souffle* is the immortal spirit of Rimbaud's cry: "I shall lose and come to regard as sacred the disorder of my mind!"

On a hot summer day in 1959, Jean-Paul Belmondo stumbled down la rue Campagne Première breathless, a bullet in his back, dropped to the pavement, smoked out the butt of his Gitane, grimaced at Jean Seberg, told her, "C'est vraiment dégueulasse," closed his own eyes, died, and entered my imagination forever. I suppose because, more than Brando, Welles, Olivier, and so on, he was what I really wanted to be then. As I saw a movie and was still young and fanciful enough to imitate, for several days at least, a fictional lifestyle (never to much good except eventually my own disillusionment), so Belmondo himself copped his lifestyle in the movies. The difference was he stuck by it. If he bought Bogart, then it was to his glory he played him to the end. "Vivre dangereusement jusqu' au bout," proclaims a movie poster on the Champs-Elysées. Patricia turns to Michel, saying,

"I want to know what's behind your mask." Michel takes his cigarette out of his mouth and, mimicking Bogart, caresses his lips with his thumb, telling us all we have to know. Belmondo alias Lazlo Kovacs alias Michel Poiccard is an image of an image in an endless hall of mirrors and nothing more. It's authentic and it consists of Bogart's integrity, to which, if in parody, Belmondo is scrupulously honest.

Breathless is more yet. It's like a soft easy edge of wind. It's sticking somebody up in a bathroom because suddenly it occurs that nothing in the world could be so natural and easy and not a "crime"; it's beating up a cowardly garage owner who needs a good beating up; it's stealing cars because people have cars and why should they have cars in the first place if I can't take them; it's killing a policeman because suddenly he wants to put me in a cage and who is he to do so because I drove too fast down a country road shooting at the sun because the sun is sitting there wanting to be shot at, in a world full of double crossers, crooks, thieves, con men, ratters, and lovers who betray because it is their nature to betray. And in the void what is it you would choose, Seberg asks, "grief or nothing?" "Grief," Michel answers, "is a waste of time. I take nothing. . . ." and on nothing, "les palais de notre chimères" (the palace of our illusions) out of imagination will be built.

Twelve years have since passed, and I've grown older into my twenties. A certain amount of adventure is behind me now, and I'm developing my own lifestyle, which, having never stolen a car or killed a policeman, in no way resembles Belmondo's. So I see *Breathless* again, not without a little irritation gnawing at me as I think how moral I've become, and what sort of social consciousness is it that leads me to condemn this flaunting young hoodlum, all the while secretly preferring, by some curious double standard, the maturer nihilism of *Weekend*. It makes sense, though, doesn't it, the dictum being that the greater the crime, the more people cannibalized, the more dignity there is to it? Is *Breathless* passé? Yes, to those of us who can only live in the present, with a narrow but penetrating view out of which revolutions are made. Godard himself will disown *Breathless* because he is a crusader, and *Breathless* is a classic for which he has no use. [Oliver Stone, 5/11/72]

Café Lumière (2003)

Dir. Hou Hsiao-hsien; Scr. Hou Hsiao-hsien and Chu T'ien-wen
103 min.

Dedicated to Yasujiro Ozu (and commissioned by Ozu's old studio, Shochiku, on the occasion of the Japanese master's centenary), *Café Lumière* is, in some ways, Hou Hsiao-hsien's melancholy rumination on the traditional Japanese family that was already in decline a half-century ago, when Ozu made his most celebrated domestic dramas. Hou's movie is introduced with the classic Shochiku logo and begins with a low-angle shot of a streetcar that might have been framed by Ozu. But for all Hou's supposed stylistic and temperamental affinities to Ozu, as well as a few affectionate quotes from *Tokyo Story*, *Café Lumière* is hardly a pastiche.

If anything, *Café Lumière* suggests an Ozu film in reverse—it's mainly ambience "pillow shots," with bits of narrative serving as punctuation. Back in Tokyo after a stay in Taiwan, Hou's young protagonist Yoko (Japanese pop star Hitoto Yo in her first movie) is subdued and opaque as she reoccupies her microscopic apartment and reestablishes contact with her equally undemonstrative family and friends. No one is particularly voluble; the lengthiest conversations are conducted over the phone. The perverse eloquence of *Café Lumière* lies in the way in which most things remain unsaid. Feelings are largely unexpressed, the better to surface in Yoko's dreams. These, it turns out, are largely mediated by Maurice Sendak's *Outside Over There*—the tale of a girl who rescues her baby sister from goblins—which Yoko realizes she read as a child.

Café Lumière is slow and quiet, with plenty of activities, mainly the eating of meals, that unfold in real time—the rapt attention given Yoko's tempura dinner recalls Chantal Akerman's *Jeanne Dielman* in its uninflected dailiness. Indeed, the movie is essentially plotless. Like a surrealist heroine, Yoko wanders the city on some mysterious project—taking photos, asking questions, and looking for vanished landmarks. (Ultimately, it becomes apparent that she is researching the life of Japan-schooled, early-twentieth-century Chinese composer Jiang Wenye, whose modernist music underscores the action.)

The metropolis may be the real protagonist—as though Hou is taking literally the title *Tokyo Story*. There's a stunningly beautiful composition of Yoko on a train, gazing out the window as the city rushes by, and she passes without seeing her friend Hajime (Tadanobu Asano). A bookstore clerk who is silently in love with Yoko, he rides the trains to gather sounds and images for a computer-based artwork.

Hou lavishes one of his few close-ups on the virtual "womb" of trains that Hajime has constructed on his laptop; despite its cramped spaces, *Café Lumière* is filmed almost entirely in middle shot. Hou's discretion would make Ozu seem forward. When Yoko visits her parents' house, the kitchen where her stepmother is shown working is scarcely more than a ribbon running down the center of the screen. And the viewer could easily miss the single sentence, half an hour into the movie, when Yoko informs the older woman that she's pregnant.

Although pegged as an author of contemplative mood pieces, Hou's originality as a filmmaker has much to do with both his handling of historical material and his daringly counterintuitive narrative structures. So it is with *Café Lumière*, where, as noted by Tony Rayns in a *Cinema Scope* piece that interestingly cites two longer abandoned versions, the ignorance of history serves as a historical marker, and most of the story tumbles out in the movie's final minutes.

Even this small eruption of melodrama is quickly subsumed in Hou's fascination with the metropolis. Yoko is last seen, as spotted by Hajime, sleeping on the train. She is dreaming perhaps of that other story, whose secret connections seem to course beneath the reflected city of waking consciousness. [J. Hoberman, 6/2/05]

Ceddo (1977)

Dir./Scr. Ousmane Sembene
120 min.

Ousmane Sembene, the Senegalese filmmaker, wears a mantle of imposing moral authority. No filmmaker of any time or place has achieved quite the same quintessential role as artistic spokesman of his nation. In American cinema, I can think only of Raoul Walsh within the system, and King Vidor without, as filmmakers with similar tap roots into the national soul when they dealt with themes of empire building and class-consciousness.

Sembene's cinema is cast in pageant form, in which the raw forces of culture, politics, and religion clash on an uncluttered stage. It is a form of public, primal art, predating the psychological concerns and the self-involvement that has so preoccupied modern Western civilization. Sembene's manner resembles that of Euripides, who, while working far outside of his character projections, invited the audience to delve deeply into the forces at work in the country.

Ceddo has the deceptive simplicity of a medieval morality play. The comparison is apt because the story is set in a seventeenth-century feudal village; while the costumes and the mannerisms remain uniquely Senegalese, the customs are reminiscent of Europe in the Middle Ages. The village, obviously a microcosm of Senegal, is introduced at the time when the influence of a white Christian priest—and his single native convert—is waning. There is a French slave trader who is important to the power structure only as an agent who can offer guns in exchange for human beings. The central concern, however, is the totalitarian putsch being engineered by a cadre of Muslims, who have converted the royal family and its councilors, but not the *ceddo* (the villagers or peasants).

A champion of the *ceddo* activates the plot by a ritualistic kidnapping of a princess (again recalling the plots of Euripides built around the "kidnapping" of Helen). His act is a formal protest against the proselytizing of the Muslims and the suppression of the villagers' ancient fetish religion. He stakes out a public arena and awaits all challengers, who are expected on horseback with their own attendants carrying the royal staff.

As in the Greek plays, the format lends itself to debates between opposing power blocs and the selection of individual champions as the spokesmen for each point of view. Sembene seems to have come to this turn instinctually. He relishes the public debate, always a highlight of his films, and the typing of individuals into champions allows him to utilize his beautiful but amateur actors to their full extent. Sembene, with wondrous simplicity, achieves an operatic orchestration of raw forces similar to Eisenstein's *Alexander Nevsky* and Kurosawa's *Seven Samurai*.

From another aspect, *Ceddo* seizes small details of the present and expands them into awesome portents of the future. A rebel nephew of the king visualizes a fully Christianized nation; the princess has a vision of life with the champion's old-time religion; scenes of branded slaves are accompanied by a soulful American spiritual. Only the Muslims, terrifying in their righteous intolerance, dare impose their future immediately on the subjugated peasants, who are prostrated, shaved, and renamed at gunpoint.

Sembene is overtly anti-Islamic in *Ceddo*, but this stance is not an abiding fixation. His whole career demonstrates that he is the true artist who is subversive on all topics. Sembene takes on both the ancient religion and French colonialism in *Emitai* (1972), and Muslim polygamy and Western imperialism in *Xala* (1974)—not with axes to grind, but with the more severe test of a great rational dramatist, testing the worth of ideas in the public forum. Sembene discourses in the face of tigers. He exposes the past and present forces at work in the Republic of Senegal for his nation's and the world's scrutiny. [Tom Allen, 2/20/78]

Céline and Julie Go Boating (1974)

Dir. Jacques Rivette; Scr. Juliet Berto, Eduardo de Gregorio, and Jacques Rivette

193 min.

Jacques Rivette's *Céline and Julie Go Boating* seems the quintessential French movie of the last fifteen years. Here, the narrative experiments of Alain Resnais and Marguerite Duras are infused with the movie-crazed energy of early New Wave films like *Shoot the Piano Player* or *Zazie* to arrive at an original and entertaining metaphor for film watching and, perhaps, film history.

Rivette was the first of the *Cahiers du Cinéma* critics to turn director, and, with the exception of Godard, he's been the most challenging and innovative filmmaker of the group. For him, *Céline and Julie* was something of a breather. It was made in the aftermath of *Out 1* (1971)—shown only once in its original thirteen-hour form—and it's far lighter, although scarcely less elaborate a fiction, than his previous New York releases. The brooding epic of beatnik paranoia *Paris Belongs to Us* (1960) turned the Left Bank into a murky, conspiratorial labyrinth, while *L'Amour Fou* (1968), a four-and-a-half-hour depiction of a theatrical couple's psychic disintegration, could've been called "The Children of Paradise Play It as It Lays." By contrast, the Paris of *Céline and Julie* is airy and verdant, and the film's plot has the ingenuous quality of a fantasy concocted by two imaginative kids during a long summer vacation.

Julie (Dominique Labourier) is a librarian and a student of the occult; the more flamboyant Céline (Juliet Berto) works as a stage *magicienne* in a seedy Montmarte cabaret, like a pouty Morticia Addams playing "the Blue Angel." Their paths cross, and they form a friendship based on playful role swapping and mutual mind reading. This rapport, with its schoolyard pranks and submerged eroticism, forms a subtext that grounds the film's whimsy: Céline can tell her friend a tall tale about some sinister doings in a mysterious house, and the place will not only exist, but Julie will have a photograph of it at the bottom of an old toy chest.

When the two take turns investigating the house, they find that they can remember what they've experienced there only by sucking on the sweets they've taken away after each visit. A film-within-a-film is a characteristic Rivette device, and under the influence of their magic candy Céline and Julie relive fragments of these blanked-out excursions, commenting and giggling as though watching a movie. The situation becomes more explicitly cinematic when they discover that the house is offering a continuous showing of the same adventure: Bulle Ogier and Marie-France Pisier slinking around in murderous competition for the affections of Barbet Schroeder, a fatuously morose widower with a young daughter. With each trip, this stagy triangle becomes increasingly unscrambled, as the heroines' high-spirited, improvisatory style alternates with the overdetermined, claustrophobic atmosphere of the haunted house. It is as though Jean Renoir and Fritz Lang were battling for control of the universe until, in a very funny final go-round, Céline and Julie intervene in the melodrama to rescue its victim.

Whenever one of the heroines appears amid the phantoms, it's in the guise of a nurse, and as they align themselves against a trio of dreary adults in a battle for a child's life, Rivette's film simulates the satisfying resolution of some forgotten but endlessly replayed nightmare.

Although Rivette's cast didn't actually improvise before the camera, they all collaborated on the development of *Céline and Julie*'s plot. The payoff is a strong sense of collective mythmaking and a film that's more suggestive than hermetic in its mysteries. But the surfeit of privileged moments—many of which should have been purged in the editing room—begins to cloy in a three-hour film already sustaining the natural leisure of Rivette's mise-en-scène and the twice-told aspect of a fairytale structure. After an evocative beginning, *Céline and Julie* runs out of gas somewhere in its second hour, and one must wait for Rivette to push his extravagant vehicle over the hump. He does, and the film—building suspense and momentum—accelerates into a brilliant, bravura finish. [J. Hoberman, 10/23/78]

The Chelsea Girls (1966)

Dir. Andy Warhol; Scr. Ronald Tavel and Andy Warhol
210 min.

After seeing Andy Warhol's new film *Chelsea Girls*, I was walking along the street and talking to myself. There was no doubt in my mind that I had just seen a very important film. But if I am going to write anything about it, people will say I am crazy.

What is *Chelsea Girls*? It is Warhol's most ambitious work to date. It is also probably his most important work to date. It is an epic movie-novel. During the four hours that the movie lasts, a huge gallery of people pass by, a gallery of complex lives, faces, fates. The film is conceived as a series of rooms at the Chelsea Hotel, two rooms projected side by side at the same time, with different people in different rooms or, sometimes, overlapping. Many strange lives open before our eyes, some of them enacted, some real—but always very real, even when they are fake—since this is the Chelsea Hotel of our fantasy, of our mind. Lovers, dope addicts, pretenders, homosexuals, lesbians, heterosexuals, sad fragile girls and hard tough girls; quiet conversations, doing nothing, telephone conversations, passing the time; social games, drug games, sex games. I know no other film, with the exception of *The Birth of a Nation*, in which such a wide gallery of people has been presented as in this film. We don't always understand what they are talking about, only short fragments of conversations really reach us clearly. As the time goes, this gallery of people and lives grows into a complex human hive. The film in its complex and overlapping structure, in its simultaneity of lives before our eyes, comes closest to Joyce. Forgive me this sacrilegious comparison—really, this is the first time that I dare mention Joyce in connection with cinema. This is the first time that I see in cinema an interesting solution of narrative techniques that enable cinema to present life in the complexity and richness achieved by modern literature.

Chelsea Girls has a classical grandeur about it, something from Victor Hugo. Its grandeur is the grandeur of its subject, the human scope of its subject. And it is a tragic film. The lives that we see in this film are full of desperation, hardness, and terror. It's there for everybody to see and to think about. Every work of art helps us to understand ourselves by describing to us those aspects of our lives that we either know little of or fear. It's there in black on white before our eyes, this collection of desperate creatures, the desperate part of our being, the avant garde of our being. And one of the amazing things about this film is that the people in it are not really actors; or if they are acting, their acting becomes unimportant, it becomes part of their personalities, and there they are, totally real, with their transformed, intensified selves. The screen acting is expanded by an ambiguity between real and unreal. This is part of Warhol's filming technique, and very often it is a painful technique. There is the girl who walks from scene to scene crying, real tears, really hurt; a girl, under LSD probably, who isn't even aware, or only half aware that she is being filmed; the "priest" who goes into a fit of rage (a real rage) and slaps the girl right and left (a real slap, not the actor's slap) when she begins to talk about God—in probably the most dramatic religious sequence ever filmed. Toward the end, the film bursts into color—not the usual color-movie color but a dramatized, exalted, screaming red color of terror.

No doubt most of the critics and "normal" audiences will dismiss *Chelsea Girls* as having nothing to do either with cinema or "real" life. Most of the critics and viewers do not realize that the artist, no matter what he is showing, is also mirroring or forecasting our own lives. The terror and desperation of *Chelsea Girls* is a holy terror (an expression that, I was told, Warhol uses in reference to his work): it's our godless civilization approaching the zero point. It's not homosexuality, it's not lesbianism, it's not heterosexuality: the terror and hardness that we see in *Chelsea Girls* is the same terror and hardness that is burning Vietnam, and it's the essence and blood of our culture, of our ways of living: this is the Great Society. [Jonas Mekas, 9/29/66]

Is *The Chelsea Girls* a "put-on?" Probably no more than *Lawrence of Arabia*.

Andy Warhol presents his material on two screens simultaneously and uses the double screen to develop the most obvious contrasts. One screen is usually synchronized with a soundtrack, while the other is silent. One screen may be in color, while the other is in black and white. One screen may show "girls," while the other shows "boys." The quotes around "boys" and "girls" are applied advisedly. The only polarities Warhol projects are homosexual and sadomasochistic. No one in Warhol's world is "straight" or "true," and the percentage of deviation is a flagrant exaggeration even for the fetid locale.

Fortunately, *The Chelsea Girls* is not concerned with deviation as a clinical subject or with homosexuality as a state of fallen Grace. Some of the more sophisticated establishment reviewers write as if everything that happens south of 14th Street comes out of Dante's *Inferno*. Warhol is not bosh, but neither is he Bosch. The Chelsea Hotel is not hell. It is an earthly, earthy place like any other, where even fags, dykes, and junkies have to go on living twenty-four hours a day. This is where Warhol has been heading through the somnambulism of *Sleep* and the egregiousness of *Empire*—toward an existential realism beyond the dimensions of the cinema. Warhol disdains the conventional view of the film as a thing of bits and pieces. Perhaps *disdains* is too strong a term for an attitude that is at best instinctive, at worst indifferent. As his scene segments unreel, the footage is finally punctuated by telltale leaders and then kaplunk blankness on the screen. This indicates that each scene runs out of film before it runs out of talk. If there were more film, there would be more talk. If there were less film, there would be less talk. How much more gratuitous and imprecise can cinema be? Goodbye, Sergei

Eisenstein. Hello, Eastman Kodak. Besides, what with the problems of projection and the personalities of projectionists, each showing of *The Chelsea Girls* may qualify as a distinctly unique happening.

Andy Warhol displays some disturbing flourishes of technique. His zooms are perhaps the first anti-zooms in film history. Unlike Stanley Kramer's zooms, which go boi-ing to the heart of the theatrics, Warhol's swoop on inessential details with unerring inaccuracy. With a double screen, the gratuitous zoom is a particularly menacing distraction to the darting eye. (Is that a girl's bare thigh? No, it's a close-up of the kitchen sink.)

A less conspicuous addition to Warhol's abracadabra arsenal is the traveling typewriter shot, which consists of a slow horizontal camera movement from left to right, culminating in a rapid return shot from right to left. What does it mean? Nothing that I can figure out. The most glaring weakness of *The Chelsea Girls* is its attempts at art through cinematic technique. The color LSD frames don't work as hallucinations; the close-ups and the camera movements don't work as comments. Nonetheless, a meaningful form and sensibility emerge through all the apparent arrogance and obfuscation.

It is as documentary that *The Chelsea Girls* achieves its greatest distinction. Warhol is documenting a subspecies of the New York sensibility. When the "Pope" of Greenwich Village talks about sin and idolatry, when a creature in drag "does" Ethel Merman in two of the funniest song numbers ever, when a balding fag simpers about the Johnson admenstruation, when a bull dyke complains about her mate getting hepatitis, it's time to send the children home. Warhol's people are more real than real because the camera encourages their exhibitionism. They are all "performing" because their lives are one long performance, and their party is never over. The steady gaze of Warhol's camera reveals considerable talent and beauty. The Pope character is the closest thing to the late Lenny Bruce to come along in some time, and his Figaro repartee with a girl called Ingrid is an extraordinarily sustained slice of improvisation. The film begins with the beautiful blond Nico on the right screen, the Pope and Ingrid on the left. The film ends with Nico on the left, the Pope on the right, and I felt moved by the juxtaposition of wit and beauty. Warhol's people are not all this effective, but they are There, and although I wouldn't want to live with them, they are certainly worth a visit if you're interested in life on this planet. [Andrew Sarris, 12/15/66]

Chinatown (1974)

Dir. Roman Polanski; Scr. Robert Towne
131 min.

I suspect that a great many people are vaguely disappointed that *Chinatown* does not cater to their nostalgia more extensively than it does. Perhaps it is considered cheating to pretend to be in the past without really working very hard at it. Certainly, *Chinatown* never evokes the films of the 1930s with any consistency. There is simply too much of a revisionist spirit in Roman Polanski (visual), Robert Towne (verbal), and Jack Nicholson (acting) to provide many reminders of the past.

It has been said quite aptly that successful films have parents (or auteurs), whereas unsuccessful films are all orphans. As it happens, *Chinatown* has been successful enough to set a great many tongues wagging as to who actually contributed what. For Polanski, *Chinatown* is a very marginally creative exercise, like *Rosemary's Baby*, rather than a personally fulfilling enterprise like *Cul-de-Sac* and *What?* It is beginning to seem that Polanski himself is the kind of marginal artist who must be saved from himself in order for his personal flair to become apparent. The hundred-proof Polanski of *Cul-de-Sac* and *What?* seems to dissolve in his absurdist acidity, but the relatively diluted Polanski of *Rosemary's Baby*, *Macbeth*, and *Chinatown* seems capable of casting a dour shadow over the proceedings. He does not so much forge these films as tilt them in the direction of his raging unconscious. Left more or less to his own devices in a personal project like *What?* Polanski tends to render his own pessimism somewhat too giddily and too chaotically. His complete lack of illusions gives him nothing on which to build. His art, left to its own devices, becomes self-consuming. He is best employed when he is destroying the illusions of others.

But it is Polanski's decision alone to tilt *Chinatown* toward tragedy that ultimately redeems the enormous contributions of the others. Yet even Polanski's intense feeling for tragedy could never have been realized without the vision of tragedy expressed in Nicholson's star-crossed eyes. I say tragedy advisedly because it is in the Nicholson character's misplaced faith in the power of truth to conquer corruption that he causes the death of his pale, guilt-ridden beloved. And only John Huston could plausibly embody the ultimate corruption of America since the 1930s. [Andrew Sarris, 11/7/74]

The hard-boiled private eye coolly strolls a few steps ahead of the audience; the slapstick detective gets absolutely everything wrong and then pratfalls first over the finish line anyway. Jake Gittes (Jack Nicholson) is neither: a hard-boiled private eye who gets absolutely everything wrong. In *Chinatown*, regarded as both the first neo-noir and the last "studio picture," the protagonist—crass and mercurial, though pillow-slipped in creamy linen—snaps tabloid-ready photos of an adulterous love nest that's no such thing. He espies a distressed young woman through a window and mistakes her for a hostage. He finds a pair of bifocals in a pond and calls them Exhibit A of mariticide, only the glasses don't belong to the victim, and his wife hasn't killed anyone. Yet when he confronts ostensible black widow Evelyn Mulwray (Faye Dunaway) with the spectacular evidence, the cig between his teeth lends his voice an authoritative Bogie hiss, and throughout, Gittes sexes up mediocre snooping with blithe arrogance and sarcastic machismo.

It's the actor's default mode, sure, but in 1974 it hadn't yet calcified into Shtickolson, and in 1974 a director, a screenwriter, and a producer (Robert Evans, who for once deserves a few of the plaudits he's apportioned himself) could decide to beat a genre senseless and then dump it in the wilds of Greek tragedy. Depravity incarnate Noah Cross (John Huston), father to Evelyn, tells the blind sleuth, "You may think you know what you're dealing with, but believe me, you don't." Ditto Oedipus—also a big jerk, but he didn't realize he was trapped in a Sophocles play any more than Jake knows he's cast in the only film Roman Polanski made in Los Angeles after Death Valley '69.

"I was absolutely adamant that she has to die at the end if the film has to have any meaning," Polanski later said of the good, vulnerable Evelyn, who directly suffers nearly every time Gittes pulls his Sam Spade act. Scribe Robert Towne never intended to harm her so grievously, but perhaps the matter was settled when Polanski—hardly a filmmaker dispensed toward wish fulfillment—based Evelyn's scalpeled eyebrows and gift-bow lipstick on memories of his mother, the first woman in his life to be taken from him and butchered.

"Los Angeles Is Dying of Thirst," screams a flyer, while Cross ambles about stealing the city's water to irrigate his own land, a scheme Towne based on a 1908 scandal. Here the rainiest of movie wings relocates to a drought-stricken outpost stranded between an ocean and a desert. Jake, who favors the phrase "That's not what it looks like," cannot see beyond these cracked, sunbaked surfaces, but *Chinatown* itself rumbles with subtext. Nicholson was then beginning an affair with Huston's actual daughter, and a few years later his home served as the scene of Polanski's enduring crime: sex with a girl younger than Evelyn Mulwray when she bore her father's child. Nihilist ironies collapse atop each other; preemptive excuses are proffered. "You see, Mr. Gits," Cross explains, "most people never have to face the fact that, at the right time and the right place, they're capable of anything." As is *Chinatown*: the last gunshot you hear is the sound of the gate slamming on the Paramount lot of Evans's halcyon reign, and as the camera rears back to catch Jake's expression, the dolly lists and shivers—an almost imperceptible sob of grief and recognition, but not a tear is shed. [Jessica Winter, 8/6/03]

Chungking Express (1994)

Dir./Scr. Wong Kar-wai
102 min.

Wong Kar-wai has created—out of colored lights, devious angles, and glorious smudged slo-mo—his own charged, dazzlingly elliptical grammar to express something about love and pain. Wong's *Chungking Express* is a lyric marvel, *Jules and Jim* for our anonymous time.

As Wong told *Time*'s Richard Corliss, the Hong Kong marketplace "has its own censorship. It requires a lot of action. So you either have a cop, a gangster or a kung fu film." With a mock bow to choice number one, *Chungking Express* has two cops. Their principal link is ordering takeout from the small all-night food stand and patrolling the labyrinthine passageways of Hong Kong's Chungking House (an arcade worthy of Walter Benjamin). Only once does one pull a gun, and this is entirely incidental. The two men could just as well drive cabs or play the market. They're working stiffs coping with heartache.

The movie divides into refracting halves, both following a man and a woman who inhabit the same sphere and move randomly toward a romantic collision. Shy people. People who prefer distance but think they don't. You could say these figures are coming together, or you could say they're in flight. When a pair ends up in a room together, they fall asleep.

Tale one centers on HK cop number 223 (Takeshi Kaneshiro) and a beleaguered drug dealer (Brigitte Lin), a moll hidden under shades, a trenchcoat, and a dated blond wig. Only at the end do we get a fleeting glimpse of what she really looks like. She could be any woman wearing Manohlo Blahnik sling-back pumps. (An understated feature of *Chungking Express* is that it's an express train of brand names: a portrait of pedestrians in a wholly commercial universe.) When the two do spend a night together, he never attempts to remove her disguise. Fear or good manners?

The second policeman, number 663 (Tony Leung), has been ditched by a stewardess who's been buzzing in and out of his life. When she drops off 663's keys at his takeout stand, the skittery countergirl Faye (pop star Faye Wong) confiscates the keys and begins secretly tidying 663's cluttered flat, conducting a romance without human contact. He notices changes but attributes them to the secret life of things. Things are his intimates.

Faye is a fabulously fey archkook—a schizy string bean defined by style, moves, and mannerisms, like her cropped head, dodgy eyes, and skinny arms that flail when she's surprised. She hides in cupboards and wraps herself inside "California Dreaming," which she blasts as she works. The movie itself works like a poignant pop song, creating a mood you'd like to crawl into. [Georgia Brown, 3/12/96]

Citizen Kane (1941)

Dir. Orson Welles; Scr. Herman J. Mankiewicz and Orson Welles
119 min.

Pauline Kael's two-part article on *Citizen Kane* ("Raising Kane," *The New Yorker*, February 20 and 27, 1970) reportedly began as a brief introduction to the published screenplay, but, like Topsy, it just growed and growed into a fifty-thousand-word digression from *Kane* itself into the life and times and loves and hates and love-hates of Pauline Kael.

My disagreement with her position begins with her very first sentence: "*Citizen Kane* is perhaps the one American talking picture that seems as fresh now as the day it opened." I can think of hundreds of "American talking pictures" that seem as fresh now as the day they opened. Even fresher. *Citizen Kane* is certainly worthy of revival and reconsideration, but it hardly stands alone, even among the directorial efforts of Orson Welles. To believe that *Citizen Kane* is a great American film in a morass of mediocre Hollywood movies is to misunderstand the transparent movieness of *Kane* itself, from its Xanadu castle out of *Snow White and the Seven Dwarfs* to its menagerie out of *King Kong* to its mirrored reflections out of German doppelgänger spectacles. Not that Miss Kael makes any extravagant claims about the supposed greatness of the film on which she has devoted so much newsprint. "It is a shallow work," she decides, "a *shallow* masterpiece."

One wonders what Miss Kael considers a *deep* masterpiece. *U-Boat 29* perhaps? The plot thickens considerably when Miss Kael drifts away from a half-hearted analysis of *Kane* to the most lively gossip imaginable about the alleged birth pangs and labor pains of the script. Bit by bit, "Raising Kane" becomes an excuse to lower the boom on Orson Welles so as to resurrect the reputation of the late Herman J. Mankiewicz. By interviewing only the sworn enemies of Orson Welles, Miss Kael has made herself fair game for Mr. Welles and his more fervent admirers.

How much of the final script of *Citizen Kane* was written by Herman J. Mankiewicz and how much by Orson Welles? I don't know, and I don't think Miss Kael does either. Undoubtedly, there will be affidavits aplenty from all sides, but literary collaboration, like marriage, is a largely unwitnessed interpenetration of psyches. Miss Kael demonstrates conclusively that Mankiewicz *could* have written the entire script unaided, but she cannot possibly know where and when and how and from whom and from what he derived all his ideas. Who among us can claim complete originality in anything? "Raising Kane" itself bears the byline of Pauline Kael and of Pauline Kael alone. Yet thousands of words are directly quoted from other writers, and thousands more are paraphrased without credit. Miss Kael deserves her byline because she has shaped her material, much of it unoriginal, into an article with a polemical thrust all her own.

Similarly, Orson Welles is not significantly diminished as the auteur of *Citizen Kane* by Miss Kael's breathless revelations about Herman J. Mankiewicz any more than he is diminished as the auteur of *The Magnificent Ambersons* by the fact that all the best lines and scenes were written by Booth Tarkington. [Andrew Sarris, 4/15/71]

Close-Up (1990)

Dir./Scr. Abbas Kiarostami
100 min.

A full decade after its making, Abbas Kiarostami's *Close-Up* emerges from the closed country of Rumored Masterpieces to no doubt pass through our cultural pipes as effectlessly as pork fat through a goose. *The* must-see Iranian Godardian knot of a movie, *Close-Up* is no crowd-pleaser, but neither is it less breathtaking than Godard in his salad days. Kiarostami's film has artichokelike layers that, once peeled, are forever resonant. How simple yet inexhaustible can a filmic text get? Here you have in vitro the ruminative spiral-evolution of Kiarostami's Quoker "earthquake" trilogy and the mysterian subtractions and realist ellipses of *Taste of Cherry* and *The Wind Will Carry Us*. Seemingly bottomless, Kiarostami's reflexivity never obscures his deep, aching concern for people. Nobody makes or has ever made movies with such mundane majesty.

Kiarostami began the movie by filming the court case against Hossein Sabzian, an out-of-work Iranian man who, posing as controversial director-celebrity Mohsen Makhmalbaf, insinuates himself into an upper-class Tehrani family's life under the pretense of casting them in a film. Ironically, Kiarostami does cast them here: entire segments of Sabzian's strange little history with the family are reenacted for the camera, and we're never clear exactly how much of what we see is true and how much is fiction. The courtroom footage is authentically "real," but that means little as the cameras emerge as important forces in how an's fate is handled by the court and his accusers. Of course, even- Makhmalbaf himself enters the reenactment fray, as himself.

The hall of mirrors is deep, but it all reflects, humanely, on both Sabzian and his prey's intoxication with movie-world fame and respect. If Godard was once the giddy Chuck Berry of self-reflexive movie-movie-ness, Kiarostami is the Dylan, moving past the bop and on to the straight goods. Indeed, his unpredictable, and unpredictably moving, investigation into the silent collision between genuine experience and cinema isn't only about the viewer's perspective, but about Kiarostami's own. But like nearly every other Kiarostami film, *Close-Up* takes questions about movies and makes them feel like questions of life, death, and meaning. He makes movies as if they were the manifest vapor trails of human need, hanging in the air even as we search. [Michael Atkinson, 12/29/99]

The Color of Pomegranates (1968)

Dir./Scr. Sergei Paradjanov

79 min.

Most simply described, Sergei Paradjanov's *The Color of Pomegranates* is a poetic evocation of the life and work of eighteenth-century Armenian troubadour Sayat Nova. Paradjanov has been an international cause célèbre since his 1974 arrest. Now fifty-eight and living in poverty, he is said to be painting, after four years in the gulag.

Paradjanov's boisterous, erratic *Shadows of Forgotten Ancestors*, an explosion of lyrical pantheism such as the Soviet cinema had not seen since the salad days of Dovzhenko, won sixteen awards abroad but tagged Paradjanov a "nationalist" at home. Once his political patrons fell from power, he had ten scripts rejected before being permitted to film *The Color of Pomegranates* in 1968. The finished work was then shelved until 1973, when it was released without fanfare in a reedited version. (Although *Pomegranates* was never made available for export, a clandestine print reached Paris in 1977.) Even truncated, it's an extraordinarily beautiful film.

Paradjanov represents eighteenth-century Armenia as the backwoods crossroads of Eurasia. Any one of its linked tableaux is a startling combination of Byzantine flatness, Quattrocento beatifics, and Islamic symmetry. It's truly amazing how Paradjanov coaxes this visionary mix of Fra Angelico and barnyard surrealism out of the most economical use imaginable of weather-beaten churches, casually tethered animals, and peasant grandmothers—punctuating his static compositions with deft jump cuts and Méliès-style movie magic. The film has perhaps three lines of dialogue in an ebb-and-flow soundtrack that alternates wailing folk melodies and choral chanting. And nothing I know has ever used the faded green and orange tones of Soviet color stock to greater effect—with its whitewashed backgrounds, *The Color of Pomegranates* looks two hundred years old already.

Some of Paradjanov's strategies—dancelike gestures, impassive performers, angels with wooden wings, a pasteboard cloud descending as a vision, the constant repetition of key props (books, silver balls, Persian rugs)—recall the poignant gravity of Richard Foreman's early theater pieces. Paradjanov seems to be illustrating Sayat Nova's verses literally, but as a filmmaker, he's so deep into Armenian folk culture, he can work with a throwaway modesty that's a quantum leap beyond second-rate surrealists and professional symbol-mongers of the Jodorowsky-Terayama mold. If from anyone, Paradjanov's hieroglyphics derive from Eisenstein. *The Color of Pomegranates* has *Ivan the Terrible*'s moldy grandeur minus the weightiness, the paradise lost exotica of *Que Viva Mexico* without the underlying hysteria. It's a truly sublime and heartbreaking film. Why settle for white bread when you can have cake? [J. Hoberman, 4/12/83]

The Conformist (1970)

Dir./Scr. Bernardo Bertolucci
115 min.

Now can begin my summer of love. The new print of Bernardo Bertolucci's *The Conformist* (1970) arrives in a torrent of silk and shadow, an eye-watering testimony to the erstwhile dash of international cinema. As with few other films, I envy the newcomer as I envy

David Niven for having made love to Merle Oberon; that Bertolucci's masterpiece—made when he was all of twenty-nine—will be the most revelatory experience a fortunate pilgrim will have in a theater this year is a foregone conclusion. And that's going *leggermente*. Fleshing out novelist Alberto Moravia's shadow-box between political compliance and personal shame with arguably the most arresting mise-en-scène ever concocted for any movie, Bertolucci has created cinema that red-inks your inner calendar. The film is set entirely on rainy city afternoons and indigo evenings; you can hardly help corresponding it to seminal mood moments in your own life.

Told in timeline flea leaps, the story follows Marcello (Jean-Louis Trintignant), a would-be sophisticate lining up with Mussolini's Fascists in the 1930s for his own, very private reasons—as the title makes clear, this is participatory politics seen as psychosocial dysfunction. Being "normal" is an ideal the fiercely closeted Marcello talks about a lot, his desire to belong spiraling out to include marriage (to the fabulously pliable and obnoxious Stefania Sandrelli) and insinuating himself into the Party by framing his old university mentor (Enzo Tarascio) and, by extension, the prof's sexy, testy trophy wife (Dominique Sanda). The motor for Marcello's lost ping-ponging between allegiances and whims (his toss-it-all yen for Sanda's bisexual flirt moves to the heart of the film and then, terribly, seems to have never been there) is an innocuous childhood accident of illegal sex and blood crime, from which spills a lifetime of searching and emptiness.

All at once, *The Conformist* is a bludgeoning indictment of fascistic follow-the-leader and an orgasm of coolness, ravishing compositions, camera gymnastics (the frame virtually squirms around, like Marcello), and atmospheric resonance—as if its decadent, twilit, art deco–noir style is itself a refutation of dictatorial social norms. The actors vogue; Vittorio Storaro's lens transforms every street and room into a catalytic baroqueness; the clothes grip the characters like iconic mantles—to a large degree, the film is an immaculate puppet play about the tension between pleasure (stylistic, sexual, etc.) and imposed duty. If all Bertolucci did was sit Storaro (again, his accomplishment may be the apex of color cinematography) and ironic-heartbreaking composer Georges Delerue at a table and give them drinks, he might've done enough. But there's a fire underneath the tailored rump of *The Con-*

formist that begs the question of Bertolucci's subsequent career—wha happen? Had he shot his load, thereafter only thinking to undress his actresses?

Not our problem, but the movie is ours: the streetlight-burnished Roman streets, the leaves blowing on Marcello's mother's seedy estate, the continental train ride with a sunset movie playing outside and casting its glow on the honeymooners, the dance hall dyke waltz cum Brueghel wedding party, the assassination on the Alpine mountain road. Count your blessings. [Michael Atkinson, 7/27/05]

Contempt (1963)

Dir./Scr. Jean-Luc Godard
103 min.

Even in the most enlightened circles, the mere mention of Jean-Luc Godard directing a million-dollar international coproduction of Alberto Moravia's *Ghost at Noon* in Rome and Capri for Carlo Ponti and Joe Levine seemed the height of improbability from the very beginning.

Once *Contempt* was completed, Levine was shocked to discover that he had a million-dollar art film on his hands with no publicity pegs on which to hang his carpetbag. Levine ordered Godard to add some nude scenes, then challenged the New York censors like the great civil libertarian he is, and finally released the film with a publicity campaign worthy of *The Orgy at Lil's Place*. The New York reviewers, ever sensitive to the nuances of press agentry, opened fire on Brigitte Bardot's backside. It strikes me that this is attacking *Contempt* at its least vulnerable point, since even if Miss Bardot were to be photographed au naturelle fore and aft for a hundred minutes of Warholian impassivity, the result would be more edifying, even for children, than the sickening mediocrity of *Mary Poppins*. [Andrew Sarris, 1/28/65]

The transition from Alberto Moravia's *Ghost at Noon* to Jean-Luc Godard's is largely the transition from a first-person novel to a third-person film. Moravia's Riccardo Molteni is obviously close to Moravia himself, and Molteni's wife, Emilia, merely an extension of Moravia's

Contempt, 1963; written and directed by Jean-Luc Godard

sensibility, a sort of subjective correlative of what the novelist feels about sex in the life of an artist. However, Riccardo and Emilia are both Italian and, as such, are closer to earthy essentials than Godard's transplanted French couple, Paul and Camille Javal, represented with Gallic perverseness by Michel Piccoli and Brigitte Bardot. Piccoli, grossly hirsute to the point of parodying the virility many artists like to assume as the mark of their métier, is denied the nobly Homeric vision of Moravia's Molteni, and the audience does not see the problem through his eyes but, curiously enough, through Fritz Lang's.

Some of the inside jokes in *Contempt* are turned against both Godard and his colleagues on *Cahiers du Cinéma*. When Bardot and Piccoli tell Lang how much they admired his *Rancho Notorious* with Marlene Dietrich, he tells them he prefers *M*. This is an anti-*Cahiers* position on Lang's own career, and Lang's description of CinemaScope as a process suitable for photographing snakes and funerals is aesthetically reactionary enough to make André Bazin roll over in his grave. Lang's kind words for Sam Goldwyn are the final confirmation that Godard has allowed Lang to speak for himself rather than as a mouthpiece for Godard. The effect of Lang's autonomy is to complete the degradation of Piccoli as a mere parrot of Nouvelle Vague attitudes toward which Godard displays mixed emotions. When Piccoli announces that he is going to look at a movie to get some ideas for a script, Bardot asks him with rhetorical scorn why he doesn't think up his own ideas. Piccoli is not even allowed to challenge the vulgar conceptions of Jack Palance's ruthless American producer, Jeremy Prokosch. Lang lines up with Homer, Palance with commerce, and Piccoli becomes a feeble echo of the producer who has set out to humiliate him.

We are not moved by what happens to the marriage of Piccoli and Bardot. We are not even particularly concerned with what happens to the ridiculous epic Palance wants Fritz Lang to direct because only a German can understand Homer. The characters keep talking about Homer's classical cosmos of appearance as reality as opposed to our atomic universe under constantly anxious analysis, but the consciously tawdry players in the film-within-a-film indicate that the great Fritz is laboring on a potboiler. Then what is so moving about *Contempt*? Simply the spectacle of Fritz Lang completing a mediocre film with a noble vision in his mind and at the edge of his fingertips. Godard appears in the film as Lang's assistant, and he repeats Lang's instructions to the camera crew, as if in this curious man who has always known how far to compromise in order to endure is hidden the real Homeric parable of *Contempt*. Where Mastroianni-Fellini in 8½ is an artist who happens to be a movie director, Lang in *Contempt* is a movie director who just happens to be an artist. [Andrew Sarris, 2/4/65]

Jean-Luc Godard's 1963 stab at a "commercial" feature, *Contempt* is at once a movie of outrageous formalism (bold colors, abstract chunks of sound) and documentary verisimilitude (cast speaking an undubbed mixture of French, English, Italian, and German). An international co-pro, adapted (with surprising fidelity) from Alberto Moravia's best-seller, shot (at Cinecittà) in Technicolor and CinemaScope, it's the story of a French writer (Michel Piccoli) who takes a job from an American producer (Jack Palance) and, as a result, loses his wife (Brigitte Bardot). The plot is distilled to anecdote in the sun-smacked Mediterranean light and further fractured by the surging melancholy of Georges Delerue's musical theme, not to mention the inserts of Bardot skinny-dipping demanded by Godard's producers. At one point, the movie is interrupted by the message that "Joe Levine is calling from New York." *Contempt* begins with a charged quote from Godard's mentor André Bazin—

"Cinema replaces the world with one that conforms to our desires"—followed by a close-up of Brigitte Bardot's world-famous derriere.

Moravia's novel was translated as *A Ghost at Noon*, and Godard's movie has the quality of a daylight haunting; an empty studio is populated by a collection of movie apparitions. The tawny nexus of desire (and token of male exchange), Bardot is never other than a platonic image of herself—although she sometimes wears the wig that Godard's then muse Anna Karina wore in *Vivre sa Vie*. Piccoli, whose stingy-brim fedora, rolled up shirtsleeves, and loosened tie suggest a refugee from the set of *Some Came Running* (Godard wanted Sinatra), has been hired to rewrite the peplum *Odyssey* being shot by a philosophically world-weary Fritz Lang (who "actually plays himself," the *New York Times* noted with surprise).

Given to big pronouncements quoted from a tiny book of wisdom, producer Palance enters the deserted Cinecittà lot in a mood of fatuous melancholy: "Only yesterday there were kings here." Beloved by *Cahiers* for his portrayal of a star in revolt in *The Big Knife*, Palance plays the producer as if reprising his Attila the Hun in the Hollywood peplum *Sign of the Pagan*.

Thanks to Lang's ill-starred production, the Olympians preside over the modern store. "I like gods, I know exactly how they feel," Palance declares in the midst of trashing the master's rushes. (A famous quotation from Louis Lumière is inscribed beneath the projection-room screen: "The cinema is an invention without a future.") Afterward, Palance coaxes an unwilling Bardot to ride in the red Alfa Romeo that serves as the story's deus ex machina. Later, back home and betoga'd in towels, Bardot and Piccoli pace and squabble through a half-furnished apartment—enacting the disintegration of their marriage in the stunning, half-hour tour de force that provides the movie with its centerpiece.

Godard called *Contempt* the "story of castaways of the Western world, survivors of the shipwreck of modernity." Thirty-odd years later, it seems like an elegy for European art cinema, at once tragic and serene. If *Contempt* is a myth about the baleful effect of the movie god on the lives of two mortals, it is also the story of Godard's victory over a similar seduction. Lashed to the mast of irascible genius, he heard the song of the sirens and lived to tell the tale. [J. Hoberman, 7/1/97]

Cutter and Bone/Cutter's Way (1981)

Dir. Ivan Passer; Scr. Jeffrey Alan Fiskin
105 min.

Ivan Passer's *Cutter and Bone* is a bitter neo-noir and an unexpected bonanza of B-movie virtues. It's a thriller but also a critique, underscoring its surgical title by performing a deft and mordant postmortem on the remains of the 1960s counterculture. Passer is a veteran of Prague Spring, so one assumes he knows something about blasted hopes and the powers that be.

Set in affluent Santa Barbara, the film harks back to the Nixon-era mode of Polanski's *Chinatown* or Arthur Penn's *Night Moves*. Bone (Jeff Bridges), an occasional boat salesman and freelance gigolo, stumbles across a squalid sex murder—the corpse is literally dumped from a Cadillac into a trashcan—which his Viet-vet roommate, the crazed and crippled Cutter (John Heard), proceeds to "solve." This leads to a grossly unequal struggle with an Olympian corporate magnate. And while Bone vacillates and bats his bedroom eyes at Cutter's long-suffering wife (Lisa Eichhorn), who floats through the film in an alcoholic haze, all three are drawn inexorably into the whirlpool.

Members of an illusionless post-hippie leisure class, this dissolute trio is ripe, verging on rancid—as expert at closing ranks against the world as they are in getting on each other's nerves. They're sympathetic, if not admirable, and sufficiently complex as characters to offset the plot's wilder pirouettes. Each embodies a mixture of countercultural virtues and 1960s burnout. As the aging beach boy whose moral unease is masked by a reflexive disengagement, Bridges projects a potent, guilty self-absorption, while the infinitely selfless Eichhorn manages a difficult balancing act between smoldering resentment and mousy martyrdom. Then there's rasp-voiced John Heard, whose one-eyed, one-armed, one-legged madman hobbles furiously through Santa Barbara like a beached version of an S. Clay Wilson pirate. This emaciated Captain Pissgums—as foulmouthed as he is paranoid—seems immediately capable of any outrage. By the end of the film, we know that he is.

Actors' film though it is, *Cutter and Bone* belongs to Passer. From the opening tryst where Bridges and Nina Van Pallandt trade casual sexual put-downs in an overdecorated hacienda-style motel room, to the bizarre pyrotechnics of Heard's last stand, *Cutter and Bone* is dense with originally orchestrated scenes. If Heard's drunken, lechy appreciation of Santa Barbara's "Old Spanish Days" parade, with its bovine cheerleaders and monstrous floats, seems the transposition of a particularly Czech form of humor, the sequence in which Heard cruelly smashes up a neighbor's car is a grotesque slapstick that's pure Americana. Passer's touch is far from heavy, and he handles his morally befuddled protagonists with an almost tender regard. The scene in which Heard unveils his mutilated body, the dissolve-bracketed single shot of Bridges and Eichhorn making love, are extraordinarily affecting in their tact.

Low-keyed and off-handed, *Cutter and Bone* percolates with odd rhythms and comic details. There's a Los Angeles sequence that's as bleakly minimal as Edgar G. Ulmer's two-set *Detour*, suffused with the sort of grim lyricism that revels in refracted light patterns on a dirty windshield. Jordan Cronenweth's accomplished cinematography conveys the essence of rot. Everything is orange-gold and subtly synthetic. The film has the burnished Naugahyde look of a sunset seen through the window of a House of Pancakes.

Intimate Lighting (1965), Passer's one Czech feature, established him as the most gifted and underrated talent of that short-lived new wave. After seeing his five uneven but also misunderstood Hollywood films, I'm beginning to wonder if he doesn't occupy a similar position here. Surely his work is due for reconsideration. [J. Hoberman, 3/25/81]

Days of Being Wild (1990)

Dir./Scr. Wong Kar-wai
94 min.

Days of Being Wild is the movie with which Wong Kar-wai became Wong Kar-wai—the most influential, passionate, and romantic of neo–New Wave directors. Wong called his second feature "a reinvention of the disappeared world."

Arguably, this is the key movie in Wong's oeuvre, as startling in its context as *Hiroshima Mon Amour* and *Breathless* were in theirs. *Days of*

Being Wild is a sort of meta-reverie populated by a cast of beautiful young pop icons—Leslie Cheung, Maggie Cheung, Carina Lau, Andy Lau, and briefly, Tony Leung—acting like movie stars. *Days* is also Wong's first film to have been shot by Chris Doyle, and the voluptuous shadows, neon color schemes, and underwater atmosphere of Doyle's cinematography would define Wong's elusive Hong Kong forever after.

Set around the same period as *American Graffiti* (or Edward Yang's retro youth epic *A Brighter Summer Day*, made in Taiwan the next year), *Days of Being Wild* makes similar use of dated cool and old cars. The very first shot smacks your eye with a redder-than-red Coca-Cola cooler. The title evokes the one under which *Rebel without a Cause* was released in Hong Kong. But this is an unfamiliar and perhaps imaginary nostalgia. In his film notes, Wong reminisces about 1960: "I used to recall, back in those days, the sun was brighter, the air fresher, with distant noises from wireless sets flowing down the streets. . . . One felt so good it was almost like a dream." For him, it was. He was born in Shanghai in 1958 and moved to H.K. with his family at age five.

Suavely achronological, *Days* opens with a tracking shot through some verdant jungle that cannot be temporally identified until the movie's gangster-flick finale. Everything else is flashback. Moving from small, humid rooms to rigorously controlled exteriors, the principals suggest a group of time travelers transported into a past that can't be inhabited. The empty stadium where Maggie Cheung works the concession counter might be ruins. The youthful demographic further abstracts the universal obsession with personal history. Leslie Cheung's character, a pomaded lady-killer and underworld tough, is the only one with a parent; that she is his adoptive mother only serves to render him more a little boy lost.

Leslie Cheung's character is searching for something unknown left behind in an unknowable time. But those familiar with Wong's subsequent films will find that his preoccupations are all in place—veiled by a delicate fog of fleeting relationships, unfulfilled longings, and missed opportunities. Here, too, are his characteristic strategies—the cast of beautiful loners, the memories delivered in voice-over, the abstractly exotic music. (Save for one Django Reinhardt piece, the Hawaiian cha-cha score comes from a compilation album by Xavier Cugat.) *In the Mood for Love* very nearly remakes *Days of Being Wild*—and *2046* even more so. In some respects, however, *Days* is a more radical achievement than those that would come later.

For one thing, there's a headier sense of simultaneity. Difficult to follow on a first viewing (although not thereafter), the movie may feel shifty as smoke, but it's composed entirely of straight cuts. The various flashbacks and flash-forwards are marked by abrupt transitions that give no indication of elapsed time. This succession of privileged moments is less evocation of the past than nostalgia for the present. Time is fragmented in the service of an Eternal Now, and yet there's a Zeno's paradox effect in which that Now instantly evaporates. Clocks are ubiquitous, and the key scene has Leslie Cheung's character seduce Maggie Cheung's by tricking her into spending a minute constructing a memory of those sixty seconds.

Wong originally wanted a *Days of Being Wild* sequel haunted by its dead protagonist. Leslie Cheung's untimely passing renders that ambition additionally poignant. But as in all of Wong's movies, you can't go home again. [J. Hoberman, 11/17/04]

Days of Being Wild, 1990; written and directed by Wong Kar-wai

Dead Man (1995)

Dir./Scr. Jim Jarmusch
121 min.

Jim Jarmusch has always been proudly idiosyncratic—a stylist at once stubborn and fey. *Stranger Than Paradise* pioneered the neo-beatnik mode of hip Americana—bleak, deadpan, borderline sentimental—that Jarmusch would elaborate in subsequent features with varied success. But the indie landscape has shifted in the 1990s, and *Dead Man* marks something of a departure—a fairy-tale Western that howls in the moonlight.

Uncompromising from the get-go, *Dead Man* opens the road with a ten-minute, pure-movie montage of nineteenth-century locomotion. A Cleveland accountant named, like the English poet, William Blake (Johnny Depp) is heading for a job at Dickinson Metalworks in the frontier town of Machine. In a fragmentary sequence that encapsulates the movie to come, Blake—a dude with lank hair, spectacles, and a vaudevillian's checkerboard suit—rides along with a changing cast of grizzled cowpokes against a wildly shifting terrain. There's no dialogue until the first of the film's several prophets (Crispin Glover) babbles a warning that all Blake will find in Machine is his own grave. To reinforce the notion, the mountain men start shooting at the buffalo grazing alongside the speeding train.

Jarmusch's *Dead Man* picks up where Kafka's *Amerika* leaves off, with the innocent young hero hurtling into the mysterious, limitless West, but it soon returns to Kafkaesque semicivilization by depositing Blake in a realm of sinister absurdity. Machine proves to be a muddy hellhole whose crummy Main Street, the province of rooting pigs and wild-eyed drifters, is marked by mountain goat skulls, dotted with coffin shops, and dominated by the hideous Dickinson Metalworks. To the amusement of the office manager (John Hurt) and his servile clerks, Blake finds another accountant already in his place and only just survives a highly unpleasant run-in with the crazed factory owner (Robert Mitchum, crouching beneath his outsized portrait like a degenerate founding father).

Wandering through the forest of the night, Blake meets the lovely

Thel (Mili Avital), named for the unborn heroine of a Blake song, who has been tossed out of the town saloon for peddling paper flowers. Thel brings Blake home, but the loaded gun she keeps beneath her pillow ("'cause this is America") results in an absurd, midtryst shootout that leaves two people dead and the wounded Blake wanted for murder. Having fled into the wilderness, the hapless accountant is saved by a beefy solemn Indian (Gary Farmer) who gives his name as "Nobody" and calls his charge "stupid fucking white man" until he discovers that his name is William Blake: "It's so strange that you don't remember anything of your poetry."

Farmer, who steals the movie from the game but necessarily blank Depp, appeared as a similarly massive and placid mystical warrior in the underappreciated *Powwow Highway*—a Western road movie that, like Jarmusch's, managed the interpretation of two historical epochs. For, although set in the 1870s and filled with creepy period details, *Dead Man* equally suggests an imaginary, postapocalyptic 1970s, a wilderness populated by degenerate hippies and acid-ripped loners forever pulling guns on each other or else asking for tobacco. Although beautifully shot in sumptuous black and white by Robby Müller, *Dead Man* resembles the grimmest of Nixon-era anti-Western movies like *Bad Company*, *Kid Blue*, and *Dirty Little Billy*—with Neil Young's discordant electric-guitar vamp providing a further abstraction of their countercultural rock scores.

On the other hand, like *El Topo*, *Greasers Palace*, and the more Christ-conscious spaghetti Westerns, *Dead Man* is a metaphysical journey. Blake is pursued through the forest by three hired killers—the meanest, a cannibal demon, sleeps with a teddy bear. At one point Blake stumbles across a trio of troll-like animal skinners, one (Iggy Pop) in drag, telling the story of Goldilocks. There are ample clues to suggest that Blake has died and that Nobody is the spirit who guides his departing soul: Nobody (not to be confused with the actual Blake's more punitive deity, Old Nobodaddy) takes peyote and hallucinates seeing the skull beneath Blake's skin.

Nobody encourages his charge to go even further beyond the law by killing as many whites as he can and thus continue writing his poetry in blood. (Blake's notoriety is clinched when a Christian gun salesman asks for his autograph on a "Wanted" poster.) The landscape grows increasingly uncanny as the pair travels even deeper into Indian country, eventually paddling by canoe toward the entry to the spirit world. Splayed out along a cold ocean beach, this terminal Indian settlement is as funky and unsettling a frontier necropolis as was Machine.

Dead Man drifts inexorably at its own pace on the River Lethe into the Twilight Zone. By the time Blake reaches his appointed destination, one's sense of Jarmusch has deepened considerably. (Rather than fey and stubborn, he seems playful and primeval.) This is the Western Andrei Tarkovsky always wanted to make. Even the references to Blake are justified. It's a visionary film. [J. Hoberman, 5/14/96]

Dead Ringers (1988)

Dir. David Cronenberg; Scr. David Cronenberg and Norman Snider
115 min.

Adapted from a novel itself based on a true story, *Dead Ringers* employs a speculum to turn the mad doctor genre inside out. David Cronenberg fans may be disappointed by the almost total absence of the director's trademark visceralia; the shocks here are purely of recognition—they provoke laughter rather than screams. Mordantly witty, the film is all the more disturbing for its chilly distance and seeming objectivity.

The story of the deaths of the twin ob-gyns broke in 1975. Emaciated and decomposed, the bodies of Steven and Cyril Marcus were found in their food-and-feces-littered Upper East Side apartment. They had died of either barbiturate overdose or acute withdrawal. Prominent surgeons and researchers, the Marcuses had a large private practice and were on the staff of New York Hospital until shortly before their nearly simultaneous demises. (Though Cronenberg shifts his location to Toronto, making the twins upper-class Anglo-Saxon rather than working-class Jewish, *Dead Ringers* is haunted and authenticated by the Marcus case.)

The headlines, though horrifying, merely confirmed the conclusion that recently politicized feminists had reached, either on their own or in gynecological self-help groups where, manipulating mirrors and specula, they exchanged choice anecdotes about experiences in the stirrups. Gynecology literalizes the only slightly veiled function of, for example, both psychoanalysis and film direction—to investigate, control, and objectify women. It's hardly surprising, therefore, that the occasional nutcase should find a haven within the institutionalized pathology of these professions. Or, as miniseries queen Claire Niveau (Geneviève Bujold) exclaims in the movie to the Mantle twins, Beverly and Elliot (Jeremy Irons and Jeremy Irons), when she discovers that she has two doctors instead of one, and that they've both been sharing her bed, "I thought I'd seen some creepy things go on in the movie business, but I really have to say, this is the most disgusting thing that's ever happened to me."

Having invented a revolutionary surgical instrument, "the Mantle Morticular," while still in medical school, the twins quickly rise to the top, where they share a thriving fertility practice and a palatial apartment. Beverly, the sensitive and retiring brother, is the dedicated clinician, while Elliot is the lecturer, the fund-raiser, and the all-around front man. While the twins seem just like other brilliant, glamorous, and rich men, their relationship is disturbingly symbiotic. They harbor the shared fantasy that, rather than merely being identical, they are Siamese twins, the definitive medical example of monster birth.

Enter Claire, a successful actress desperate to have a baby. The Mantles discover what Claire's previous doctors have failed either to notice or report—that she has a "tripartite womb." This is the film's only foray into the fantastic, and Cronenberg manages to downplay it so that it passes for the mere exception that proves the rule. Fascinated, Elliot fucks Claire and then passes her on to the reluctant "Bev"—who, identifying with Claire as a fellow mutant, falls horribly in love. As the new symbiosis threatens his attachment to "Elly," Bev's anxiety mounts apace. Under her Victorian lace blouses, Claire is tough, disciplined, and self-knowing. She can afford an occasional S and M indulgence or week of pill popping. Not so Bev. Two downs and he's dreaming of a remake of *The Brood*, in which a voracious Claire bites through a bloody mess of fetus and umbilical cord tying him to Elliot, belly to belly.

Irons's delicately nuanced interactions with himself are even more of an acting tour de force than Bob Hoskins's manic intimacies with Roger Rabbit. He plays the twins not as diametrical opposites, but as complementary partial personalities. Irons's characterizations are so subtle that if Bev and Elly were protagonists of separate films, we might easily pass each performance off as just Irons brilliantly playing Irons. Which makes the doubling all the more uncanny, particularly when Cronenberg employs computerized split-screen effects, so that both brothers—and the camera—move in tandem. Irons has total responsibility for making the crucial shift in the film's tone from social farce to the desperate sadness of the last third. His "Poor Elly, poor Bev" moment, as the twins acknowledge their mutual plight, is extraordinary.

Cronenberg's discreetly formal mise-en-scène (austere gray-blue granite sets, punctuated with crimson surgical uniforms) undercuts the potential melodramatics in the film's dynamic of separation and loss, dominance and submission.

Dead Ringers seems bound for misinterpretation. Many will find Cronenberg's dismantling of an honored (though always slightly suspect) patriarchal professional intolerable. (It's mostly women who've been laughing at the previews.) Others will mistake the critique of misogyny for the thing itself.

Dead Ringers suggests that the future of the species may be controlled by self-defined "mutants." You go giddy on the irony—and fall into the abyss. [Amy Taubin, 9/27/88]

The keynote address in what has become—rising out of the neurotic bath of 1970s exploitation films—one of world cinema's most original and discomfiting visions, this 1988 masterwork by David Cronenberg has aged into a kind of subterranean sacredness. Name another film that takes as many risks, runs its astonishing course with such a steady hand, and has as much to say about brotherhood and corporeal transience. Derived from a true story about a pair of gynecologist twins who committed suicide together, but marinated in Cronenberg's unique physio-anxiety, the film tracks Jeremy Irons as two dislocated doctors with an avant-garde practice whose warped symbiosis becomes infiltrated by a third party (Geneviève Bujold, as a sensible-minded hophead who has the audacity to like one of the identicals and not the other), and who begin spiraling into a crazed dream world of mutation-phobic dementia, pharmaceutical zombiehood, and body panic. To watch Irons not merely inhabit two characters in the same frame but also manifest the dizzyingly complex dynamic between them—their history, dependencies, fears—is to see the thespian equivalent to splitting the atom. Proportions of wit, fear, weakness, hostility, and kindness vary from brother to brother, never quite adding up to 100 percent, while during the film's shattering, mordant birthday celebration, the differences between the twins become lost in a sleepwalking barbiturate swoon. [Michael Atkinson, 6/29/05]

The Decalogue (1989)

Dir. Krzysztof Kieslowski; Scr. Krzysztof Kieslowski and Krzysztof Piesiewicz
550 min.

The breakdown of traditional (read "quaint") moral imperatives is a subject rubbed in our faces with every film we see. Vengeance is mine, sayeth the godfather. Thou shalt not rat on thy pals. But since in real life most of us are deprived of the authority provided by organized crime, we find ourselves employing other, more undefined, codes of conduct. An investigation into actual ethical behavior is what Polish director Krzysztof Kieslowski has presumed to undertake in *The Decalogue*. This tough-minded work—one of the few masterpieces of recent time—consists of ten hour-long dramas, each based on one of the Ten Commandments. Made for Polish TV, *The Decalogue* might be called a philosopher's soap opera or an immensely entertaining grammar of morals.

Given the length and the daunting scope of *The Decalogue*, I'm condensing my reflections into ten reader-friendly categories.

1. *The commandments*. Even those retaining a firm grasp of their Sunday or Hebrew school lessons will find it hard to tell which commandment fits a given episode. Many commandments—about stealing, adultery, honoring father and mother, having no other god—apply to most. The work's implicit question: Breaking the commandments as casually as we do, what codes do we actually follow?

2. *The apartment complex*. The episodes are unified by their setting in a Warsaw housing development—according to the director, the

"nicest" apartments in the city. Here taxi drivers, physicians, and professors reside classless, side by side. Some quarters are quite posh—leather and chrome—others are threadbare. The tenant with the most valuable possessions turns out to have the drabbest habitat. People jog, use computers, watch *Sesame Street*, listen to stereos, have affairs, build greenhouses on the balconies. This city in miniature becomes a perfect place to examine the contemporary social contract.

3. *Broken glass*. Even adult Poles, who pride themselves on living without illusions, find that there are still some that remain to be shattered. The exquisite, cryptic opening shot of episode one seems at first like an abstract image or camera trick. What the picture actually shows is the line on a river between ice and moving water. One day a boy goes to bring a bottle of milk inside and finds it frozen, the glass broken. (Breaking glass becomes a recurring image in the series.) Is the river frozen solid enough to skate on? He and his father gather data necessary for the calculations. The father, a popular professor of computer science, is an enlightened man; he believes in reason. According to his formula, the boy can go skating. When the ice breaks, his first reaction is, "It shouldn't have."

4. *Grief and guilt*. Beginning with the failure to save a brilliant child, *The Decalogue* explores the effects of various kinds of loss—of loved ones, sexual potency, a large fortune, life as it was. Guilt is contagious. Secrets are brought into the light, opened for inspection. In the end there are new secrets.

5. *Angel*. A thin young man with reddish blond hair appears in eight of the sections. Bundled up, sitting by a fire at the edge of the frozen river, he's the first figure we see in *The Decalogue*. Repeatedly, he sees tragedy about to strike but doesn't intervene. Kieslowski is the man who directed *Camera Buff*, about a worker with a movie camera who threatens authority simply by being a true, accurate witness. Here the stranger also suggests a witness in the his-eye-is-on-the-sparrow sense.

6. *Intimacy*. One of the most noticeable differences between this and American movies and TV is the level of acting. Since the direction

favors close-ups, faces are crucial. They aren't cosmeticized or photographed to look their "best." (Once the ideal of screen beauty is scrapped, the whole notion of "best" gets redefined.) A number of Polish stars appear in the cast (notably Krystyna Janda of *Interrogation*), but they blend seamlessly with the others. The overall impression is one of transcendent modesty and a degree of realism, of humaneness, we almost never see on-screen.

7. *Sex/Love*. Some of the best sections—two, three, six, and nine—are about sex and the relations between lovers, husbands, and wives. Four explores the temptation of incest between a teenage girl and her father (or stepfather; we never learn which he is). Yet sex is never represented in the distracting way that it usually is.

8. *Parenthood, mystery of*. A recurring question: who is the real mother, the real father? In a number of the episodes, children are in the dark about their real parents. (In *The Decalogue*, the adultery commandment gets a workout.) Many in the older generations are estranged from their children, regret never having children, or have otherwise lost them. If the prevalence of the paternity theme makes this into a theological issue, the stories' tenderness also emphasizes the sacredness of children.

9. *"The child is alive."* This is the key line from segment eight, which, as far as I'm concerned, marks the series' emotional high point. It's a section that "contains" many of the others—both by referring to characters from other parts and by introducing a historical frame. An aging but vigorous ethics professor encounters a younger woman, a Jew, whom she declined to save in 1943. Elizabetha comes from New York to confront her failed guardian and to thank the couple who had been willing to adopt her. What she's unprepared for is the degree to which history has placed East Europeans in ethical danger, as well as the depth of character, and sometimes the terrible vulnerability, developed by crisis.

10. *Poland/America*. "What a strange country this is," observes Elizabetha when she begins to grasp the maze of grief she's wandered into. [Georgia Brown, 11/6/90]

The Devil, Probably (1977)

Dir./Scr. Robert Bresson
95 min.

Like every feature Robert Bresson has directed, *The Devil, Probably* is a drama of faith so uncompromising as to border on the absurd.

Chic yet austere, as flat and stylized as a medieval illumination, *The Devil, Probably* is a vision bracketed by the void. It's a movie that begins (and ends) in total darkness, presenting itself as an interlude during which abstract creatures flounce purposefully in and out of frame. As these Yves St. Laurent angels flit through Paris on predestined missions of celestial mystery, the youthful hero, Charles (Antoine Monnier), rushes headlong toward his end—suicide or murder?—in the star-studded Père Lachaise cemetery.

Bresson's near-classic *j'accuse* begins with Charles's death; the rest of the narrative is an extended flashback covering the past six months. The movie is set in a generic student milieu where longhaired panhandlers play their flutes and bongos by the Seine, while sinister political activists plant pornographic photos between the pages of books sold in a church concession stand. A university dropout, the androgynous, aristocratic Charles has captivated a posse of grave young hippies with the purity of his despair. (Nonactors all, the principals are extraordinarily beautiful objets d'art, with Monnier himself the great-grandson of Henri Matisse.)

Bresson may loathe the notion of a mechanical world, but each action in his film provokes an equal and opposite reaction. The oddly named Alberte leaves her doggedly adoring Michel, an ecological activist, to comfort Charles. Her sacrifice prompts Charles, who is nothing if not a studied sybarite, to take up with Edwige—but, really, he's in love with the idea of death. Although Alberte becomes concerned when she finds a vial of cyanide in his backpack, not everyone is so tolerant. Charles has a casual tryst with a third girl who kicks him out of her apartment upon discovering that he tried to drown himself in her bathtub.

For his circle, Charles exudes a magnetic passivity. With his blank, accusatory look, he's a living reproach to a corrupt, polluted world.

Viewers may find him insufferable because, in implacably rejecting the social order, he's repudiating them as well. On the other hand, however mopey and sanctimonious, he's transfigured by the purity of his adolescent rejection. Press reports suggest that when first released in France, *The Devil, Probably* was seen as so dangerous an incitement to suicide that it was nearly prohibited for those under eighteen. Indeed, this evocation of glamorous youth cult nihilism could be Bresson's belated, caustic answer to Antonioni's *Blow-Up*. (Alternately, as Richard Roud pointed out, the entire movie could be read as a case study of homosexual panic.)

The Devil, Probably maintains its formal rigor through Bresson's geometric interest in fragmenting his actors—isolating their feet or truncating their gestures. The close-ups of hands trafficking in drugs by the Seine affords the sort of transaction he revels in. Still, the movie is not altogether devoid of acerbic humor. Charles adopts a heroin addict and brings him (along with a portable phonograph and a record of Monteverdi) to crash on the floor of Notre Dame; the junkie immediately takes the opportunity to rob the poor box. The greatest scene has Charles and Michel riding a city bus—their trip interspersed with cutaways to the inner working of the exit door, the machine for collecting money, the rearview mirror. They are talking, of course, about It (death, despair, the end of the world), and, as if scripted by Bertolt Brecht, the other passengers join in the conversation. "Who's in charge?" someone finally asks, setting up for the inevitable punchline, "The devil, probably." The sequence is majestically punctuated—it ends when the bus hits something, we never know what.

The Devil, Probably is a fiercely irascible movie, and part of its kick is watching Bresson invoke the modern world. Mainly, this takes the form of eco-disaster. Michel's involvement with the Association for the Safeguard of Man and His Environment allows for the interpolation of 16mm documentary footage of air pollution, oil spills, garbage mounds, and the deformities of Minimata—not to mention the clubbing of a baby seal. At the same time, the film is contemptuous of politics. Charles turns his back on an underground meeting at which the youthful speaker opens his oration by proclaiming "destruction"; it hardly seems coincidental that when the movie begins, Charles is found lying dead beside the tomb of France's postwar communist leader, Maurice Thorez. (One wonders whether Bresson was cognizant of the Jim Morrison cult also centered on the Père Lachaise.)

The corruption of the adult world is absolute. Politicians lie, professors obfuscate, priests hypocritically try to make themselves relevant. At Edwige's request, Charles visits a stylishly grim shrink who questions him about his sex life and childhood, then makes a few facile pronouncements. The inference is that Charles is too smart for this disgusting world: "My sickness is seeing clearly." (Is this the voice of the filmmaker?) In a burst of transcendent sarcasm, Charles pulls out an advertising flyer and—announcing that in "losing life, I would lose . . . "—begins to recite a litany of consumer catchphrases.

When Charles expresses his fear of killing himself, the shrink taunts him with the observation that in ancient Rome, the suicidal hired their own assassins. Meeting him after this session, his friends think that Charles has been cured—and in a sense, he has been. Logic prevails. Like a rocket burning off its heat shield as it plunges to earth, *The Devil, Probably* incinerates all affectation in tracing Charles's single-minded march toward oblivion. That we never know his final interrupted thought only underscores Bresson's voluptuous pessimism: Charles is us. [J. Hoberman, 11/18/94]

Distant Voices, Still Lives (1988)

Dir./Scr. Terence Davies

85 min.

For some, a few years of childhood create a mystery they spend most of the rest of their years trying to solve. The British filmmaker Terence Davies appears to be one of these. In his wrenching *Distant Voices, Still Lives*, Davies invents a cinematic means of time travel and—in the service of mourning—a language to talk with the dead.

Born in 1945 into a Liverpool working-class family, Davies is the youngest of ten children (seven of whom survived); in the film, which takes place during the hard times of the 1940s and 1950s, there are only three children: two girls, Eileen and Maisie, and their younger brother, Tony. Davies has scrupulously re-created the era, using houses and lanes, Liverpool pubs and Liverpudlians, that dovetail with sense memory. Forsaking primary colors, he's achieved a picture with a tonal range mainly of browns (with ghostly sea-greens, pale blues, and roses) that may suggest tinted sepia photos or simply the atmosphere peculiar to the foreign climate of the past.

For all the detail re-creation, the movie is impressionistic and elliptical, moving cryptically backward and forward in time. Some audiences, apparently, find Davies's movie opaque and leave unmoved; others (I am one) come away stricken, overcome by grief.

Distant Voices, Still Lives is conceived as a diptych and divides into two discrete sections shot two years apart. *Distant Voices*, the first film, centers on the father (Pete Postlethwaite) and is circumscribed by his death and funeral. *Still Lives*, the second film, shows family members arrested, *transfixed* really, in a melancholy, if turbulent, afterlife. Dad's rage hovers over the children's efforts to get free. In both sections, one of the children marries—first, the embattled, fiery Eileen (Angela Walsh), then the softer, more inward Tony (Dean Williams)—and each breaks down crying after the wedding. It's only a supposition, but receptivity to Davies's movies may divide according to the type of father one had.

I could just as well say, what type of mother. In one scene in Davies's picture, the mother (Freda Dowie) sits out on an upstairs windowsill washing the window, while down below one of her daughters chants, "Don't fall, Mum. Please don't fall!" A child's infinite concern—constant trepidation woven with protective fantasies—for an endangered parent is graphically evoked here. In this case the danger is real (equally vivid concern develops out of a mother's depression)—not that Mum will fall, but that she will be beaten to death.

This scene elides with another where Dad starts beating Mum until she's invisible on the floor, and he's still hitting her. One of the girls' voices is heard asking Mum why she'd married their father and in reply receives that terribly basic and poignantly frivolous "reason": *"He was a good dancer."* Ella Fitzgerald has all the while been singing "Taking a Chance on Love," and on and on it goes, determining, it would almost appear, the length of this harrowing scene. "Rainbows bending now, we'll have our happy ending now . . . " she sings, until discrepancy grows beyond unbearable.

Each unhappy family develops its own outlets from unhappiness—some form of giddiness, lightness of being, that allows members to soar free temporarily. For the movie's family, it's singing, and the sisters, in particular, sing their hearts out. Even Granny sings, and Pa croons "When Irish Eyes Are Smilin'" while currying a horse. Song lyrics become speech for the language-impoverished. "If You Knew Susie," "Up a Lazy River," "I Love the Ladies," "Buttons and Bows"—where the words are meaningless, the sheer energy of the singing lifts the singers out of depression. The local pub might sound like the jolliest corner in England, with the singing usually led by the intrepid Eileen or her sassy friend Micky (Debi Jones).

The film opens with the sound of thunder and the voice of a radio announcer reading a weather report. It's pouring outside a working-class row house, its brick that grimy yellow-gray peculiar to endless English city blocks. The milkman has left several bottles to one side of the door. A woman (the mother) comes out for the milk. As the camera follows her slowly, though only as far as the entry hallway (where it turns 180 degrees), we hear a couple's voices from somewhere inside, and soon a woman's voice begins to sing "I Get the Blues When It's Raining."

This front door, and the staircase just inside, become parts of a recurring tableau. Davies likes duration—holding a "still life" or using measured traveling shots that redefine visual excitement. Focusing on doors and windows, he's trying to find a way inside. In an early scene, Tony, wearing an army uniform, puts his fist through a window in order to confront his father. Later, we see an earlier encounter at the door. The child Tony, locked out by his father, knocks and asks, "Can I come in, Dad?" "There's no place for you here," says Dad. Mum watches silently from an upstairs window as Tony runs away.

Davies's family battle complements the one in D. H. Lawrence's *Sons and Lovers*. Configurations differ, but both stories are about how children inherit allegiances, and about the debilitating-energizing intensity that artists contend with. In Davies's film, the children grow up with the cycle of sorrow far from completed.

After generations of bitter relations, men and women have no visible means of attaining a lasting rapport. Falling in love is a ruse. Men tend to be either brutes or vague, beaten boys, passionate only about football. Women wind up bitter shrews or saintly sufferers. Songs lie, and still, the dream of (re)union survives in the singing. Love, you understand, is a many-splendored thing. [Georgia Brown, 8/15/89]

Do the Right Thing (1989)

Dir./Scr. Spike Lee
120 min.

The effect of motion pictures on human behavior is a question that's been debated for nearly a century, but *Do the Right Thing* is being treated in some quarters as a blueprint for catastrophe. The experience of this movie is complicated and perhaps chastening, but is also skillfully organized and not exactly unpleasurable. *Do the Right Thing* is bright and brazen, and it moves with a distinctive jangling glide. Set on a single block in the heart of Brooklyn on the hottest Saturday of the summer, it offers the funniest, most stylized, most visceral New York street scene this side of Scorseseland.

Lee is a deft quick-sketch artist. His Bed-Stuy block—a dank pizza stand, a Korean grocery, a storefront radio station, a half-dozen decrepit brownstones—is as humid as a terrarium and as teeming with life. Taunted by a moving chorus of heedless high school kids, the tormented, borderline Radio Raheem (Bill Nunn) stalks the neighborhood with a humongous boombox. Meanwhile, a retarded stammerer (Roger Guenveur Smith) peddles a double portrait of Malcolm X and Martin Luther King Jr. The irascible Mother Sister (Ruby Dee) stares contemptuously out her window at the beer-sozzled busybody known as Da Mayor (Ossie Davis), as a trio of street corner philosophers shoot the breeze beneath their portable beach umbrella, badmouthing Mike Tyson, the Korean greengrocer, and the proud but foolish Buggin' Out (Giancarlo Esposito), an irate hiphopster looking for a fight. Someone opens the hydrant. The cops turn it off. People get on each other's nerves. Da Mayor saves a kid running for the Mister Softee truck. The sun starts going down; you're waiting for the catastrophe.

Do the Right Thing has a surplus of data; it's filled with low angles and crowded, panoramic frames, the characters peering over each other's shoulders like good and bad angels in a medieval morality play. Everyone interacts with everybody else, the diminutive hero Mookie (played by Lee) threading his way among them, delivering pizzas, dispensing advice, dropping in on his girlfriend. The other unifying presence is Mister Señor Love Daddy, the DJ who broadcasts twenty-four hours a day. If Mookie is a black everyman, Mister Señor Love Daddy is the celestial spirit of the neighborhood, at one moment offering a celebratory litany of black artists, at another calling time out to end a cathartic montage of ethnic slurs.

Lee, himself, isn't quite so mellow; his portraits are affectionate but not exactly flattering. Few black filmmakers have ever been this bold, and it's telling that in a movie as filled with intricate checks and balances as this, he would make the most obnoxious, least articulate character the ultimate victim. Everyone has his or her own agenda. Mookie is introduced counting his money, then nuzzling awake his sister Jade (the filmmaker's sister, Joie Lee) as Sal (Danny Aiello) pilots his battered white Cadillac toward his "famous" pizzeria, warning his squabbling sons, "I'm gonna kill somebody today."

Given a weary dignity by Aiello, the patriarch Sal is a complex creation. Crude but hardworking, the pizza man is the movie's sole embodiment of the American Dream. It's Sal's fantasy that his sons will someday inherit this empire of nourishment—in a moment of generosity, he even declares that there will always be a place for the hired hand Mookie. Sal's success is comprehensible, his paternalism has a human face.

A daring mix of naturalism and allegory, agitprop and psychodrama, *Do the Right Thing* begins with a Brechtian call to "wake up." The choppy, fragmented narrative seems much smoother on second viewing, once you get the spiral structure. The flow is teasingly eruptive: Lee designs his production numbers with an eye toward MTV. The movie opens with a surge of rock-video energy and a burst of prurient militance as Rosie Perez in boxer shorts pugnaciously gyrates to Public Enemy's "Fight the Power." This anthem has an irony that only becomes apparent when the film is over.

Lee has already taken a fair amount of criticism for sanitizing his street scene. But the real issue is not the absence of drugs or street crime; the real issue is racial solidarity. No black character on this street may exploit another for economic gain. Thus, no black character can operate any sort of business or hold any real authority. No black character, save Mookie (and the ethereal Mister Señor Love Daddy), is shown to be gainfully employed. Where *School Daze* offered a critique of black racism and class conflict, *Do the Right Thing* presents no essential divisions within the black community. Discontent is signaled by the endless series of personal turf wars, the movie touching lightly on the pain in having your sense of self bound up in a pair of sneakers or a radio, the relative merits of this major league pitcher or that pop music superstar.

There are a number of powerful black personalities in American show business, but Lee is unique, having gone further on his own terms than any other black filmmaker in American history. In addressing racism and racial violence, while refusing to take an unambiguous stance for (white) civil order, Lee risks being blamed as the messenger of bad news—if not as an outright demagogue. Joe Klein, *New York*'s expert on race relations, predicts that while white liberals debate *Do the Right Thing*'s message, "black teenagers won't find it so hard. . . . *white people are your enemy.*" In spite of this hysterical accusation of cinematic wilding, it seems obvious that (1) most black teenagers don't have to see *Do the Right Thing* to have feelings about white people; (2) there is no monolithic, unthinking response to this film anyway; and (3) the vast majority of Lee's fans would probably rather star in his next movie than torch the bijou where it's shown.

Do the Right Thing, 1989; written and directed by Spike Lee

But even if black teenagers are angry enough to burn it down, Spike Lee didn't invent that destructive rage or American racism. Did George Bush need *Do the Right Thing* to get himself elected by running against Willie Horton? Americans spent the past eight years under a Teflon smile button whose pleasure it was to deny that racism *ever* existed in America—let alone that it might actually be a live social problem.

The ending of *Do the Right Thing* is certainly upsetting (and upsettingly incoherent), but its pathos and self-defeat are real. In the absence of an organized movement, honest political leadership, and a realistic sense of American life, the alternative for those this system denies will be to fight whatever comes to hand, even if they are only the powers that *seem* to be. [J. Hoberman, 7/11/89]

Dogville (2003)

Dir./Scr. Lars von Trier
178 min.

The Scarlet Letter, D. H. Lawrence noted, "isn't a pleasant, pretty romance. It's a sort of parable, an earthly story with a hellish meaning." So too Lars von Trier's *Dogville*.

A beautiful fugitive, suggestively named Grace (Nicole Kidman), is harbored, then exploited and nearly crucified by the denizens of an American small town until, in a convulsive finale, she brings down upon them God's wrath. For passion, originality, and sustained chutzpah, this austere allegory of failed Christian charity and Old Testament payback is von Trier's strongest movie—a masterpiece, in fact.

Working with a handheld camera on a nearly bare soundstage, von Trier represents his town as a nearly life-size schematic plan. Less a narrative than the scaffolding on which a story might be constructed, *Dogville* is divided into nine chapters (and a prologue) and infused with the fathomless sarcasm of John Hurt's insinuating voice-over. It's the blueprint for a movie given form by the mind's eye. Although described as filmed theater, *Dogville* feels more like filmed radio.

The terrific, oddball cast includes Ben Gazzara as a blind man in proud denial, Lauren Bacall as an acerbic shopkeeper, and Philip

Baker Hall as a hypochondriacal doctor. Blair Brown, Patricia Clarkson, Chloë Sevigny, and Stellan Skarsgård are also seen to excellent advantage, as is Paul Bettany, who plays the nominal hero, a smug do-gooder and writer manqué. But the movie belongs to Kidman, who delivers another remarkable performance—acting natural in an almost absurdly diagrammatic setting while playing a character who seems naturally good.

Grace arrives on the eve of the vernal equinox; the Fourth of July marks her glorious integration into Dogville's polity. Blossoms fill the air as the townspeople hold their Independence Day picnic and together sing the patriotic hymn "America the Beautiful." Some sort of cosmic drama is about to unfold at the dead end of the Rocky Mountain road: "God shed his grace on thee." It's a beautiful moment. Speaking for the town, the blind man thanks Grace for showing them who she is. All too soon, however, she will show them who they are. The appearance of a police wanted poster precipitates a moral crisis that reaches its climax with autumn. Running nearly three hours without a single boring minute, *Dogville* builds in suffering to the apocalyptic conclusion. The fugitive is punished—not least for her various good deeds. At this point, the movie does become painful. God shed his Grace and has now returned—in the form of gangster king James Caan.

Is Grace a political refugee? A fallen angel? A guilty moll? While *Dogville* was in production, von Trier suggested that his political inspiration was Denmark's new restrictions on immigration. When the movie premiered in Cannes, however, it was taken personally by some American critics as an affront. Indeed, *Dogville* is set in a realm one might abstract from Hollywood movies. Von Trier populates his community with stock figures and, as Arthur Penn did in *Bonnie and Clyde*, evokes Depression America with a few cloche hats, Model T's, and a bit of FDR.

Dogville travesties Thornton Wilder's *Our Town* and glosses its evil twin, Shirley Jackson's "The Lottery," in which the inhabitants of an idyllic New England town hold an annual ritual to stone one of their citizens to death. But the most interesting of von Trier's inspirations—referenced for maximum impact at the movie's end—is Jacob Holdt's multimedia presentation *American Pictures*, an unsettling mix of *The Lower Depths*, *On the Road*, and the Book of Revelation that played continuously for years in Copenhagen. Holdt's visceral sense of America as an unjust, racist, violent society—blighted by the primeval curse of slavery and defined by its black underclass—lurks under *Dogville*'s surface to explode with magnum force as the movie ends.

Von Trier's tale of martyrdom and hypocrisy could hardly seem un-American to anyone familiar with Hawthorne or *Sister Carrie* or Mark Twain's *Letters from the Earth* or the prophetic scolding of Bob Dylan's *John Wesley Harding* or the resentment of Clint Eastwood's *High Plains Drifter*. Although he's famously never been here, von Trier has imagined an America that, in its iconography and concerns, seems almost a contribution to American literature—in this case, to the specific genre of the jeremiad.

America, as we are often told, is the most Christian nation on earth; *Dogville* creates a space within which to wonder what exactly that means, specifically when two Hollywood deities sit in the backseat of a chauffeured automobile pedantically debating the definition of arrogance, discussing the quality of mercy, and parsing the nature of human nature. Abused by the good "Americans" of Dogville, Grace pays them back with some exceedingly rough "American" justice.

Dogville has a horrifying denouement, but the movie saves its catharsis for the end credits—a devastating juxtaposition of pop music and photographic evidence. It's a nasty joke, but David Bowie's "Young Americans" is so stirring—and who could laugh at these images of naked distress? The town's hitherto unseen dog turns real at the end and so does von Trier's America. [J. Hoberman, 3/24/04]

Donnie Darko (2001)

Dir./Scr. Richard Kelly
113 min.

Donnie Darko, the first feature by twenty-six-year-old writer-director Richard Kelly, is a wondrous, moodily self-involved piece of work that employs *X-Files* magic realism to galvanize what might have been a routine tale of suburban teen angst—okay, borderline schizophrenia. Part comic book, part case study, this is certainly the most original and venturesome American indie I've seen this year.

Kelly begins fiddling with normality from the opening scene, the evening of the 1988 presidential debate, wherein a sitcom family gathers in the dining room to partake of a delivered pizza. "I'm voting for Dukakis," the oldest Darko sister announces, mainly to cause her father to choke on his slice. A discussion regarding the candidates' respective economic policies quickly degenerates into vulgar abortion jokes and the revelation that middle child Donnie (Jake Gyllenhaal) is off his medication and receiving messages from outer space.

Clearly, we are dealing with an advanced life form. The mysterious forces of the universe demonstrate their power most vividly in the snoozy aftermath of the Bush-Dukakis dustup, when Donnie is summoned from his bedroom out into the night. Waking the next morning somewhere in the middle of the local golf course, he returns home to discover that a plane engine has inexplicably fallen from the sky and crashed through his bedroom ceiling. Convinced that the world will end in twenty-eight days, Donnie continues to experience alien visitations in the form of a monstrous toothy rabbit named Frank.

Signs of a parallel universe abound. An unhappy fat girl roams through Donnie's high school. His gym class impassively watches a videotape on "fear management." A beatnik English teacher assigns her students to read "The Destructors," Graham Greene's jaundiced story of teenage nihilism. Smiling and mumbling to himself, socially maladroit Donnie manages to hook up with a new girl (Jena Malone) who has the Grimm name of Gretchen and a lurid family story to match. Meanwhile, the town suffers a few curious plagues: the school is flooded, a home burns down. Donnie's shrink ups his meds and embarks on a regimen of hypnosis.

With Drew Barrymore as Donnie's English teacher, Patrick Swayze as a demonic motivational speaker, and Katharine Ross as Donnie's therapist, the casting is both showy and inspired. Holmes Osborne is a sympathetically smooth and spineless paterfamilias; Mary McDonnell, his wife, full of false cheer, carries hilarious intimations of early 1991 and the Gulf War, through her status as Dances with Wolves's righteous mate, Stands with a Fist. But the movie rests on the hunched shoulders of its spaced-out protagonist. Jake Gyllenhaal refuses to make direct contact with the camera. At once goofy and poignant, frozen and shambolic, he convincingly portrays Donnie's eccentric genius. Gyllenhaal's sidelong performance allows him to take spectacular delusion in stride—he tries to kill Frank when the rabbit appears in his malleable bathroom mirror, and he hallucinates ectoplasm extravagantly emanating from his father's chest.

Although the big influence would seem to be Paul Thomas Anderson's *Magnolia, Donnie Darko* is steeped in 1980s pop culture. The metaphysics are largely derived from *Back to the Future,* there's a particularly strange and funny allusion to *E.T.*, and in one of the most haunting scenes, Donnie and Gretchen watch *Evil Dead* in an empty theater. The sub–Toni Basil routine performed by Donnie's kid sister and her dance group, Sparkle Motion, has been as lovingly choreographed as the soundtrack has been assembled.

The events of September 11, 2001, have rendered most movies inconsequential; the heartbreaking *Donnie Darko,* by contrast, feels weirdly consoling. Period piece though it is, Kelly's high-school gothic seems perfectly attuned to the present moment. This would be a splendid debut under any circumstances; released for Halloween 2001, it has uncanny gravitas. [J. Hoberman, 10/24/01]

Earth (1930)

Dir./Scr. Aleksandr Dovzhenko
75 min.

The great Soviet filmmaker Aleksandr Dovzhenko (1894–1956) was both a sophisticated revolutionary artist and a Ukrainian tribal bard; his name epitomizes a cine-lyricism so passionate as to verge on pantheism.

Dovzhenko, the son of illiterate peasants, became a village schoolteacher, studied economics during the Russian Revolution, and entered the Soviet diplomatic service before reinventing himself as a graphic artist. Breaking into movies in 1926, he made his debut with a short slapstick satire, *Love Berry*. Compared to his peers Eisenstein and Vertov, Dovzhenko proved to be a man of many genres. His first feature, *Diplomatic Pouch* (1927), was a spy thriller, as was his 1935 *Aerograd*; his breakthrough came with the political folk tale *Zvenigora* (1927) and was consolidated with the grotesque and frenzied war film

Earth, 1930; written and directed by Aleksandr Dovzhenko

Arsenal (1929). Some fifteen years later, Dovzhenko was documenting the German invasion of the Ukraine.

After the critical attacks on his enraptured, startlingly aestheticized tractor-paean *Earth* (1930) and beginning with his first sound film, *Ivan* (1932), Dovzhenko was largely constrained to Stalinist biopics, including *Shchors* (1939) and *Michurin* (1948). But even his most doctrinaire movies are marked by personal eccentricities, including his last, the unfinished and blatantly propagandist *Farewell, America* (1950).

Dovzhenko suffered more frustration than persecution during the Stalin period, but his current reputation rests mainly on his last three silent features. *Zvenigora* is a masterpiece of magic realism made well before the term was invented. *Arsenal*'s powerful use of repetition, cartoonish images, mad angles, fondness for close-ups, and frenzied parallel action suggests a talented Eisenstein follower's attempt to blast his mentor off the screen.

The astonishingly beautiful *Earth* is unlike anything else in movies. Drafted to make a film on rural collectivization, Dovzhenko produced a myth presenting the creation of the kolkhoz as a natural phenomenon, part of a cosmic cycle of birth and death. Murdered by a crazed kulak (or wealthy peasant), *Earth*'s young hero is a martyr to the fertility of harvest. Released amid the campaign to liquidate the kulaks, *Earth* is ultimately a pagan myth made to celebrate a tragic social experiment, as exotic now as a Mayan temple or a Sienese altarpiece. [J. Hoberman, 5/8/02]

Eraserhead (1977)

Dir./Scr. David Lynch
89 min.

It is the future, I think, which is the setting for *Eraserhead*, the current midnight offering of the Cinema Village. It was written, produced, and directed by David Lynch, whose forty-five-minute film *The Grandmother* surfaced seven years ago. *Eraserhead* is a murky piece of post-nuclear guignol concerning a catatonic young couple who live together in a depressing miasma rendered unbearable by the cries of their hideous mutant offspring. Life with "baby"—a mewling, eye-rolling first cousin to the skinned rabbit from *Repulsion*—eventually drives the wife home to her lunatic parents and the bemused husband to scissor-wielding infanticide. Fans of the Sex Pistols may enjoy the simpering putty-faced creature who lives in the hero's radiator, singing in a rain of squishy protoplasm 'bout how fine things are in heaven.

Eraserhead's best scene has the hero visiting his in-laws. Their apartment looks like it was furnished by brain-eaters from *Night of the Living Dead*, dinner is a platter of synthetic mini-chickens stuffed with slime, and Lynch's portentously deliberate style suggests Bresson or Straub directing a film for Larry (*It's Alive!*) Cohen. Though its special effects are impressively nauseating, *Eraserhead* (which was partially funded by the American Film Institute and Sissy Spacek) is far too arty for 42nd Street; and so here it is, until mid-November, looking for a cult. *Eraserhead*'s not a movie I'd drop acid for, although I would consider it a revolutionary act if someone dropped a reel of it into the middle of *Star Wars*. [J. Hoberman, 10/24/77]

The Evil Dead (1981)

Dir./Scr. Sam Raimi
85 min.

The Anthology Film Archives would have been the ideal place for the world premiere of *The Evil Dead*. It cannibalizes *The Exorcist*, *Night of the Living Dead*, *The Day of the Triffids*, *The Texas Chainsaw Massacre*, and a Three Stooges classic, *A Plumbing We Will Go*. The script is balderdash; most sane adults, if they sit it out, will be revolted by the splattery climax. Why write of it?

For three good reasons—three new, young, impressive talents: Tom Sullivan, the creator of the stop-motion and makeup effects; Tim Philo, who performs fluid wonders with a home-rigged "Shaky-Cam" apparatus; and twenty-one-year-old director Sam Raimi. Raimi and a classmate at Michigan State formed a production company in Detroit and made a half-hour version of *Dead* to show to potential backers—then took what money came in and ran to shoot the feature on location in Tennessee.

Of economic necessity, the film observes an Aristotelian unity—it all takes place in and around a cabin in the woods that has been rented for a weekend by five college kids. They find a tape recorder and a book bound in human flesh, the property of a former tenant who had been researching Sumarean funeral incantations. When a tape is played, it conjures demons that promptly take possession of four of them. The only means of dispossession is dismemberment. The survivor is played by Bruce Campbell, who is not only the star but the coproducer, and therefore seems entitled to dismember the rest of the cast.

In Wes Craven's 1977 splatterfest *The Hills Have Eyes*, a *Jaws* poster was much in evidence, as if to say that *that* was fantasy and *Hills* was reality. In the cabin of the *Dead*, there is a torn poster for *The Hills Have Eyes*—but in Raimi's film the trees have genitals, as one of the girls discovers as soon as she sets foot in the woods alone and a kinky demonized pine wraps her in branch bondage and has its leafy way with her.

The movie's palette is richer than you'd expect in a sleazoid horror film. Exteriors are in melancholic autumnal tones, corpses are awash in pastel reds and greens, like putrid bon-bon assortments painted by some demented Renoir. Philo's camera is on the prowl during most of the film—these dogged, well-organized movements manage to impose some formal cohesion on the vacuous proceedings. The climactic "meltdown," during which teenage zombies age two thousand years in two minutes, is remarkable. In the case of one poor creature, it's as if Ivan Albright's painting for *The Picture of Dorian Gray* had twitched to life, only to deliquesce altogether after a spasm of stop-motion fireworks. [Elliott Stein, 5/3/83]

F for Fake (1974)

Dir./Scr. Orson Welles
85 min.

In *F for Fake* (1974), Welles shaped François Reichenbach's candid footage into a loose-limbed but tautly built cine-essay on "two world leaders in fakery": the prolific art forger Elmyr de Hory and his biographer Clifford Irving, who himself counterfeited the autobio of Howard Hughes. Bearded and bedraped, Welles serves as self-amused emcee to their strange inventions, and far from passing judgment on these charismatic tricksters, the director admires them as fellow artists and comrade tale-tellers, whose exploits reflect his own adventures in faking it (bluffing his way into the Gate Theatre in Dublin as a hungry teenager, panicking millions with *War of the Worlds*, being William Randolph Hearst . . .). Maybe the *F* also stands for the finger given to Pauline Kael ("I'm a charlatan," Welles declares early on, a note of embittered challenge in his voice). Still, *F for Fake* is chiefly a sly, spry comedy, a playful minuet of secrets and lies but, as you'll see, no broken promises. [Jessica Winter, 2/18/04]

Simultaneously slapdash and Borgesian, Orson Welles's late-career nonfiction board game of a movie may be, by ordinary standards, the most off-putting, coy, and self-satisfied object the man ever created. (It first saw festival showings in 1974.) But it's also a film that creates its own scale of experience, a sleight-of-hand exercise that asks unanswerable

F for Fake, 1974; written and directed by Orson Welles

questions of itself even as it presents perfectly obvious mysteries before us. Beginning with footage from a BBC doc, Welles dances around art forger Elmyr de Hory, his lying biographer/Howard Hughes scamster Clifford Irving, Hughes's duplicitous intercourse with the world, and the filmmakers' own canard-filled biography; accepted notions of authenticity, fakery, experthood, aesthetic value, and narrative are not only debunked but redefined. [Michael Atkinson, 5/4/05]

Faces (1968)

Dir./Scr. John Cassavetes

130 min.

I saw John Cassavetes's new film, *Faces*, three months ago, at a midnight preview. The invited audience hated it; they thought it was boring and much much too long. I thought it was great. It was a very moving film, an original film, a difficult-to-make film. But I was in a bad spot. I remembered my experiences with *Shadows*. I figured, if I'll start praising the film, Cassavetes will think that his film must be too experimental—why else would I like it? So he will start reshooting it, to make it more commercial, more like "real" cinema. Or if I start defending its length, which I thought was perfect, he may start chopping it. So I decided to keep quiet until the film goes out into the world.

Now Cassavetes's film is out, and it's getting rave reviews. I'm free to say whatever I like. I am free to say that *Faces* is a very very good movie. It's a merge between Warhol and Chekhov. What Warhol does with nonprofessionals, Cassavetes did with professionals. And when you have the special talent of Cassavetes, his Chekhovian touch—his professional actors succeed in breaking through the usual Hollywood acting techniques and open to the camera a different, unfilmed-yet reality. The cinema of Cassavetes is the cinema of emotions. Not the emotions that you see in cinema every day—fear, suspense, shock—no, Cassavetes is somewhere else. There may be suspense and shock and tension in the lives of his characters—but he concentrates on the everyday, "horizontal" reality, on the human content that reveals itself through the moment-to-moment relationships, responses between two people. [Jonas Mekas, 9/26/68]

Faces should be seen with a degree of tolerance for its rough edges and raw nerve endings. Scenes go on and on with Warholian exhaustiveness (though not exhaustion). And writer-director John Cassavetes lets all the players laugh their heads off to the point that nervousness is transformed into purgation.

Strange, different, but is it good? The notion of art as selection and compression gets short shrift in *Faces*. All in all, there are only seven master scenes with three very brief transitions and virtually no parallel editing for contrast or irony. No one seems to be cut off and nothing seems to be cut. Even at its best, *Faces* cannot be considered a triumph of cinematic form, and the formalist in me has been resisting the eccentricities of Cassavetes ever since *Shadows* a decade or so ago.

Ultimately, however, *Faces* emerges for me as the revelation of 1968, not the best movie, but certainly the most surprising. After its somewhat strained beginning, *Faces* not only works; it soars. The turning point is the first desperately domestic conversation between Marley and Lynn Carlin, a conversation swept along on its banal course by gales of nervous laughter; a conversation accompanied by physical withdrawal behind the luxurious barriers of space, walls, doors, and furniture; a conversation that in its lacking topical details and symbolic overtones is perhaps closer to aimless soap opera than to deliberate drama. But it works in ways that are mysterious to behold, as if for once a soap opera was allowed to unfold out of its own limited logic for two hours without interruptions for commercials or station identification. What we have in *Faces* is not only a failure to communicate but a reluctance to terminate, and this reluctance is one of the reasons *Faces* achieves an otherwise inexplicable intensity of feeling that transcends the too easily satirized milieu of affluently superficial Southern California. Although it is concerned almost exclusively with the lecherous delusions of pickups and pick-me-ups, *Faces* is never sordid or squalid. Cassavetes stays with his tormented, alienated characters until they break through the other side of slice-of-life naturalism into emotional and artistic truth.

All through the movie, people are intimating that they want to be alone with each other even though they have been conditioned to function only in a crowd. They are driven to sex not by desire but by an adolescent bravado that they know instinctively is spiritually futile, but they still pay lip service to the ideal of intimacy, the very ideal their society has degraded in its dirty jokes and infantile inhibitions. The characters in *Faces* start off as a lineup of emotional cripples, but somehow they all make it to the finish line with all their souls intact. If this be actors' cinema, long may it flourish. At the very least, Cassavetes deserves full credit for staging the spectacle with both conviction and compassion. [Andrew Sarris, 11/28/68]

Fight Club (1999)

Dir. David Fincher; Scr. Jim Uhls
139 min.

Let us triangulate. David Fincher's *Fight Club* is not a brainless mosh pit. Nor is it a transgressive masterpiece. As provocations go, this malevolently gleeful satire (closely adapted from Chuck Palahniuk's confrontational first novel) is extremely funny, surprisingly well-acted, and boldly designed—at least until its steel-and-chrome soufflé falls apart.

Sometimes a skyscraper is only a skyscraper and a gun only a gun, but not here. Set amid the repressive trappings of ubiquitous phallocracy, *Fight Club* means to be one sustained psychosexual ejaculation. Edward Norton, who plays the nameless protagonist-narrator, is introduced sucking on a revolver. The rest of the movie flashes back to detail just why and how this conformist have-not learned to stoke his testosterone levels and free his inner lad by playing body-slam with the primal horde. Meanwhile, Fincher flaunts his own mastery with a series of sleekly impossible, digitally contrived camera moves.

Fight Club unfolds in the deadpan, five-minutes-into-the-future environment invented by J. G. Ballard. Ballardian, too, is the narrator's job as a corporate "recall coordinator"—an occupation that sends him flying all over the country studying car wrecks and imagining midair collisions. Living inside an Ikea catalog above the same generic city Fincher devised for *Seven*, this nerdy insomniac spends his evenings cruising support groups. His favorite, naturally, is the one for men with testicular cancer, where he develops a moist rapport with a hormonally whacked ex-wrestler (Meat Loaf) and a more ambivalent relationship with another "tourist," this one female.

A kohl-eyed, chain-smoking goth rag doll living in a hovel with a dildo on the dresser, Marla (Helena Bonham Carter) is virtually the movie's only woman. *Fight Club* is boys' night out with a vengeance; the narrator's life really changes when he finds himself in a plane seat next to Tyler Durden, a vision of wildness played by Brad Pitt in red leather jacket, plaid shirt, checked pants, and orange shades. Pitt, as demonstrated in *12 Monkeys*, can be a highly charismatic maniac. After the narrator's condo explodes, he moves in with his volatile new ego-ideal, the two pals shacking up in a dank, decrepit Victorian that seems the natural efflorescence of the city's toxic waste dump.

Although Tyler's quaint job as a projectionist has bearing on the movie we are watching, the Norton character is even more captivated by his roommate's reckless taste for bare-knuckled violence. Soon the two are making a spectacle of themselves, staging nocturnal fistfights in the parking lot outside their neighborhood bar. With its gurgling savoir faire and voluptuously decayed mise-en-scène, *Fight Club* could be *Brazil* with bloody Chiclets.

For all its sadomasochistic celebration of aggro fun and cosmetic bruises, *Fight Club*'s gross-outs are mainly metaphysical. The narrator and Tyler steal fat from a liposuction clinic to make cosmetic soap. ("We were selling rich women their fat asses back to them.") Inevitably, Tyler's heavy-metal existentialism begins to attract followers. Soon, he's not only freaking out the local wiseguys with the bizarre Ramrod Club he's running down in their basement but pulling more extravagantly antisocial pranks—smashing cars, blowing up show windows, terrorizing 7-Eleven clerks.

Fight Club makes much of its tormented male characters' sense of abandonment: "We're a generation of men raised by women. . . . We are God's unwanted children." Unable to fight their fathers, they slug each other. In the movie's key scene, the narrator confronts his boss and proceeds to punch himself into a bloody pulp. As this self-administered beating suggests, *Fight Club* makes even the Nietzschean will-to-power a joke. Here's a question for daytime TV: is it possible to play Oedipus in a world without Dad? [J. Hoberman, 10/26/99]

Flaming Creatures (1963)

Dir. Jack Smith

45 min.

Jack Smith's *Flaming Creatures* (1963) has publicly surfaced again after seven and a half years in legal limbo. Despite its suppression and despite the fact that Smith has remained underground, his aesthetic progeny are everywhere apparent—most recently, the Cockettes of San Francisco and Jackie Curtis's *Vain Victory*, more generally in the work of Warhol, Morrissey and the Factory Superstars, the Playhouse of the Ridiculous (and its progeny), Ronald Tavel (who in a recent *Voice* interview compared Smith to Ezra Pound), the several artists who have been doing one-madman theater pieces in Soho this season, and in phenomena like the current Carmen Miranda revival (though, characteristically, Smith remained true to Maria Montez's more subtle and Arabian embodiment).

The initial impact of *Flaming Creatures* upon New York artists and writers was great. Smith was compared in print to Milton, Dante, Hieronymus Bosch, Wagner, and Josef von Sternberg. Prints were confiscated by the state, Jonas Mekas and others arrested at a screening. It was the first shocking manifestation of an aesthetic vision subsequently marketed as Camp, and later made palatable as Nostalgia. *Flaming Creatures'* forty-five washed-out, dated minutes depict a place where a cast of tacky transvestites and other terminal types (some costumed as recognizable genre faves—a Spanish dancer, a vampire, an exotic temptress), accompanied by recordings of popular music, shrieks, and snatches of Hollywood soundtracks ("Ali Baba is coming! Ali Baba is coming!"), dance, grope, stare, posture, and wave their penises with childlike joy. The marriage of Heaven and Hell presented with playful depravity. Gregory Markopoulos was only slightly exaggerating when he commented that *Flaming Creatures'* early audiences were astounded when their secret Hollywood fantasies burst upon the screen.

Photographically, *Flaming Creatures* is as visually sensual and as exquisitely mannered as *Shanghai Express* or *The Devil Is a Woman*. The film transcends artiness (not that Sternberg doesn't also) with the intoxicated energy and the mortal clowning that characterize the fragrant, faded Kodachrome rolls of a New Year's Eve costume ball in 1952. Despite painstaking care apparent in each composition and set-up, *Flaming Creatures* is put together with willful home-movie casual crudeness—a triumph of sensibility over craft. The flaming creatures are Smith's perfect film stars—actors so bad that they can't play anything other than their inspired selves (or any role other than their own)—who, rather than vanish into their parts, project their personalities. "A bad actor is rich, unique, idiosyncratic, revealing of himself. . . ." Warhol's conception of Superstars comes directly out of this—Mario Montez makes a stunning debut in *Flaming Creatures*.

Whereas a foreign classic like *Breathless* (1960) uses American pop cultural clichés with sophisticated Old World romantic ennui (Camus-the-Shamus), *Flaming Creatures*, Fleischner, Smith, and Jacobs's *Blonde Cobra* (1959–1962), and the 8mm films of the Bronx Mozarts, George and Mike Kuchar, are insane regurgitations of ten to twenty years' prolonged overexposure to radio and the movies. Jacobs called his early unfinished work *Star Spangled to Death*. (What *Breathless* has in common with *Flaming Creatures* or *Blonde Cobra* or *Hold Me While I'm Naked*, aside from a common Rossellini heritage, is that they are all representative of the ontological drive toward the nature of film and/or the movies by the fourth, by my reckoning, generation of filmmakers, and in this respect they are all romantic, as opposed to the more formal work of Michael Snow, Ernie Gehr, and others.) Though it is to some extent a meditation on Hollywood and Tin Pan Alley forms, *Flaming Creatures* is too obsessive to share the ironic condescension toward the mass culture of democracy that characterizes the capitalist realism of second-rate pop artists like Roy Lichtenstein or the more clever creations of Madison Avenue.

Smith, like a four-dimensional Kurt Schwitters, takes for material things at hand—the refuse and relics of his civilization—and presents them as phenomena without overt comment, though in new contexts. (This is virtually an anthropological metaphor for the job of the artist as bricoleur, old rag and bone man with a movie camera.) Using Tin Pan Alley, old *National Geographic*, thrift shop, and socially rejected human trash, Smith celebrates the commonplace with a vengeance.

All last year Smith put on weekly plays at midnight in his loft, half of which was devoted to a massive assemblage that included empty bottles of pagan punch and old tin cans, a toilet, a crutch, half a mannequin, a large heart-shaped candy box, a few commercial signs (Free All Day, U.S. Gypsum), and a rubber dinosaur, strewn with Christmas tinsel and bathed by colored theater lights from above. Despite the heap's seeming chaos, it became increasingly structured during the course of the three- or four-hour performance (even more so on subsequent viewings), much of which was Smith making minor adjustments or vacuuming while wrapped in a shawl. At a well-attended performance of "Gas Stations of the Cross Christmas Spectacular" (there were fifteen or twenty people sitting in a rickety grandstand, including a Serbo-Croatian professor who was moved to declare that this was two years ahead of what they were doing in Europe), a Japanese destruction artist spontaneously somersaulted into the assemblage. Smith, keeping his temper with some difficulty, spent the next hour painfully restoring his trash to its former state.

Smith is exemplary for his use of music as a thing in itself and not as commentary or for background, though he often creates intersections between image or action and sound (or art and life) that are totally left field and weirdly hilarious. (One play was briefly recessed at about 3 A.M. while the audience shared a joint. Stoned, I perceived Smith go to his coffin-enclosed phonograph and play Merle Haggard singing, "We don't smoke marijuana in Muskogee. . . .")

Other films by Smith, *Normal Love* (1964) and *No President* (1969), are unavailable—if they still exist. *Flaming Creatures* is the brilliant overture to a body of work that has continued to grow despite (or rather because of) its lack of recognition. [J. Hoberman, 2/3/72]

The Flower Thief (1960)

Dir./Scr. Ron Rice
70 min.

Taylor Mead of *The Flower Thief* is the happy innocent, the unspoiled idiot. He has a beautiful flower soul. He will go to heaven like all children do. The idiot and the child are unspoiled by the conventions, laws, and ideas of the world. The idiot today is the only character through which a poet can reveal the beauty of living. Salinger chose children. The entire beat generation chose idiocy. The idiot (and the beat) is above (or under) our daily business, money, morality. It is bad, it is pretty bad when we have to learn from the idiot, but that is exactly where we are today. All wise men have gone mad.

That's why *The Flower Thief* is one of the most original creations in the recent cinema (or in any other art, for that matter). There is nothing revolutionary about it, no world-shaking techniques. It is the simplest, the humblest movie there can be. It is almost as innocent and idiotic in its techniques as it is in its content. It is like Taylor Mead himself: you take him as he is or you reject him as he is; you can't improve upon his imperfections or his idiocy (child's mind, one critic said), you can't criticize him. *The Flower Thief* is one of those few films in which the sloppiness is part of its content: it is difficult to criticize it on technical grounds without destroying its very content.

So there he is, Taylor Mead, the idiot, the child, the poet, the modern hero, Ron Rice's child, walking across the screen, slowly, step by step, in his sport shoes, no hurry, no urgent business, no stock markets to crash, no telephones to answer. He walks across the garbage cities of Western civilization with his mind pure and beautiful, primeval, unspoiled, sane, a noble idiot, classless, eternal. I image Diogenes very much like Taylor Mead, sitting there in his old barrel, enjoying the sun. [Jonas Mekas, 7/19/62]

Flowing (1956)

Dir. Mikio Naruse; Scr. Toshirô Ide
117 min.

Late Chrysanthemums (1954)

Dir. Mikio Naruse; Scr. Sumie Tanaka and Toshirô Ide
101 min.

The simultaneous opening of films by Mikio Naruse at the Film Forum and the Public Theater is another step forward in the acceptance of this brilliant, downbeat director, a contemporary and peer of Yasujiro Ozu and Kenji Mizoguchi. Although neither is a masterpiece, both *Late Chrysanthemums* (1954) and *Flowing* (1956) offer good introductions to the director, who once recalled, "From the youngest age I have thought that the world we live in betrays us." *Late Chrysanthemums* has the more flamboyant characterizations, *Flowing* the more nearly perfect structure.

If Naruse has finally caught on, it's in part because his movies exhibit certain classic Hollywood values that no longer exist. Like Sirk or Ozu, Naruse was a director of family dramas, or "women's films." His material resembles Ozu's, but his is an altogether tawdrier, less transcendent, unhappier world. The paradigmatic Naruse figure is a woman alone, living in what Audie Bock calls a "condition of trapped awareness." Although Naruse, like Ozu, is less interested in drama than in states of being, compared to him Ozu is a sentimental Pangloss. "Ozu's widows," Bock points out, "are not permitted to need money or think about remarriage, and no one in an Ozu film is permitted to dislike his job or be openly exploited by his family members." In Naruse's world as in life, however, money is a problem, widows are ambivalent, jobs can be demoralizing and so can families. Furthermore, there is usually no resolution.

Naruse exhibits an extraordinary empathy for his protagonists, yet (unlike Mizoguchi, who specialized in "fallen women" melodramas) he never sentimentalizes them. An uncanny ability to operate between the maudlin and the mordant is only one of Naruse's mysteries. Although the evidence on the screen shows him to have been a brilliant director of actresses, by most accounts he is said to have hardly directed at all. "More than merely reticent," his "refusal to talk was downright malicious," recalled Hideko Takamine, the actress most associated with Naruse. "Even during the shooting of a picture, he would never say if something was good or bad, interesting or trite. He was a completely unresponsive director. I appeared in about twenty of his films, and yet there was never an instance in which he gave me any acting instructions."

Was Naruse then an illusionist who created performances as well as films in the cutting room? *Flowing*, in particular, is so densely edited, it could be the formal precursor to Nagisa Oshima's 1966 *Violence at Noon*, a tour de force that has something like two thousand cuts in ninety-nine minutes. Naruse never holds a shot for emphasis—his deceptively artless restraint makes even Ozu seem affected. The typical Naruse film is an open-ended accumulation of ordinary events and recurring incidents. Elusive and teasing, his movies are constructed of hints, private rituals, and half-explained intrigues, bound together by the mysterious circulation of ephemeral bits of paper (tickets, letters, photos). "Flowing" is an apt meta-title for Naruse's work; his cinema, Kurosawa observed, is "like a deep river with a quiet surface disguising a fast-raging current underneath." Kurosawa was describing Naruse's ability to imbue a complex montage with the fluid impression of a single take, but the metaphor is more encompassing. There are unplumbed depths of fatalism and resignation just below the deceptively placid surface of any Naruse film.

Late Chrysanthemums and *Flowing* are both about geishas—a subject particularly well suited to Naruse's interests. On one hand, the geisha is a metaphor for a traditional, if not archaic, Japan; on the other, her relative freedom (and the price she pays for it) throws the situation of Japanese women into bold relief. Then, too, the geisha is an extreme model for any kind of social role-playing. As Ian Buruma has written, the geisha is "the ultimate human work of art. . . . Everything she does is stylized according to strict aesthetic rules. Her 'real self' (if there is such a thing) is carefully concealed (if that is the word) behind her professional persona." It's this paradoxical "real self" that concerns Naruse; as professional performers, his geishas are largely obsolete.

Kin (Haruko Sugimura), the protagonist of *Late Chrysanthemums*, is a retired geisha who lives alone except for a deaf-mute maid. The part would scarcely seem foreign to the post–World War II Joan Crawford; a hardboiled career woman (even if she does transact most of her business at home), Kin is a real estate speculator who has amassed a considerable fortune. Not that she does anything ostentatious with her riches. Investments aside, Kin's chief source of amusement is lending money to her less enterprising geisha "sisters" and engaging them in sour banter. (Among these former colleagues is Yuko Mochizuki, the Japanese cinema's archetypal self-sacrificing mother, here cast against type as a feckless cleaning woman forever cadging off her more ambitious daughter.)

The first film ever made about geishas out to pasture, *Late Chrysanthemums* is said to be one of the few projects Naruse initiated himself; despite its flowery title, the world it presents is utterly bleak. Money is the universal topic of conversation; virtually every relationship is a commodity. (One wonders if this is Naruse's view of post-geisha Japan.) Far less romantic than Mildred Pierce, Kin believes that men and children all eventually abandon you—and events prove her right. The film's drama, so to speak, has two grown children leaving their ex-geisha mothers and two of Kin's old flames drifting back into her life. That she despises one and has a secret fondness for the other ultimately means less than that both men simply want to borrow money from her. Joan Crawford might have risen up in fury, but because this is Naruse, the film reaches its climax with the impulsive burning of an old snapshot and ends simply with Kin looking for something in her pocket that is no longer there.

Old-fashioned as Naruse's movies may be, they are the opposite of escapist. Oblique, open-eyed, and relentless, the film they most suggest is a thin membrane over the void. [J. Hoberman, 12/3/85]

Gertrud (1964)

Dir./Scr. Carl Theodor Dreyer
119 min.

Carl Dreyer has lived long enough to know that you live only once and that all decisions are paid in full to eternity. Some critics have attacked Gertrud herself as a Hedda Gabler character consumed by her destructive demands for perfection in others. The difference between the two, however, is the difference between a genuine idealism, however intolerant, and foolish fantasizing. Dreyer did not create the character of Gertrud. He "merely" adapted a play to the screen. Yet no mere adaptation could capture the lyrical intensity and lucid interiority of this film. "But this isn't cinema!" snort the registered academicians with their kindergarten notions of kinetics. How can you have cinema when two people sit and talk on a couch as their life drifts imperceptibly out of their grasp? The academicians are right, of course. Dreyer simply isn't cinema. Cinema is Dreyer.

Gertrud, 1964; written and directed by Carl Theodor Dreyer

That wildly beating heart struggling against its mortal coils, that fierce resignation one encounters in a character who realizes too late that love is the only meaningful issue of life, the only consolation of memory. Admittedly, there is something cold and merciless and implacable in Dreyer's vision of life, and the audience may be put off by the film's intolerant attitude toward inadequacy. But Dreyer should not be tagged as an elitist. He grasps and treasures what he has held despite his tortured awareness of what he has lost. The tenacity of his art is summed up in the ceremonial style Gertrud maintains to the last flickering light of her life; to the last conversation on a couch; to the last warm, human encounter before the meaningless mists of eternity enshroud her. *Gertrud* is the kind of masterpiece that deepens with time because it has already aged in the heart of a great artist. [Andrew Sarris, 6/2/66]

Glen or Glenda? (1953)

Dir./Scr. Edward D. Wood Jr.

65 min

They've tacked on an extra "n" and dropped the lurid question mark, but I couldn't be more pleasantly stunned to see the title *Glenn or Glenda* defacing the marquee of a first-run theater if Edward D. Wood Jr., the auteur of this 1953 Bela Lugosi vehicle (aka *I Changed My Sex*, aka *I Led Two Lives*, aka *Transvestite*), were to posthumously receive next year's American Film Institute "Life Achievement" award.

Wood (1922–1978), whose last recorded opus was an 8mm "home study" segment of *The Encyclopedia of Sex*, is best-known to sci-fi buffs and connoisseurs of *mishegaas* for his monumentally inept *Plan 9 from Outer Space* (1959). He's the ultimate cult director, the terminal manifestation of "expressive esoterica." If Edgar G. Ulmer was the poet of Hollywood's Poverty Row, Wood was the Barnum of its Bowery. In addition to the pitifully burned-out, emaciated Lugosi, his bargain-basement films feature such showbiz oddities as Criswell the TV prophet, Tor Johnson the four-hundred-pound Swedish wrestler, and Vampira the beatnik ghoul girl. No more oddball than the least of his entourage, the mustachioed Wood was said to affect women's pantsuits, spike heels, and angora sweaters. Former coworkers remember him as an alcoholic prone to brag that he'd worn a brassiere and panties beneath his World War II combat fatigues.

Like *Freaks* and *Ecstasy*, *Glen or Glenda?* stopped playing 42nd Street around the time Russ Meyer's *Immoral Mr. Teas* galvanized the grindhouse circuit with real T and A. Since then, its reputation has been strictly underground. Eons ahead of its time, the film is a passionate defense of transvestism—and thus free expression—cast in the mode of a half-heartedly "scientific" exploitation flick. Wood's narrative is based on two case histories, which are recounted (with Foucauldian aptness) by a shrink to a cop. In the first, the tormented Glen—forever ogling the lingerie displays on Hollywood Boulevard—gets married and lives happily ever after with his wife's wardrobe. In the second, a disgruntled GI goes all the way and gets a sex-change operation. Formally, the entire film is structured to resemble an anterior parody of *Mon Oncle d'Amérique*, with Lugosi in the role of Professor Henri Laborit. Like Laborit, Lugosi never interacts with the other characters but remains cloistered in his laboratory (casually littered with smoking test tubes, human skulls, a crystal ball), kibitzing the action in cutaways. Every few minutes, he barges into the plot, cackling like a madman, to shriek, "Bevare! Bevare! The story must be told!" or darkly wonder, "Vat are little boys made of? Is it puppy dog tails? Big fat snails? Or maybe *Brassieres! High heels! Garters!*"

Nothing I've ever seen quite resembles the grotesque quality of this film, in which every significant moment—and there are many—is underscored by the same flash of stock footage lightning, and where everyone from a bearded lady to the cop on the beat sits around glomming the identical dog-eared tabloid headlined: "World Shocked by Sex Change." (The end of the film is announced when this well-thumbed paper lands in the garbage.) As if the plot and Lugosi's (improvised?) rantings weren't enough, Wood fills the movie with turgid dream sequences, incoherent montages, and didactic asides making much of the fact that women's clothing is more comfortable than men's. Perhaps anticipating the viewer's objection that if God had wanted men to wear brassieres, he would have given them less perfunctory breasts, Wood cuts to a shot of traffic on the freeway as the shrink narrator observes: "We're not born with wheels . . . " In short, *Glen or Glenda?* is so weird as to be ineffable. The appropriate reaction is less mirth than awe. [J. Hoberman, 5/20/81]

Gun Crazy (1949)

Dir. Joseph H. Lewis; Scr. MacKinlay Kantor and Dalton Trumbo
86 min.

Brisk, percussive, a veritable primer for intelligent camera placement and a film of great plastic beauty besides, Joseph H. Lewis's *Gun Crazy* has been mythologized as classic noir, an archetypal B, the real *Bonnie and Clyde*. The French love it.

This is the kind of movie they don't make any more—and it's as if they never did. From the moment the tabloid title (an improvement over the original *Deadly Is the Female*) screams up on the screen, *Gun Crazy* has the flavor of a Bowery hallucination. The first scene is a kind of d.t. nightmare of living in the gutter, looking at the stars. Rain drenching a studio Main Street, the camera dollies back to reveal its position inside a gunstore display window. A kid transfixed by the sight of a naked .45 shatters the glass, grabs the gun, runs off, and slips on the curb as the object of his desire skids to rest at the feet of a handy lawman.

After a vague public-service frame, which serves to place young Bart's gunlust in an institutional context—and seems the most obvious fingerprint left by the blacklisted Dalton Trumbo—*Gun Crazy* blasts off into the world of the id. The grown Bart, played by John Dall, learns to sublimate his mania—sort of—when he falls for a dame as crazy as he is. As the carnival sharpshooter Annie Laurie Starr, Welsh actress Peggy Cummins makes a sensational entrance—packaged in a snug cowgirl outfit, swiveling her hips, and advancing toward the crouched camera, a sixgun blazing in each hand. Dall is beyond smitten. He challenges her to a contest; she offers her pinky ring for a stake. They flip revolvers back and forth, take turns using each other as props, flash big slow smiles, the whole scene played in a state of sexual arousal so blatant it could short-circuit the air-conditioning of any theater that shows it.

Visually, Dall and Cummins make a superb team. Gangling and open-faced, he has a farmboy's goofy smile; lush red lips emblazoned on the pasty oval of her face, she reeks of curdled wholesomeness. Impassive and sexy, wearing the beret that Arthur Penn swiped for *Bonnie and Clyde*, Cummins's affect is totally disorienting. As they switch from showbiz to stickups, her mounting excitement is complemented by his giddy sense of unreality: "Everything's going so fast, it's all in high gear, as if it weren't me," he complains. Her response is ours: "When do you have time to think about this?"

It's been observed that Cummins gets no point-of-view shots—she's totally objectified, a pure sociopath. But her psychology is implicit in her actions (as is his); once the movie gets going, it's amazingly economical. The montage transitions are virtual ideograms: Dall and Cummins in a mountain idyll, Dall and Cummins visiting Vegas, Dall and Cummins entering a pawnshop. Lewis starts one scene with a close-up of hamburgers sizzling on a grill, maneuvering the camera to peer down the end of a tunnel-like diner where the couple spend their last two bits, then opens the next sequence with a bullet shattering a gumball machine.

Gun Crazy was built for speed, and no movie has ever made better use of an automobile. For much of the film, Lewis just plants his camera in the back seat of a car and lets it ride—Dall and Cummins plunging headlong into the landscape, as wrecked police cars recede in the rear windshield. The most cited sequence is the four-minute take, camera waiting in the car while Dall jumps out to pull a bank job, then swiveling to observe Cummins coldcock a cop. The set-piece is the intricate robbery of a meat-packing plant (what could be more appropriate than these slabs of dead flesh?); the lovers celebrate their getaway by careening 360 degrees around the parking lot before burning rubber down Main Street.

"We go together," Dall tells Cummins, "like guns and ammunition." Yeah, like sex and violence, love and death. After pulling the meat-plant job, the pair plan to split up—they drive off in separate cars, then, at the exact same moment, reverse gears, back up, embrace, and depart together, leaving the unused getaway car in the middle of the road. From then on, the movie is concerned with coming full circle, reprising earlier incidents on the highway to doom. The couple make their final escape into the mountains, speeding past work crews, crashing through barricades, pushing farther than the road itself, until their car itself begins to disintegrate around them and they're lost in the swamp, in the fog, as aren't we all.

Despite Trumbo (and unlike such socially conscious analogues as *You Only Live Once*, *They Live by Night*, *Bonnie and Clyde*, and *Thieves Like Us*), *Gun Crazy* seems to have no particular agenda other than to live fast, die young, and leave a good-looking corpse. Paul Schrader, who championed the film two decades ago in his incarnation as editor of *Cinema*, captured its appeal for the 1960s cineastes: "In no film has the American mania for youth, action, sex and crime been so immediately portrayed. There are no excuses for the gun craziness—it is just crazy." [J. Hoberman, 5/21/91]

Halloween (1978)

Dir. John Carpenter; Scr. John Carpenter and Debra Hill
91 min.

It's useless to take a lofty view of an instant schlock horror classic, but there are reasons why John Carpenter's *Halloween* stands with George A. Romero's *Night of the Living Dead* and, before that, with *Psycho*.

The resemblance of *Halloween* to the Romero film—an assault on credibility couched in documentary prose—is the utter implacability of the antagonist, a faceless psychopath of terrifying strength and preternatural ubiquity who lays siege to two households of teenagers. Otherwise, *Halloween*, a study in warm colors, dark shadows, and ceaselessly tracking dollies, owes more to the expressive possibilities raised by Vincente Minnelli in the Halloween sequence of *Meet Me in St. Louis* than to any films in the realistic school.

Psycho comes to mind because of the knife-wielding madman, and more important, because Carpenter has attempted to stretch the shower sequence into as much of a feature film as the traffic will allow. That means there are plenty of pauses—rest stops that Carpenter fills with a wholesome portrait of small-town Haddonfield, Illinois, and an abundance of in-jokes about babysitters, the local police, and kids on trick-or-treat night watching traditional (not quite schlock) movies like *The Thing* and *Forbidden Planet* on TV. The trio of teenage girls in *Halloween* are victims truly worth caring about. They speak more intelligent dialogue and are more attractively contemporary than the hundreds of blithering idiots in all the youth films this year.

Yet *Halloween* is a movie of almost unrelieved chills and of violence, conjuring up that unique mix of subliminal threat and contrapuntal physicality employed by Hitchcock. Carpenter isn't a disciplined director of narrow strategies and high aims like Hitchcock, but he does blow imitators like Brian De Palma off the screen. Carpenter's free, eclectic use of the subjective shot is enough to drive purists crazy: he uses it, though, as the basic resource of an unabashedly devious visual labyrinth in which every blank space, curve, and corner poses a threat. *Halloween*, after all, is a schlock film—the old one about the masked psycho ignited by any sign of pubescent sexuality. It would seem that Carpenter's duplicitous hype is the most honest way to make a good schlock film.

Perhaps more accurate parallels to *Halloween* would be the frisson of the final jump in *Wait Until Dark*, the ominous trompe l'oeil sentinels of *The Innocents*, and the zany cinematic control of Mario Bava in *Black Sunday*. Put them all together and you have *Halloween*, the trickiest thriller of the year. [Tom Allen, 11/6/78]

The Heart of the World (2000)

Dir./Scr. Guy Maddin
6 min.

The Heart of the World is the celluloid equivalent of concentrated juice. Guy Maddin packs nearly every human emotion (and then some) into five supercharged minutes. Commissioned by the Toronto Film Festival as one of ten short "preludes" to be screened before the main features, *The Heart of the World* was designed to withstand repeated viewings—and it does.

The Heart of the World, 2000; written and directed by Guy Maddin

Maddin has called the movie the "world's first subliminal melodrama." What it suggests is the trailer for an imaginary Soviet silent film, rereleased with a dubbed soundtrack—a mad flicker of densely edited, artfully distressed-looking footage accompanied by crazed piano music and occasional sound effects. Suitably overwrought subtitles explain that two brothers—one a mortician, the other an actor playing a Rasputin-like Jesus Christ in some sort of pageant—both love Anna, a comely "state scientist"-cum-flapper who has studied the earth's core and just discovered that the planet is "dying of heart failure." Orgy! Apocalypse! Rapid-fire shots of constructivist sets and huge crowds! Has Anna been duped into marrying some lecherously slobbering capitalist swine?

If you've seen his features *Archangel* or *Careful*, you know Maddin is a kind of movie antiquarian who delights in invented traditions and genres. He's also a master of low-budget pastiche and outrageous sight gags—here, these include a cannon in the shape of a dildo and the world's heart, which, in its ominously intermittent throbbing, suggests nothing so much as the rubber octopus in an Ed Wood movie. [J. Hoberman, 2/21/01]

A History of Violence (2005)

Dir. David Cronenberg; Scr. Josh Olson
96 min.

A History of Violence, with its Hitchcockian "wrong man" theme and continual implication of the viewer, is as coolly distanced as its title would suggest. In the film's first minute, a scarily hard-bitten killer walks on camera and perfects the flat perspective by straightening a chair. A work for hire, as well as David Cronenberg's biggest budget ever, freely adapted by Josh Olson from John Wagner and Vince Locke's graphic novel, *A History of Violence* manages to have its cake and eat it—impersonating an action flick in its staccato mayhem while questioning these violent attractions every step of the way.

Cued by Howard Shore's unobtrusive Western score, *A History of Violence* illustrates, as its title suggests, the return of the repressed—or, if you prefer, the vicissitudes of an overdetermined superhero destiny. A pair of cartoonishly chiseled normals (Viggo Mortensen and Maria Bello) live with their CGI-perfect children in a Disneyland-idyllic

A History of Violence, 2005; directed by David Cronenberg; written by Josh Olson

small town that might have been designed for the game players of Cronenberg's *eXistenZ*. In one romantic scene, Mortensen and Bello pretend to be teenagers; in their next tryst, they no longer know who they are. In between, the couple and their kids have been irrationally terrorized by a series of criminals, most impressively by Ed Harris's mutilated gangster.

Tense and atmospheric, with a real sense of animal menace, *A History of Violence* is a hyperreal version of an early-1950s B movie nightmare—albeit one where the narrative delicately blurs dream and reality, the performances slyly merge acting with role-playing, the location feels like a set, and blood always oozes from lovingly contrived prosthetic injuries. Each lie builds on another. Innocuous interaction is rife with hints to turbulent inner lives and violent fantasies. Innocent scenes are booby-trapped to explode on a second viewing. One child is shot; another wakes up screaming to be told by her father, "There's no such thing as monsters."

It's the monsters that keep *A History of Violence* from projecting a world as hermetic as the madman's mind in Cronenberg's misappreciated *Spider*. The violence is amazingly staged and increasingly cathartic. But whether directed at high school bullies or cold-blooded killers, it never fails to rebound uncomfortably on the spectator. Cronenberg's tone is too disconcertingly dry to be ironic and too scary to register as absurd. By the time William Hurt appears as a godfather from the City of Brotherly Love, *A History of Violence* has succeeded in incriminating virtually all of its characters in its particular "history," not to mention the audience (and maybe the species, too). Only in the light of that recognition can Superman return to Smallville and seek his place at the table. [J. Hoberman, 9/21/05]

Horse Thief (1986)

Dir. Tian Zhuangzhuang; Scr. Zhang Rui
88 min.

With his astonishing *Horse Thief*, thirty-three-year-old Tian Zhuangzhuang represents the aesthetic vanguard of the new Chinese cinema. The child of two prominent movie actors, Tian (like his fellow innovator Chen Kaige) was sent into the countryside during the Cultural Revolution, joined the army to escape the work brigade, and entered the Beijing Film Academy when it finally reopened in 1978.

Like other "fifth generation" directors, Tian made his first films in provincial studios and took a radically new approach to China's non-Han ethnic minorities. Set in Tibet, *Horse Thief* instantly conjures up its own enigmatic world—full of masked demon dancers and mummified totems, with the flutter of sacred banners and the spinning of prayer wheels giving the superbly oblique action a primal backbeat. The dialogue is sparse, but the movie is far from silent. Ambient sound is often strategically replaced by a sensational mix of growled prayers and tolling tubular bells; this dense aural montage is matched by startling jump dissolves and multilayered superimpositions.

Produced for the innovative Xi'an studio, *Horse Thief* makes only token concessions to bureaucrat-think. Like all minority-language films, it's dubbed into Mandarin, while a tacked-on title situates the essentially timeless (but also contemporary) action in "1923," well before the occupation of Tibet. According to Xi'an studio head Wu Ianming, the only cuts ordered by the film ministry were the elision of the corpses from three "sky burials"—like Parsis and Jains, Tibet Buddhists raise their dead up to heaven by exposing human remains to carrion birds.

Horse Thief opens with one sky burial (a cluster of circling vultures intercut with a crimson row of chanting monks), and ten minutes into the movie you suspect that you've already seen more Buddhist ritual than appeared in all Chinese films combined. The elliptical narrative concerns the perverse apotheosis of the hardboiled horse thief Norbu who, although pious (he gives most of his loot to the local temple), is cast out by his clan and compelled, along with his family, to wander to his doom. *Horse Thief* lacks the overt political boldness of Chen's *Yellow Earth*—it may be that making a feature in Tibet is a statement enough, let alone one that takes so flamingly neutral a view of the local sacraments. Still, like Chen's *Big Parade*, *Horse Thief* articulates a conflict between the individual and the collective against a backdrop of overwhelming political pageantry.

Economical yet spectacular, Tian fills the screen with a field of flickering candles or a blizzard of paper prayers scattering into a valley.

(Later, snow will fall on a kindred green void as Norbu holds his dead child.) *Horse Thief* recalls the sort of ecstatic ethno-lyricism with which progressive Czech filmmakers of the 1930s embraced the backward Carpathians, but Tian's visionary insistence lofts him to the headier realm of such anthropological aesthetes as Sergei Paradjanov, Robert Gardner, and Werner Herzog. Its vast, empty landscape accentuated by a dramatic use of CinemaScope, the movie has an epic sweep—it suggests a Western told from a Native American point of view.

Doubly exotic in our context, *Horse Thief* is doubly unorthodox in its own: at once a corrective to the Han-chauvinist representations of national minorities and an affront to the stylistic conventions of the traditional Chinese cinema. Even more than *Yellow Earth*, *Horse Thief* is the movie that should put the new Chinese cinema on the world map. [J. Hoberman, 1/12/88]

The House Is Black (1963)

Dir./Scr. Forugh Farrokhzad
22 min.

In 1962, beloved and controversial poetess Forugh Farrokhzad went to Azerbaijan and made this short film on the grounds of a leper colony, presaging in twenty-two minutes the entirety of the Iranian new wave and the international quasi-genre of "poetic nonfiction." It's a blackjack of a movie, soberly documenting the village of lost ones with an astringently ethical eye, freely orchestrating scenes and simply capturing others, while on the soundtrack Farrokhzad reads her own poetry in a plaintive murmur—this in the same year as *Vivre sa vie* and *La Jetée*. (Chris Marker has long been a passionate fan, as has Abbas Kiarostami, whose *The Wind Will Carry Us* owes its title and climactic verse to Farrokhzad.) It was the only substantial piece of cinema Farrokhzad ever made. Five years later, having already attained near legendary status in Iran for her writing, she was killed in a car crash at the age of thirty-two, guaranteeing her posthumous fame as a feminist touchstone for generations of angry Persian women. [Michael Atkinson, 2/23/05]

I ♥ Huckabees (2004)

Dir. David O. Russell; Scr. David O. Russell and Jeff Baena
106 min.

In a career that otherwise defies classification, the writer-director David O. Russell has found humor where others fear to tread or never think to look. *Spanking the Monkey* (1994) is a comedy about mother-son incest; *Flirting with Disaster* (1996), a comedy about adoption and adultery; *Three Kings* (1999), a comedy about the moral confusion of war. A euphoric bungee jump into the abyss of the Big Everything, *I ♥ Huckabees* is by far his boldest: a comedy about the meaning of life, the nature of reality, the mystery of consciousness, and the elusiveness of infinity. It poses questions seldom spoken out loud and generally not heard at your local multiplex: "How am I not myself?" and "Is existence a cruel joke?" and "What happens in a meadow at dusk?" and "Do you love me, with the bonnet?"

Balancing an almost unfeasible multitude of ideas at any given moment, *Huckabees* defies lucid synopsis. Poet-activist Albert (Jason Schwartzman), a fervent campaigner against suburban sprawl, hires "existential detectives" Bernard and Vivian Jaffe (Dustin Hoffman and Lily Tomlin) to investigate a coincidence that he hopes will illuminate an underlying truth about his life. Variously aiding and complicating the client's psychic "dismantling" are Brad (Jude Law), a slippery exec who muscles in on Albert's coalition on behalf of Huckabees, a Target-like department store; Brad's girlfriend and Huckabees model Dawn (Naomi Watts); Albert's fellow patient Tommy (an amazing Mark Wahlberg), a firefighter enraged about September 11, 2001, and the evils of the petroleum economy (perhaps a holdover from *Three Kings*, where Wahlberg's character was forced to drink crude oil by an Iraqi torturer); and the frosty Caterine Vauban (Isabelle Huppert), a French philosopher who offers a seductive nihilist alternative to the Jaffes (her business card promises "cruelty, manipulation, meaninglessness").

If Russell's blithely profound mishmash of screwball Sartre and zany Zen seems incongruous, it's because movies have historically consigned existential musings to the more passive and agonized sectors of art cinema. *Huckabees,* like Russell's other films, is furiously active, bordering on unhinged, and its farcical tone proves ideally suited to philosophical striving. The movie acknowledges that to undertake such a quest is often to risk ridicule, even as it reconnects existentialism to a rich tradition of absurdity. In a sense, its insistence on the inadequacy of any one school of thought goes right to the core of existentialism.

Huckabees may be the most heartfelt cinematic reaction yet to 9/11—especially in Wahlberg's character, it crystallizes the free-floating confusion and despair of the post–9/11 world and shows a bracing willingness to dive in. A furiously depressed election-year howl of liberal-left impotence that somehow lands on a grace note of provisional optimism, it's a film that positions the very act of constant questioning as a life-saving rebellion. [Dennis Lim, 9/29/04, 2/23/05]

I Was Born, But . . . (1932)

Dir. Yasujiro Ozu; Scr. Akira Fushimi and Geibei Ibushiya
100 min.

One of the rare, joyful movie experiences. Ozu re-creates his childhood. The childhood of two boys whose parents move into a new neighborhood. Ozu works with very carefully selected details and with perfect execution. The feelings, thoughts, games, relationships of the two boys and their friends are outlined with realism, humor, and growing social consciousness. There are lines in this movie on the subject of schools, education, rich, poor that sound exactly like reading *Rat* (my favorite underground paper since women took over its editorship). Which goes to prove, for the millionth time, that a genuine and inspired artist transcends the temporary—his work becomes eternally relevant. *I Was Born, But . . .* is as true and as moving and timely today as it was in 1932. As Buddha used to say (in case you are wondering, I'm quoting from Buddha's unpublished works, soon to come out): One should never underestimate the power of Art. [Jonas Mekas, 4/23/70]

I'm Going Home (2001)

Dir./Scr. Manoel de Oliveira
90 min.

Manoel de Oliveira's *I'm Going Home* is a highly literary—or, at least, a highly intertextual—work, as well as an uncharacteristic one. It shows the ninety-three-year-old Portuguese master in a surprisingly humanist mode. Indeed, the story of an aging actor's bereavement may be as close as Oliveira has come to making a commercial movie.

A rueful hurdy-gurdy provides the recurring theme. *I'm Going Home* opens with Gilbert Valence (Michel Piccoli) onstage, more whining about than raging against the dying light as the title character in Eugene Ionesco's absurdist intimation of mortality, *Exit the King*. This raggedy production is the first of the movie's three lengthy quotations. Oliveira's staging is more avant-garde than the play's; he willfully contrives to have Piccoli turned away from the camera. Something is happening backstage; after his curtain call, Valence is informed that his wife, daughter, and son-in-law have been killed in a car crash—leaving him only his twelve-year-old grandson.

Oliveira does not invite the viewer to mourn Valence's loss. The filmmaker's concern is with the actor's transformation. "Some time later," per a formal title, we see the old man alone in a dark room on a beautiful day. Nevertheless, he can still smile, sign autographs, and riff with café waiters. Indeed, Valence is back onstage, playing Prospero in *The Tempest*. On impulse, he even buys a pair of expensive brogue shoes. These become one of the movie's key metaphors. Oliveira grants them a lengthy close-up even as Valence's pushy agent, who is hoping to land his client a role in a cheesy made-for-TV movie, suggests that he has become too isolated. "Don't forget, I act—I'm constantly in someone else's shoes," Valence tells him. All is vanity. Leaving the meeting, the actor is mugged by a junkie who absconds with his footwear as well as his wallet.

A ninety-three-year-old can scarcely be unacquainted with loss. Oliveira's camera placement is blithely distanced. (The frequent scenes shot through shop windows effectively convert the action to pantomime.) Pointedly set on the eve of the millennium, *I'm Going*

Home is restrained, precise, and unobtrusively wry. Luxuriating in "empty" moments, Oliveira is more interested in habitual behavior than in human misery. The big dramatic turn comes when Valence is called for an urgent meeting with an American director (John Malkovich) who is on location in France shooting an English-language version of the original unadaptable text, James Joyce's *Ulysses*. The actor playing Buck Mulligan has come down sick, and Valence is thrown into the breach.

Piccoli, a relative youth at seventy-six, albeit a saturnine performer with no shortage of joie de vivre, enjoys a role that allows him full range: doddering monster, wise enchanter, genial celebrity, stubborn artist, doting grandfather, and, finally, miscast actor. Grossly made up in a wig and a pasted-on mustache, Valence is hopelessly wrong for the part of Mulligan, even before he opens his mouth and his heavily accented, garbled English clashes with the rest of the cast's brogues. Valence stumbles through the role, perhaps closer to Ionesco's pathetic monarch than he would like to admit. To add to the dry comedy, most of the scene is played out in the mirror of the director's impassively appalled reaction.

New beginning or false start? It's suggestive that the film within the film never gets beyond *Ulysses*' first few pages. Escaping the studio, Piccoli is warmly affecting and so is this adroitly minimalist movie. Take the title as you will—Oliveira's confidence is exceeded only by his serenity. [J. Hoberman, 8/14/02]

In a Year of 13 Moons (1978)

Dir./Scr. Rainer Werner Fassbinder

124 min.

Rainer Werner Fassbinder's *In a Year of 13 Moons* takes its place with *The Bitter Tears of Petra Von Kant* (1972) and *Fox and His Friends* (1975) as films in which Fassbinder confronts directly the dramatic and psychological consequences of "deviant" behavior. In many ways, the transsexual Elvira (formerly Erwin) Weishaupt in *13 Moons* is one of the most hopelessly alienated characters Fassbinder has ever conceived.

Petra Kant and Fox were at least partially sheltered by a milieu in which their sexual predilections were the norm rather than the exception. Elvira, played by Volker Spengler, does not really fit anywhere in the curiously anomalous atmosphere of Fassbinder's Frankfurt, Germany, in 1978. Elvira's very first misadventure is grotesque and disconcerting. Adorning herself/himself in men's clothes, she/he goes cruising along the river bank to pick up a young boy. When her date opens her fly and discovers no male organ, he calls over his hustler pals, and they beat Elvira/Erwin up for misrepresenting the merchandise. After this abjectly absurdist humiliation, it seems inconceivable that any such character could continue to function throughout a feature-length film. But Elvira's degradation is just beginning. Her actor-lover slaps her around a bit, drags her before a mirror to demonstrate how hideous she has become, and then brutally abandons her. After falling off the hood of her lover's speeding-away car, Elvira is tended to by Zora, a kindly prostitute friend, in one of the film's few merciful interludes. Eventually, the last five days of Elvira's tortured existence parade before us in ever more intricately developed encounters. There are no flashbacks as such, but the past of Elvira/Erwin begins to cast its dark shadow on the present. Erwin Weishaupt worked for a time in a slaughterhouse, and Elvira/Erwin revisits one such establishment to reacquaint herself/himself with the matter-of-factness of the job. Far from recoiling in horror from a spectacle that may disturb many viewers, Elvira seems to find solace in the plight of the doomed beasts: "It's blood and death that gives an animal's life meaning."

Fassbinder has dedicated the film to a friend who committed suicide, and he and Spengler seem to share a spiritual rapport in achieving an uncompromisingly lyrical intensity. As if to move even further from the clinical toward the poetical, it is established that Erwin obtained the sex-change operation not because of any hormonal promptings or even out of any gay predilection, but because of a very specific affection for a "straight" man, who casually (and thoughtlessly) remarked that Erwin would be his type if he (Erwin) were a woman. Despite being a husband and a father, Erwin took the surgical route to womanhood, but all in vain, as it turned out. Meanwhile, the object of his affections has become a powerful real estate tycoon with a hilariously demonstrated enthusiasm for Martin and Lewis movies. But every encounter undertaken by Elvira/Erwin ends in an emotional dead end. She/he was doomed from birth, through early traumatic years in an orphanage to the painful vaudeville of sex-role reversals, and we bear witness to the almost unrelieved pain and suffering of this uncomfortably androgynous victim. Yet for the truly discerning cineaste, *In a Year of 13 Moons* ends up as a truly exalting experience. More than ever before, Fassbinder has taken me so far outside myself that I do not think that my sensibility can ever be completely "straight" again. Undoubtedly, Fassbinder's film will not find conspicuous support from the more sybaritic spokesmen for gay liberation. Too much gloom and doom and all that. But it will be difficult for anyone, straight or gay, to argue that Fassbinder does not work on his superficially unsavory subject from the inside out, instead of vice versa. And Spengler provides a performance of such exquisite gravity and resilience as to call forth every last impulse of compassion in the viewer's psyche. [Andrew Sarris, 6/16/80]

In the Mood for Love (2000)

Dir./Scr. Wong Kar-wai
98 min.

Wong Kar-wai may be the most fetishized—as well as the most fetishizing—of contemporary filmmakers, and with *In the Mood for Love* he takes this form of worship as his subject. Boldly mannered yet surprisingly delicate, this wondrously perverse movie not only evokes a lost moment in time but circles around an unrepresentable subject.

Mood is the operative word. A love story far more cerebral than it is emotional, *In the Mood for Love* invests most of its passion in the act of filmmaking . . . mainly by subtraction. Oblique events unfold in a sort of staid delirium. There may be no distinction between creating the memory and making the movie—"the past was something he could see but not touch," it is explained of the lead character—except that *In the Mood for Love* is structured on a principle of selective amnesia. The movie's presumptive title song is scarcely the only absent element.

Wong's story is set, mainly among displaced Shanghainese, in the Hong Kong of the early 1960s—the period and the milieu of the filmmaker's own childhood. Mrs. Chan (Maggie Cheung) and Mr. Chow (Tony Leung) simultaneously rent rooms in adjacent apartments in the same crowded building and are forever bumping into each other in the narrow corridor. Through a series of parallel conversations, they deduce that his wife and her husband—who are several times heard, but whose faces are never shown—are having an affair, seemingly on their frequent business trips abroad. As a result, Mrs. Chan and Mr. Chow are often alone and consequently drawn together.

This overdetermined symmetry is Wong's version of the urban romance epitomized by the 1928 silent picture *Lonesome*, in which a young couple meet, fall in love, and then lose each other in the mass-society frenzy of a Coney Island Saturday night only to discover that they actually live in adjoining rooms in the same anonymous boarding house. Wong begins where *Lonesome* ends and, in a sense, works the story backward as well as forward. (At times, Mrs. Chan and Mr. Chow pretend that they are their own adulterous spouses, rehearsing confrontations that may never take place.) With its blatantly manufactured coincidences, *In the Mood for Love* works both as experimental character drama and as ritual in transfigured time.

A largely fluid succession of short, often shot-length scenes interspersed with tantalizingly incomplete interactions between its two stars, *In the Mood for Love* is rhythmically a matter of dramatic elision and elongated privileged moments. Wong is never more modernist than in his willingness to create a narrative out of trivial dailiness, the storyteller's equivalent of the painter's negative space. If the relationship between his two elegantly unhappy and impossibly beautiful losers is sexually consummated, the audience will never know it. *In the Mood for Love* is a family romance without a primal scene.

Because the stars almost never touch, the air between them accrues an electric charge. The slightly slow-motion interludes, accompanied by Michael Galasso's stringent, wistful score, allow for the enraptured contemplation of Cheung's moving form—seen from the perspective of her affably depressed admirer—as she recedes slowly into the past. There is a sense in which the movie is all about the pensive languor with which the actress models her *qipao*. *In the Mood for Love* has many clocks but no temporal signifiers. The viewer learns to tell time by the leading lady's dresses—she wears a new one in every scene. (The size of her closet is another off-screen mystery.)

Studied as it is, *In the Mood for Love* might have felt airless or static were it not for the oblique editing. Every artful contrivance is fuel for the fire, ashes of time scattered on the wind. "That era has passed" is the closing sentiment. "Nothing that belongs to it exists anymore." Is *In the Mood for Love* Sirkian? Proustian? Can we speak of the Wongian? This forty-three-year-old writer-director is the most avant-garde of pop filmmakers (or vice versa). Poised between approach and avoidance, presence and absence, *In the Mood for Love* is both giving and withholding. Governed by laws as strict as the old Hollywood production code, it's rhapsodically sublimated and ultimately sublime.

When Mr. Chow finally decides to leave Hong Kong, the camera finds him in his office, and the image almost freezes on a gesture. Similarly, the narrative itself disintegrates into a remarkable series of vignettes—a scene predicated on a phone call placed to Singapore, a fleeting glimpse through a Hong Kong tenement door. The coda—set, with wild extravagance, in the jungle city of Angkor—is almost too lovely. The monumental merges with the ephemeral, as the stately camera tracks through the empty ruins of someone else's eternity. [J. Hoberman, 1/30/01]

Irma Vep (1996)

Dir./Scr. Oliver Assayas

97 min.

The agony and the ecstasy of making a movie isn't the freshest croissant in the café, but Olivier Assayas's *Irma Vep* sure makes it seem so. This latest feature by the forty-two-year-old festival-god was shot, in Super 16, like an on-set documentary—at once self-deprecating and megalomaniacal, it's a jagged, speedy rap fueled by cigarettes, coffee, and insomnia.

A wry and witty piece of work, *Irma Vep* puts business first, holds the art for last, and keeps stardom at center screen. Hong Kong action diva

Maggie Cheung descends, straight from a twelve-hour flight, into a churning maelstrom of production-assistant hysteria. Cheung, known as Maggie and essentially playing herself, has arrived in Paris to take the title role of the black-clad cat burglar Irma Vep in a remake of Louis Feuillade's 1915 serial, *Les Vampires*. The original cult film, a baroquely paranoid tale of criminal conspiracy, is to be updated, with some trepidation, by René Vidal, a burned-out New Wave auteur (Jean-Pierre Léaud).

For a French cineaste, *Les Vampires* is a cultural childhood lost—representing both an impossible innocence and a virtually forgotten commercial dominance—and *Irma Vep* has the atmosphere of a cheerful haunted house. René whispers cryptic phrases—he's his own oracle—while Léaud's mere presence effectively populates the movie with spectral performances for Godard and Truffaut, especially in the latter's movie-making movie *Day for Night*.

René is acutely aware that it is impossible to re-create Feuillade's unself-conscious poetry, but, unburdened by such history, his star radiates sweetness and grace. Maggie is enthusiastic, hardworking, modest, and—never less than professional—somewhat baffled by the backbiting antics of her French colleagues. At the same time, as poured into her latex bondage suit, she's the universal fetish object of desire. "You want to touch her, play with her—she's like a plastic toy," the production's hyperfrazzled AC/DC costumier Zoë (Nathalie Richard) confides. This longing is compounded by interpolated scenes of the Feuillade original (Irma's abduction and unmasking), as well as the presence of Maggie's body double, also in black latex.

Trapped in the phantom zone, temperamental René storms imperiously out from a screening of his dailies, leaving his colleagues in consternation and Maggie abandoned, forced to catch a ride to a crew party on the back of Zoë's moped. Anyone who has seen Assayas's sensational *Cold Water* knows that this director can choreograph a bacchanal. But in the theory-crazed world of *Irma Vep*, the revelers can't stop talking about movies—or even looking at them. Someone has commandeered the VCR to show the post–May 1968 faux Godard agitprop *Classe de lutte*, an even stranger fossil than *Les Vampires*—as well as another movie about movies. The image of a flickering

Steenbeck image is underscored by the militant slogan: "Cinema is not magic: it is a technique and a science."

A different sort of cine-romantic, Assayas may beg to differ with that Marxist formulation, although, as Maggie is gracious enough to demystify her own stardom, so *Irma Vep* exudes a restrained cinephilia that repeatedly questions itself. While waiting for René to return, Maggie is interviewed by an obnoxious French film buff who drones on (in English) in praise of John Woo ("*Bullet in the Head*—I think it's a great, great film") and Arnold Schwarzenegger, dismissing French cinema as snobbish, passé, and "nombrilistic" (a wonderful Franglaise coinage for "navel-gazing").

The self-parody is layered and even dialectical. Just as *Irma Vep* switches off between French and English (the latter serving as lingua franca), so the scene in which temperamental René admires a mad bit of HK swordplay in Maggie's vehicle *The Heroic Trio* also serves to play "natural" Maggie off his mannered postures. Richly hybrid, *Irma Vep* opposes decadent French auteurism with insouciant Hong Kong pop, pits Gallic play against Hollywood materialism, and juxtaposes the urge to recycle the movie past with the desire to represent the moment.

The idea of remakes extends even to the soundtrack, which includes Luna's hipster cover of the gloriously absurd Brigitte Bardot–Serge Gainsbourg duet "Bonnie and Clyde," while, as if in counterpoint, the action is interspersed with a number of gratuitous "pure" film interludes—a conversation shot on a crowded metro, a few minutes of Zoë dancing in a strobe light. *Irma Vep* is lighter than earlier Assayas, but it ends marvelously with a taste of René's vision—an act of aggression that, combining kinesis and mystery, achieves a primitive essence of cinema.

I wouldn't want to jinx the miraculous revival of a low-budget, free-wheeling, film-smart French cinema but—*zut alors!*—if it's not already here. *Irma Vep* isn't only about making movies, it demonstrates that making real ones is still actually possible. [J. Hoberman, 5/6/97]

Jeanne Dielman, 23 Quai du Commerce, 1080 Bruxelles (1976)

Dir./Scr. Chantal Akerman
201 min.

At very long last, Chantal Akerman's *Jeanne Dielman, 23 Quai du Commerce, 1080 Bruxelles* is receiving a commercial opening in New York. Andrew Sarris isn't reviewing this film, and I doubt that Pauline Kael will either. The *New York Times*, at least, *has* to see the movie, but it'll be most surprising if *Time*, *Newsweek*, or *New York* magazine bother to send anyone down to investigate Akerman's truly legendary 1975 feature.

Jeanne Dielman is—to put it baldly—a great movie and one that in film circles, at least, hardly languishes in obscurity. Made by Akerman (and an all-woman crew) when she was twenty-five, *Jeanne Dielman* has long been a touchstone for feminist film theorists.

The film, which runs nearly three and one-half hours, details a three-day stretch in the life of a compulsively organized, petit bourgeois Belgian widow (Delphine Seyrig)—a paradigm of efficiency who promptly scours the tub after bathing, finishes every morsel on her plate, doesn't even need a radio to keep her company, and turns one trick an afternoon to support herself and her teenage son. The operative word in the description is *details*: Akerman makes a spectacle unique in film history out of Seyrig's daily chores—cleaning, folding, straightening, cooking, shopping, and fucking. By the middle of the movie, her routine is so familiar we know something's amiss merely because she forgets to place the cover on the soup tureen where she keeps her earnings. And when she overcooks the potatoes, we're being primed for the narrative's lurid denouement. The static, often symmetrical compositions are invariably presented from Akerman's eye level, with the camera usually placed parallel to the wall. In other words, Akerman's geometry surpasses even the orderliness of her protagonist's life. Shots are orchestrated so that the setups slowly rotate around Seyrig as she progresses through her household tasks, which are characteristically rendered in real time.

Seyrig inhabits her role so absolutely—even to the clumsiness of her potato-peeling—that she more than justifies the deliberate pedantry of the film's full title. She appears in virtually every shot. This in a film that goes beyond Ozu in eliminating camera movement, background music, fades, or optical effects. There is very little dialogue, and, most extraordinarily, Akerman further eschews the classic rhythm of shot-countershot (reverse angles to show point of view) that French theorists say "sutures" the spectator to the screen.

Despite (and, of course, because of) its rigor, *Jeanne Dielman* is a supremely sensual film. Almost as much as it's about anything, this is a movie about the quality of recorded light and sound. Babette Mangolte's unlit cinematography is exceptionally fine, and Seyrig is forever walking in and out of rooms switching fixtures on and off while our eyes grow accustomed to savoring the same spaces as differently illuminated during the course of the day. At the same time, Akerman builds up the soundtrack into a little symphony of clicks, splashes, and slams. *Jeanne Dielman* is as monumental a formal film as Michael Snow's *La Région Centrale*; Akerman's landscape, however, is radically other. Seyrig's slow-motion breakdown, her leap into an abyss beyond the kitchen sink, packs an emotional wallop entirely different from the products of earlier (mainly male) avant-gardes.

The Belgian-born and based Akerman lived in New York in 1972, at the moment when "structural" film was at the height of its local prestige. The lessons of pre-Morrissey Warhol—the power of duration, the effect of monotony, the wonder of people simply "having," as the Hindus say, "their being"—had only recently been absorbed, while the impact of *Wavelength*'s overdetermined narrative structure was still fresh and immediate. Assimilating Warhol and Snow, Akerman made their discoveries the vehicle for her own interests, using their formalism to produce one of the most absolutely lucid movies ever made.

Obviously, *Jeanne Dielman* has its European precursors as well. The best known is Straub-Huillet's *Chronicle of Anna Magdalena Bach*, but there's also the Hamburg-based avant-gardist Hellmuth Costard's *Die Unterdrückung der Frau ist vor allem an dem Verhalten der Frauen selber zu erkennen* ("The Oppression of Woman Is Primarily Evident in the Behavior of Women Themselves"), an hour-long film of a male hippie doing a housewife's chores. But whether Akerman was inspired, influenced, or just anticipated by Costard is moot. *Jeanne Dielman* is the film that changed the face of contemporary European cinema.

Akerman has always resisted characterization of *Jeanne Dielman* (or any of her other films) as "feminist." Yet no other movie in recent years has so bluntly hyperbolized Western woman's traditional lot. On the other hand, *Jeanne Dielman* is also a work that lends itself to a multiplicity of readings. Until its climax, for example, this is a film where sex is something that happens behind closed doors—in great measure, *Jeanne Dielman* is a movie about representing what can't be shown, what can't even be felt.

Then, too, the film is a lethal travesty of melodrama—a deadpan resurrection of the ultimate weepie plot—using a situation that was a chestnut when Mizoguchi (or even Ruth Chatterton) discovered it. In affect, *Jeanne Dielman* resembles late Hitchcock, but what Hitch uses to set the table, Akerman turns into virtually the entire film. As in *Psycho* or *The Birds*, Akerman reveals the sinister in the commonplace, but she does so to a far more astute social purpose. Finally, the movie's climax—which is that, literally—suggests something perhaps fundamental about the relation of narrative to both male and female sexuality. At once spectacle and antispectacle, *Jeanne Dielman* not only criticizes the dominant mode of representing women but challenges the dominant mode of representation itself.

Here's something for the ads: if you see only one supposedly "difficult" movie—ach, make that only one movie—this year, see *Jeanne Dielman*. [J. Hoberman, 3/29/83]

This reviewer was a bit miffed last week to find himself listed on the front page of the *Voice* as the member of a de facto conspiracy against a French film entitled *Jeanne Dielman, 23 Quai du Commerce, 1080 Bruxelles*. (Try fitting *that* on a Main Street marquee sometime.)

Inasmuch as Hoberman has decided to taunt his colleagues for their insensitivity to great art, he is coy in the extreme in not revealing that he is assigned films such as *Jeanne Dielman* as a matter of editorial policy at the *Voice*. Also, Hoberman has attended enough *Voice*-sponsored "meet your advertisers" luncheons to understand that he and I are not covering the movie scene for the old *Partisan Review*. As it is, we both get considerable (and very welcome) leeway in our assignments. Still, it is generally understood that I get first crack at the turf north of 14th Street and he south of 14th Street. This is not to say that I never see movies that I happen not to review. To the contrary, I have been straining to catch *Jeanne Dielman* for eight years. Now, thanks to the very helpful Film Forum, *Jeanne Dielman* has found its ideal home in the arty precincts of Soho, and it is very much worth seeing, if only as an indication of where a certain sector of the cinematic avant-garde and a certain faction of radical feminists have been suspended for the past eight years. The *Voice*'s own front-page splurge on *Dielman* seemed to be divided along these lines, with Hoberman self-consciously supplying the avant-garde hype and B. Ruby Rich the ultrafeminist hysterics. Ironically, *Dielman* strikes me as neither particularly avant-garde nor particularly feminist. Even Manny Farber and Pat Patterson, its most articulate and most eloquent champions, place it in a box-frame tradition with such noble precedents as the works of Bresson and Ozu. Chantal Akerman is certainly not a minimalist in the manner of early pre-Morrissey Warhol. Besides, minimalism has become a commonplace of the video scene. Nor is *Jeanne Dielman* at all monomaniacal in its technique in the manner of Michael Snow.

Indeed, nothing in the panegyrics of Hoberman and Rich prepared me for how pretty and how French *Dielman* is. The performers seem to have graduated from the Robert Bresson academy for nonacting. The bright colors evoke Godard, Delphine Seyrig's hauntingly abstracted expressions the Resnais of *Last Year at Marienbad* and *Muriel*. And right next door to *Jeanne Dielman* is Fassbinder's *Why Does Herr R. Run Amok?*, another saga of petit bourgeois banality degenerating into homicidal madness.

What is more surprising still, at least from any feminist rationale, is the pinched, remarkably unsentimental characterization of Dielman herself. The Saturday afternoon Soho audience laughed on many occasions *at* rather than *with* Dielman's ridiculously excessive fastidiousness. The big trick of the film is the casting of the soft-voiced, soulful-looking Seyrig in a role that otherwise suggested a shrewish yenta. There is very little dialogue, not a smidgen of joyous conversation, and absolutely no chatter or patter. The eerie silences thus make the framed and sustained compositions seem even more painterly to the viewer's increasingly restless eye. Every article of furniture, every piece of bric-a-brac, every texture, every surface is scanned endlessly for clues to the glacial progression of the narrative.

Two brilliant sequences are alone worth the price of admission and duration (three hours and eighteen minutes being close to two hours too long). In one of the film's bizarre "babysitting" episodes, Seyrig picks up a screaming infant, which seems terrified of her, and, as we have already had intimations of her impending breakdown, we are in turn terrified that she is going to retaliate against the infant in some gruesome way. Akerman's most brilliant coup of mise-en-scène occurs in a coffee-house tableau in which Seyrig, finding her favorite table occupied and her favorite waitress out, sulks at the adjacent table, on the edge of the frame, while an intellectual-looking older woman toils away on her notebook in the center of the frame. My hunch is that most of us identify more with this otherwise unknown woman than with the wretchedly trivial and apparently mindless protagonist.

Some feminists may get a rise out of Seyrig's murdering a "john" who may or may not have aroused her sexually. (*Jeanne Dielman* is the kind of movie in which viewers do not so much wonder about characters as wonder whether they should wonder.) Even at the end, however, Akerman shows less feeling for the broken-down petit bourgeois machine that Dielman has become than Kubrick displayed for the doomed HAL in *2001*. In the final analysis, I respect *Jeanne Dielman* as a whole and even admire parts of it, but I do not feel that it breaks out of its formal shell into the realm of exquisite feeling that I have found over the years in the great works of Bresson, Godard, and Fassbinder.

There, Hoberman, I've seen *Jeanne Dielman* and taken a stab at commenting upon it. I do like difficult films, honest. Perhaps I wouldn't have been so sensitive about your supercilious comment if on that very week I had not been caught reviewing Tom Selleck in *High Road to China*, one of my more unrewarding, mainstream, white-bread assignments, while you and Rich were freaking out on art-house acid downtown. [Andrew Sarris, 4/5/83]

JLG/JLG (1995)

Dir./Scr. Jean-Luc Godard
62 min.

Like Rembrandt, the great, grizzled Godard ages in his studio, a mirror propped before the easel. His newest self-portrait, *JLG/JLG*, is at turns—and as usual—sedate, silly, and sublime. From the beginning, Godard's films have always been speculums and speculations, self-portraits in convex lenses, and, as an aging Fritz Lang put it in *Contempt*, where his project was nothing less than *The Odyssey*, "You must always finish what you have started."

As Roger Leenhardt put it in *A Married Woman*: "At any rate, one must love young wise men and old fools." (The rhetoric then was a lot plainer.)

When he was a young wise man, Godard was always enthusiastically inviting his elders (Lang, Melville, Brice Parain, Francis Jeanson, etc.) into his class as guest lecturers. Now in *JLG*, holed up in his tidy house in Rolle, Switzerland, Godard himself is his own elder, puttering with tapes, bent over his notebooks, the lamplight glowing as softly as any diva could desire. To those of us growing old along with Godard, the spectacle is especially poignant, not just because we, too, are conspicuously drooping, but because Godard, sixty-four this year (Will you still need me? Yes!), was always synonymous with youth and vitality and audacity.

A goodly portion of *JLG/JLG* is charged with death, absence, silence. The landscape (usually without figures) will be familiar to anyone who's followed the films made since Godard's move from Paris: the large lake like an inland sea, placid meadows and ordered woods, the gentle bend of a road through trees. But here the frost is on the pumpkin. The waves now lash, not lick, the shore. Stubble in the fields and on the chin.

The film's opening shots, however, are interiors—furniture and paraphernalia without their master, everything so neatly composed. (There's Brigitte, the housekeeper.) Prominently set out is a photo of Jeannot, as the boy was called; a shadow of the artist-as-cameraman falls on the wall behind. In regard to the boy's "slightly distressed look," says the shadow's voice-over, "I was already in mourning for myself." It also observes, "He possessed hope, but didn't know it was important to know who possessed him."

The question asked in *JLG* isn't so much who possessed the boy as what: first, books and paintings, then films. Except for a small off-screen voice murmuring, "I'm Anne-Marie," the who isn't addressed in terms of family or loved ones but in terms of artistic forebears. A creature of his times, only more so, Godard presents himself as technology's wild child belatedly nourished by giant faces projected on screens.

If *JLG*'s opening images are ravishingly serene, eventually, of course, the film caroms off into gagaland: Godard in a ski hat and a white lab coat teething on his stogie; the house being invaded by Cinema Center inspectors while Cassandra, a young woman in cutoffs, dusts the bookshelves. The boy can't help it.

But even at its lightest, the film's dominant mood is fever: partly, a sense of too much to assimilate, too little time and space. The lust to include, to list, to catalogue (to possess), of course, has always been there in Godard, becoming over the years one of his most endearing qualities. He's like *Les Carabiniers*'s oafish warriors Ulysses and Michelangelo, who return from the war and proudly dig out their horde of picture postcards. Touchingly, they've brought back the world.

Cinema, image, as world. Each of Godard's films is a small museum lovingly tended.

Speaking of Homer, at one point in *JLG* Godard stands on a tiny spit in the lake, a parody Odysseus, and then turns and wades ashore. Except that instead of coming home to his first hot bath or a go-round with the suitors, there's the feeling that Godard remains perpetually in exile, if not from home per se, then from human contact and from cities and their stories. Like a Russian poet confined to his dacha, he seems to be pacing the hectares, impatient for the great mediocre culture outside to fall of its own dead weight. [Georgia Brown, 5/10/94]

Johnny Guitar (1954)

Dir. Nicholas Ray; Scr. Philip Yordan
110 min.

Before there was Jerry Lewis, there was *Johnny Guitar*. Nicholas Ray's 1954 Western—a luridly operatic mix of Freudian sexual pathology and political subtext, featuring Joan Crawford's grim, glam gunslinger—was dismissed by American reviewers but embraced by *Cahiers du Cinéma* as an auteurist cause célèbre: "Le cinéma c'est Nicholas Ray," in Jean-Luc Godard's exuberant formulation.

Like all cult films, *Johnny Guitar* is a pop-cultural magpie's nest, conflating *Casablanca*, *Sunset Boulevard*, and *The Ox-Bow Incident*—not to mention Jean Cocteau. This blatantly theatrical Western immediately confounds the generic imperative with a forty-minute interior scene played by Crawford as though it were Shakespeare. The most dogged of stars (the original Demi Moore), Crawford was making her first Western since 1928. She demanded the man's role, essentially switching parts with nominal hero Sterling Hayden. "Feminism has gone too far," the *New York Herald-Tribune* began its review.

Packaged by super-agent Lew Wasserman, whose clients included Crawford, Ray, novelist Roy Chanslor, and screenwriter Philip Yordan, *Johnny Guitar* followed the second wave of the House Un-American Activities Committee's (HUAC) Hollywood hearings. Although saturated in Cold War atmospherics, the movie is less allegory than distillation; its plot turns on vigilante justice, xenophobia, and guilt by association. Ray was a former communist. So was Hayden, already regretting the "friendly" testimony that saved his career. Yordan fronted for blacklisted writers. Ward Bond, a leader of the right-wing Motion Picture Alliance for the Preservation of American Ideals, played a wealthy rancher who heads a lynch mob. He and Mercedes McCambridge, as the resident demagogue, are out to burn Crawford's witch.

The on-screen tension between the actresses was exacerbated by McCambridge's marriage to Crawford's ex, and Crawford's star fits drove her director nuts. "The atrocity *Johnny Guitar* is finished and released, to dreadful reviews and great financial success," Ray wrote to a friend. "Nausea was my reward." Sartre could not have put it better. [J. Hoberman, 8/13/03]

The King of Comedy (1983)

Dir. Martin Scorsese; Scr. Paul D. Zimmerman
109 min.

Martin Scorsese's *The King of Comedy* is not a comedy that will have you falling off your seat from the force of your belly laughs. Much of the time, you may not even feel like chuckling or smiling. You may instead be wincing from the pain of unpleasant recognition as you watch Robert De Niro's inspired, uncanny rendering of Rupert Pupkin, bridge-and-tunnel creep, autograph hound, and stand-up comedy stiff who nonetheless enfolds himself in his grandiose fantasies more fanatically than Norma Desmond ever dreamed of doing even at her looniest. Pupkin kidnaps a late-night TV host (Jerry Lewis) and holds him hostage in a bid to secure a guest appearance on his show. De Niro's is one of the most honest pieces of acting I have seen in an American movie, and he and the film will probably be punished for it. In *King of Comedy*, the talk-show world is played comparatively straight. Rupert Pupkin is not one of Woody Allen's clever schnooks who is tricked up to seem wittier and nobler than the powers-that-be, thus feeding his audience's fantasy that everyone above them is a fool and a knave. From Jerry Lewis as Jerry Langford, the Carson-like talk-show host, on down, all the establishment types that Pupkin encounters are wiser and more considerate than he is. Paul D. Zimmerman's surprisingly clear-eyed script even gives what should have been a very funny curtain line to an FBI agent. Shelley Hack as Jerry Langford's briskly efficient production assistant could have been reduced to a bitch or a bimbo so that Pupkin could gain some sympathy, but she wasn't. She is just a nice girl doing a tough job, and Pupkin is an unusually obnoxious pest.

Yet Scorsese shows himself capable of an enormous compassion, not only for Pupkin but for all the Pupkins in the world, and for the more than a little bit of Pupkin that is in all of us. When Pupkin tries to pick up the pieces of a grotesquely abortive high school "romance" with the cheerleader-turned-barmaid (played with perhaps a Pirandellian poignancy by De Niro's very talented estranged wife, Diahnne Abbott), I was much closer to crying than laughing over the desperately blazing hope that was trying to break through the thick film of cynical resignation over the girl's eyes. Mean Streets indeed! Scorsese has never forgotten what it feels like deep down inside to be left behind in the American rat race.

But he has not found much solace at the top, either. Jerry Langford's life, for all its creature comforts, is in some ways bleaker and lonelier than Rupert Pupkin's. Pupkin at least has his fantasies to keep him going. Langford must subsist entirely on a diet of reflex professionalism, instinctive suspiciousness, and galloping paranoia. Granting that

Marilyn Beck's account of the casting of Jerry Lewis as Jerry Langford is essentially correct, and that Lewis is, in effect, "acting" Johnny Carson, there is a very satisfying reversal of type involved here, and the consequences of this reversal verge on myth-making genius. [Andrew Sarris, 2/15/83]

As talk-show host Jerry Langford, Jerry Lewis has given Martin Scorsese his first dramatic performance. Actually, Lewis is not so much De Niro's costar as his straight man; it is De Niro who plays the self-appointed "king of comedy." Dressed in garish polyester, he's grown a pencil-thin mustache and slicked his hair into a razor-sharp pompadour for the role of Rupert Pupkin, a thirty-four-year-old messenger and autograph hound, still living in his mother's Union City basement, who constructs an obsessional fantasy around Langford. "I find comedians fascinating," says Scorsese. "There's so much pain and fear that goes into the trade."

Pain and fear—and the convulsive desire for public recognition—are Martin Scorsese's meat. Not even Woody Allen has chosen to dramatize his neuroses more flagrantly. Unlike Allen, however, Scorsese offers no apologies. Racism, misogyny, selfishness, and paranoid fury are right up front. More than any studio director, he resembles an avant-garde filmmaker like Yvonne Rainer, who unpacks her mind and fissures her persona with each feature, then figures it out later. Except, of course, Scorsese's subject is macho.

With De Niro as his alter ego, Scorsese has created a memorable gallery of jittery, psyched-up loners: Johnny Boy, Travis Bickle, Jimmy Doyle, Jake La Motta. As embodied by De Niro, *homo scorsesian* is a frustrated outsider fueled by a highly combustible combination of guilt, jealousy, and delusions of grandeur. Ellen Burstyn plays a female, suburban variation of the type in *Alice Doesn't Live Here Anymore*, but Scorseseville is mainly a man's world. Women are unknowable Others, children the promise of destruction. The family is at once a sacred value and something to flee like the plague.

Rupert Pupkin may be less violent than Travis Bickle or Jake La Motta, but he's no less possessed. Although he has never performed for an audience, Pupkin demands the TV show watched by half of America each night as the launching pad for his career. "To have drive is what counts!" Scorsese exclaimed in an early interview. "Anything to meet people to generate events toward your goal." Pupkin personifies this crazed pragmatism: rejected by Langford's aides and thrown out of Langford's weekend house, he ultimately gets himself on *The Jerry Langford Show* by kidnapping its star.

Originally, Scorsese wanted Johnny Carson for the role of Jerry Langford. When Carson demurred, Scorsese approached Jerry Lewis. There is a sense in which Robert Pupkin's pathology hyperbolizes the profoundly ambivalent relationship Americans have with the aristocracy of winners who, presented on TV or paraded through the pages of *People* magazine, live their lives as public drama. Among other things, the mild gossip purveyed by the news and entertainment media promotes the socially cohesive illusion of an intimate America where everyone knows (and everyone cares) about each other. Part of Rupert's motivation is simply a hunger for intimacy with Langford, the celebrity he idolizes, impinges upon, violates, and ultimately supplants. Rupert imagines he "knows" Langford personally just from years of watching him on television and nights spent waiting for his autograph. Moreover, he comes to feel that Langford actually owes him something for this "unselfish" loyalty.

In *The Fall of Public Man*, Richard Sennet suggests, "It is the complete repression of audience response by the electronic media" that produces "a magnified interest in persons or personalities who are not similarly denied." *King of Comedy* takes the rage and the wounded narcissism implicit in such denial as a fulcrum for an oedipal drama. Splitting its sympathies between the "have" Langford and the "have-not" Pupkin, the film offers a both-sides-now dialectic of American celebrity. [J. Hoberman, 2/15/83]

Kiss Me Deadly (1955)

Dir. Robert Aldrich; Scr. A. I. Bezzerides
106 min.

Genres collide in the great Hollywood movies of the mid-1950s thaw. The Western goes South with *The Searchers*; the cartoon merges with the musical in *The Girl Can't Help It*. Science fiction becomes pop sociology in *Invasion of the Body Snatchers*; noir veers into apocalyptic sci-fi with Robert Aldrich's 1955 *Kiss Me Deadly*.

Kiss Me Deadly tracks the sleaziest private investigator in American movies through a nocturnal labyrinth to a white-hot vision of cosmic annihilation. From the perversely backward title crawl (outrageously accompanied by orgasmic heavy breathing) through the climactic explosion, the film is sensationally baroque—eschewing straight exposition for a jarring succession of bizarre images, bravura sound matching, and encoded riddles.

Mike Hammer plays with fire and (literally) gets burned. Jagged and aggressive, *Kiss Me Deadly* is an extremely paranoid movie—with all that implies. The mode is angst-ridden hypermasculinity. Fear of a nuclear holocaust fuses with fear of a femme fatale. Hammer pursues and is pursued by a shadowy cabal—a mysterious "They," as they're called in the film's key exchange, "the nameless ones who kill people for the Great Whatzit."

Hammer's quest is played out through a deranged cubistic space amid the debris of Western civilization—shards of opera, deserted museums, molls who paraphrase Shakespeare, mad references to Greek mythology and the New Testament. A nineteenth-century poem furnishes the movie's main clue. The faux Calder mobile and the checkerboard floor pattern of Hammer's overdecorated pad—a bag of golf clubs in the corner and Hollywood's first answering machine built into the wall—add to the crazy, clashing expressionism.

Among other things, *Kiss Me Deadly* served to kiss off Mickey Spillane, the most successful American novelist of the Cold War. Filling a function now satisfied by talk radio, Spillane created a character who was God's Angry Man. Mike Hammer was a self-righteous avenger—judge, prosecuting attorney, jury, and executioner in one. His antagonists were gangsters and communists. At the end of *One Lonely Night*, he exults that he "killed more people tonight than I have fingers on my hands. I shot them in cold blood and enjoyed every minute of it. . . . They were Commies."

Hammer knows why his "rottenness was tolerated." His mission was "to kill the scum . . . I was the evil that opposed other evil." As played by Ralph Meeker, Hammer exhibits a surplus of macho individualism, aggravated by sexual repression and crass self-interest, that is so exaggerated it ultimately becomes a criticism of itself. This ends-justifies-the-means brutality had its contemporary political manifestation in Senator Joseph McCarthy, described by one colleague in suitably Hammeresque terms as a "fighting Irish Marine [who] would give the shirt off his back to anyone who needs it—except a dirty, lying, stinking Communist. That guy, he'd kill." In late 1954, after McCarthy was under Senate investigation, the *Saturday Review* published an essay bracketing Hammer and McCarthy. The same analogy occurred to Aldrich. In some interviews he called Hammer "a cynical fascist" and Spillane "an anti-democratic figure," arguing before the MPAA Code Administration that the film demonstrated that "justice is not to be found in a self-anointed, one-man vigilante."

Aldrich's early Hollywood associations were distinguished, and they put him in a potentially precarious situation. He served as an assistant director for Jean Renoir, Lewis Milestone, William Wellman, Joseph Losey, and Charles Chaplin; he worked closely with leftists Abraham Polonsky, Robert Rossen, and John Garfield. Given the company he kept, Aldrich expected to be named during the Hollywood witch-hunt but wasn't; perhaps he was too unimportant or too well connected. When he teamed with producer Victor Saville to make *Kiss Me Deadly*, Aldrich hired A. I. Bezzerides, another Hollywood fellow traveler, to adapt the novel. Bezzerides imbued *Kiss Me Deadly* with a surplus of cynicism and free association: "I wrote it fast, because I had contempt for it. It was automatic writing. Things were in the air at the time and I put them in."

Shortly before its scheduled opening in May 1955, *Kiss Me Deadly* was condemned by the Legion of Decency. Never reviewed in the *New York Times*, *Kiss Me Deadly* was banned in Britain; in France, however, the newly founded *Cahiers du Cinéma* made it a cause célèbre. Aldrich was hailed as "the first director of the atomic age." Young critics Truffaut and Godard repeatedly cited the movie, whose traces can be seen in *Shoot the Piano Player* and *Alphaville*. *Kiss Me Deadly* is the masterpiece of Aldrich's most delirious and iconoclastic period. [J. Hoberman, 3/15/94]

Landscape in the Mist (1988)

Dir. Theo Angelopoulos; Scr. Theo Angelopoulos, Tonino Guerra, and Thanassis Valtinos

127 min.

At fifty-two, Theo Angelopoulos is a cinematic master who is virtually unknown here. A manic culture doesn't sit still to meditate and dream, and so, to our detriment, we're now supporting one kind of cinema only. During the 1980s, Angelopoulos made three related films—*Voyage to Cythera* (1983), *The Beekeeper* (1986), and *Landscape in the Mist*—a series often compared to Wim Wenders's road trilogy. But Wenders's heroes are youngish hipsters, whereas Angelopoulos usually makes films with obsessed, aging protagonists. As a Greek, Angelopoulos appreciates ruins—flesh as well as stones.

In the sublime *Landscape in the Mist*, two grave children, Voula (Tanya Palaiologou), age twelve or so, and Alexander (Michalis Zeki), seven or eight, run away to find the father they've never known. (The child performances are incredible—not a coy false note.) Their mother—whom we know only as an intruding voice and a light at their bedroom door—has always told them that he lives in Germany. She's made up the story to protect herself. One bleak, wintry day the kids set out from Athens, stowing away on trains, hitchhiking, walking. Angelopoulos never gives us the sun-drenched, picturesque, touristy Greece. Freezing rain lashes the highways and the hillsides, and beaches are bare and harsh. Yet with his cinematographer Ghiorgos Arvanitis, he provides some of the most exquisite compositions you'll ever see.

The children meet up with a series of father figures who, one way or another, let them down. The most engaging encounter is with the playful Orestes (Stratos Tzortzoglou), a member of a theater troupe (roughly the same group as in Angelopoulos's politically savvy *The Travelling Players*). Voula falls in love with him, but he, too, disappoints. Basically, the journey describes a progressive shedding of illusions. At the end, the kids reach the border, but what actually happens in the stunning last scene is one of those debatable film moments. Uniting the trilogy is a vision of a blue tree in the mist.

Angelopoulos may be a landscape realist, but he's also a dedicated surrealist, a maker of dream images. He has something of Magritte's or Wallace Stevens's way of suggesting an alternate universe and a means of seeing into it. One of his trademark shots shows characters concentrating on events outside our view, before we know what's there. This focus on looking expresses desire and inner vision. Metaphysical directors aren't much in vogue, but as far as I'm concerned, we could use a change of pace occasionally. [Georgia Brown, 9/18/90]

The best European film of the 1980s? The greatest Balkan film ever made? Yes and yes: Theo Angelopoulos's underseen, underworshipped epiphany redefined the art film, hijacking the Antonioni/Tarkovsky long-take syntax and winnowing away its metaphysics, emerging with a heart-stopping odyssey of wintery orphanhood and breathless images. A young sister and brother launch out into the industrial Greek hinterlands to find a rumored father who doesn't exist, and the passage of their journey is, for us, an ordeal by sympathy, monolithic visions, adult monstrosity, and effortless metaphoric torque.

Most of Angelopoulos's incredible films are epochal translations of history into visual experience—time grows gargantuan, landscapes change, masses of people engage in social surge—but here, in a film alone in a filmography of epic trilogies, the movements, the images, and the symbology begin and end with children, lost in the war field of grown-ups. From the giant statue's hand rising from the sea to the catatonia on a snow-shrouded highway, any single scene could change your life, or at least what you expect from cinema; a single, lengthy shot of a parked truck, while catastrophically upsetting, might also be the sharpest critique of viewer omnipotence ever created. A master of apocalyptic orchestrations, Angelopoulos never married his ambitious pyramid-making to human experience this perfectly before or after, but then, nobody else has come very close, either. [Michael Atkinson, 12/14/05]

Late Chrysanthemums (1954)

See Flowing

Love Streams (1984)

Dir. John Cassavetes; Scr. Ted Allan and John Cassavetes
141 min.

John Cassavetes's final film, all too rarely screened and still underappreciated, is at once a culmination of the director's obsessions and his most atypical work. It's a movie that gives up its mysteries slowly—flirting with theatricality, inserting dream sequences, concluding on a brazenly surreal enigma. Cassavetes stars as Robert Harmon, a tough-guy novelist with unorthodox research methods. Gena Rowlands, magnificent as ever, is Robert's sister, Sarah Lawson, a divorcée who turns up at his doorstep with two taxis full of luggage and an entire barnyard menagerie. An emotional live wire and by default a social rebel, the embarrassingly demonstrative Sarah is kindred spirit to *A Woman under the Influence*'s unhinged housewife Mabel Longhetti and *Opening Night*'s aging stage star Myrtle Gordon. All are women with a raw-nerved, overwhelming capacity and need for love. The enormously moving interplay between Cassavetes and Rowlands gets at the heart of the performative spectacle unique to his films: an interaction beyond words and gestures, predicated on the invention of a shared language so hyperbolic and specific and almost inexplicable, it must be love. Indeed, the movie—as its title suggests—performs an anatomy of its subject. More explicitly metaphysical than the other great Cassavetes films, it nonetheless shares their view of love as a way of life and a form of madness. [Dennis Lim, 11/16/05]

The Lovers on the Bridge (1991)

Dir./Scr. Leos Carax
125 min.

Les Amants du Pont Neuf was three years in the making and, now known as *The Lovers on the Bridge*, has taken twice that long to get an American release. Written and directed by then enfant terrible Leos

Carax, this wildly romantic antiromance was attacked for its shameless extravagance and praised for more or less the same reason.

The Lovers on the Bridge is as exalted as it is ridiculous—an outrageously contrived paean to freedom, a crazy mixture of scabby naturalism and rock-video mescaline staged on a movie set worthy of Stroheim. Carax expended most of his budget reconstructing a chunk of Paris—including the Pont Neuf, the quays along the Seine, the facade of the Samaritaine department store, and part of the Ile de la Cité—as the backdrop for the grand passion that consumes two of the world's scruffiest lovers, the half-blind street-artist Michèle (Juliette Binoche) and the alcoholic street-performer Alex (Denis Lavant). Making their home on Paris's oldest bridge, the couple create their own world, and so does the movie. They embrace on the grass in the glare of whizzing headlights and stroll through a city lit only by the strobe of a subterranean disco.

In his most grandiose gesture, the filmmaker re-creates the fantastic fireworks display that marked the two-hundredth anniversary of the French Revolution as, drunk and cackling, the lovers sprawl on the Pont Neuf, shooting at the sky with the revolver Michèle keeps in her paintbox. The director's trademark shot—let's call it a Caraxysm—is a convulsive rock-scored lateral pan alongside his running, capering hero. Here, Alex and Michèle cavort across the bridge, alone in an exploding world as the music switches from Franco rap to an ecstatic Strauss waltz. It's a tremendous scene—one of the peak movie moments of the decade—and Carax manages to top it off with an inexplicable shot of Michèle waterskiing on the Seine in a stolen powerboat.

Beatifying the lower depths, Carax reverses Chaplin's *City Lights*. Here the tramp would rather have the woman he loves go blind than for her to leave him. (In another stunning image, Alex tries to set the world on fire.) But the movie, too, doesn't go anywhere, being itself a sort of bridge. There's no setup and, even invoking *L'Atalante*, Carax can't conjure a closing to match the middle. Still, even suspended in midair, *The Lovers on the Bridge* remains a glorious binge—as half-cracked and heedless as its protagonists. [[J. Hoberman, 6/30/99]

M (1931)

Dir. Fritz Lang; Scr. Thea von Harbou and Fritz Lang
110 min.

A template for *Jaws*, the *Psycho* of its day, Fritz Lang's *M* seems scarcely less immediate than when it was first released in Germany sixty-six years ago.

Lang's first talkie was also the original example of a filmed case history. *M* is the movie that introduced the enduring cinematic subject of criminal pathology. After an unforgettably disturbing sex crime, a serial psycho killer (Peter Lorre) terrorizes Berlin, himself pursued by two parallel investigations—one carried out by the police, the other (more efficiently) by the denizens of the city's underworld.

M opened here in 1933, the year the Nazis came to power and both Lang and Lorre left Germany. "It is regrettable that such a wealth of talent and imaginative direction was not put into some other story, for the actions of this Murderer, even though they are left to the imagination, are too hideous to contemplate," the *New York Times* wrote. Slightly less squeamish, the *Daily News* reviewer correctly noted that in treating a previously taboo subject, *M* had invented a new formula ("one which I hope will never be repeated, since it is too harrowing an experience to sit through"). In demonstrating the power of suggestion (as well as of montage), *M* managed to be both explicit and restrained.

What you see in *M* is not necessarily what you get. From the very first sequence in which a group of children chant a grisly nursery rhyme, Lang revels in sound as a formal element, using it to undermine the authority of the visual. Sound—not sight—is privileged. Sound establishes the central clue, while creating the off-screen space that functions as the movie's zone of danger; sound leads to the murderer's discovery, and sound provides him with his great scene. In the movie's still-astonishing climax, the childlike, compulsive killer is allowed to speak—or rather, shriek—for himself ("Always I am followed—soundlessly!") in a soliloquy that still inspires a disconcerting mixture of pity and horror.

Lorre, the *New York Herald Tribune* thought, had given "the most terrifying performance in screen history." Some years later, in preparing for the most extensive mass murder in European history, the Nazis exploited *M* by appropriating the scene of Lorre's panicked capture for *The Eternal Jew*—the vilest and most virulent of anti-Semitic pseudodocumentaries—while paraphrasing it at the end of their fictional extravaganza *Jud Süss*. [J. Hoberman, 6/17/97]

The Magnificent Ambersons (1942)

Dir./Scr. Orson Welles
88 min.

Orson Welles was not only a genius—he played one on the screen. The most lavishly gifted Hollywood director of his generation, this all-around showboat both lived and dramatized the self-serving Promethean spectacle of the outsize artistic temperament laid low by the constraints of commerce.

Having begun his career with a movie that continues to top critics' polls as the greatest ever made, Welles suffered a suitably outsize sophomore jinx. *The Magnificent Ambersons*, however different in tone and subject from *Citizen Kane*, gave every indication of being a comparable precocious masterpiece. Then it ran into a perfect storm of historical and studio interference, surviving today as a magnificent ruin.

Adapted from Booth Tarkington's barely remembered Pulitzer Prize–winning novel about social change in turn-of-the-century Indianapolis, *The Magnificent Ambersons* was in production when the Japanese bombed Pearl Harbor in December 1941. Less than two months later, patriotic Welles took off on a war-related mission to Latin America that would result in his unfinished documentary *It's All True*. *Ambersons'* original 131-minute cut was entrusted to editor Robert Wise. The movie tested poorly with audiences, and the RKO brass deemed it too long and too gloomy; *Ambersons* was re-edited in Welles's absence, or, should we say, it was butchered.

Thus, the movie became the sacred relic of Welles's martyrdom. About fifty minutes were cut, and new material was indifferently filmed and inserted along with several crass reaction shots designed to break the flow and make obvious what particular characters were feeling. The last half was reshuffled in preparation for a new, horribly botched ending, and then—with a new management team in place at the studio—the version we know was dumped into release on a double bill with a Lupe Velez vehicle, *Mexican Spitfire Sees a Ghost*. (Legend has it that Welles left a print of the original cut behind in Brazil; were it ever to turn up, this lost ark would rival *Greed's* still-missing reels as the greatest archaeological find in movie history.)

"It was a much better picture than *Kane*—if they'd just left it as it was," Welles famously told Peter Bogdanovich decades later. But even still, *The Magnificent Ambersons* is a pretty sensational movie. The film language is more fluid and adept than *Kane*'s, the expressionist lighting is more rigorously modulated. The astonishingly choreographed Christmas ball that serves to introduce the major characters is arguably the greatest set piece of Welles's career. The highly rehearsed ensemble, which complemented a contingent of Mercury Theater regulars (Joseph Cotten, Agnes Moorehead, Ray Collins) with RKO cowhand Tim Holt, retired silent star Dolores Costello, and then-unknown Anne Baxter, is sensational.

Detailing the decline of a wealthy family and the much deserved "comeuppance" delivered its scion, Georgie Minafer (Holt, with an uncanny resemblance to the young, petulantly entitled George W. Bush), *The Magnificent Ambersons* is unusually somber for a Hollywood movie. What American secrets are being hidden here? The Amberson mansion is a miniature Xanadu, with Welles's camera relentlessly craning up or prowling around its gloomy grand staircase. Filled with dark nostalgia for the artist's Midwestern boyhood, *Ambersons* may be Welles's most personal film—he would maintain that Tarkington had based the character of the automobile inventor (Cotten) on his (Welles's) own father.

Welles had adapted *The Magnificent Ambersons* as a radio play two years earlier (assigning himself the role of Georgie), and not even *Kane* made more effective use of dramatic sound. Again, and with greater subtlety, there are Welles's trademark overlapping dialogue and his construction of aural "deep space," a brooding Bernard Herrmann score, and the clever deployment of a naturalistic Greek chorus. Most remarkable, however, is the voice. *The Magnificent Ambersons* is the lone Welles feature in which the maestro does not grace the screen.

Still, he is overwhelmingly present in the insinuating invisibility of his tender, omniscient narration. The movie is haunted by Welles's voice, by his youth, and by a sense of a lost America that he would never again visit—and mainly by its own lost possibilities. It might be unfolding in his mind's eye—or inside the snow globe Kane dropped. [J. Hoberman, 2/18/04]

The Man with a Movie Camera (1929)

Dir./Scr. Dziga Vertov
80 min.

When people, like the neophyte Houston film critic whose letter arrived yesterday, ask me my "all-time favorite movie" or "the greatest movie ever made," I brace myself for a look of blank incomprehension and say, Dziga Vertov's *The Man with a Movie Camera*.

Say what? Released in 1929, at the end of the silent era, *The Man*

The Man with a Movie Camera, 1929; written and directed by Dziga Vertov

with a Movie Camera is the epitome of machine art, the grand summa of the Soviet futurist-constructivist-communist avant-garde. This kaleidoscopic city symphony—conjoining Moscow, Kiev, and Odessa into one metametropolis—may be the most densely edited movie ever made. Vertov matches the rhythms of a single day to the cycle of life, and the mechanisms of moviemaking to the logic of industrial production. Made without intertitles, employing strategies of visual analogy and associative montage so intricate they have yet to be named, *The Man with a Movie Camera* is at once a Whitmanesque documentary-portrait of the Soviet people, a reflexive essay on cinematic representation, and an ecstatic ode to human labor as a process of transformation.

More than any movie I know, *The Man with a Movie Camera* celebrates the sensory bombardment of twentieth-century urban life. You can never step into the same river twice nor, given its exhilarating tempo, can you see the same *Man with a Movie Camera*. The split screens and superimpositions, shock cuts and variable-speed motion aside, the editing is so dense that there are never less than a half-dozen things going on. The visual rhymes and perceptual jokes are so intricately cross-referenced that the placement of each shot involves multiple chains of meaning. A kind of cinematic *Ulysses* (considered by Vertov to be "the film that broke free from the tutelage of literature and the theater . . . 100 per cent cinematography"), *The Man with a Movie Camera* need be seen only once to be understood and enjoyed, but it demands to be studied on an editing table to be fully appreciated.

Designed to rid viewers of their habitual way of watching motion pictures by revealing the ways in which the camera and the film editor construct reality, *The Man with a Movie Camera* has the remarkable effect of encouraging the spectator to identify with the filmmaking process. Perhaps this is what Vertov had in mind when he later wrote, "The method in which I work is the most unexplored in the cinema. My methods demand superhuman efforts of organization, technique, way of life and so on. It is the most thankless way to work. Believe me, it is really hard: yet I hope that one day I shall achieve the victory of realism over formalism and naturalism, and become a poet who can be understood not by a few people but by millions." [J. Hoberman, 11/28/95]

Man's Favorite Sport? (1964)

Dir. Howard Hawks; Scr. John Fenton Murray and Steve McNeil
120 min.

I recently watched for the second time Howard Hawks's *Man's Favorite Sport?*, a film that was universally ridiculed when it appeared in 1964 and that I myself hadn't much liked. This time I was delighted and deeply moved by the grace and humor with which the story is told, and moved by the reverberations of a whole substratum of meaning, of sexual antagonism, desire, and despair.

The two layers, narrative and allegorical, interweave in such a way that the cruelty is constantly tempered by compassion and the ridiculous is redeemed by risk and anguish. As a result, the intrigue is not only richer, but the humor is funnier. In describing a layer beneath the surface, I don't mean to suggest that Hawks is a subconscious artist. The control and precision, the economy and follow-through of a Hawks film is assurance that he has mastered his material, that he *knows* it in a way that is more than intuitive but short of theoretical.

In *Man's Favorite Sport?* he gives us Rock Hudson and Paula Prentiss as primordial man and woman, Adam and Eve in the lush, hazardous Eden of a hunting and fishing resort.

Hudson works as a salesman in the sporting goods department of Abercrombie and Fitch. He has written an authoritative book on fishing, although he has never gone fishing in his life and finds the idea repugnant. His professional standing, therefore, is a hoax. Or, in the vocabulary of sexual allegory to which the film implicitly alludes, Hudson is a virgin, who has written a "how-to" book on sex while harboring a deep, fastidious horror of it. His masculinity is a lie. (Interestingly, he is engaged but has never told his fiancée he can't "fish.")

Prentiss, an aggressive, outdoorsy girl (the female equivalent of a man's man), arrives on the scene to browbeat Hudson into entering a fishing competition at the lodge where she works. But one can't help noticing certain things. Although Prentiss seems strident and overbearing in her action, there is something in the way Hawks directs her behavior—her soft, nervous gestures and the odd rhythm of delivery—that suggests vulnerability. And although Rock Hudson seems inoffensive and gentle—just a man trying to mind his own business and have peace—there is something flaccid and unresponsive about him, a self-satisfaction that is untested and therefore undeserved. Prentiss, in a remarkable performance, is the girl we knew at college, smart and good at everything but terrified of (and therefore hostile to) men. Yet she is competent (even sexually, in the film's metaphor), and it is she who must take the initiative in Hudson's sexual initiation.

Hawksian comedy, as Peter Wollen and other critics have pointed out, is the underside of, and compensation for, the action drama. Heroism and danger are replaced by adolescence and sexual failure, the way falling in a dream compensates for our overweening aspirations. The progression, in drama, from life to death, giving birth to an ideal, becomes in the comedy a progression from death (Hudson's inertia) to life with the burial of a false ideal.

Without giving a play-by-play analysis, I will mention several of the loveliest and most complex images:

In a small clearing—his own Garden of Eden—Hudson tries unsuccessfully to pitch his (pink) tent, while Prentiss and her girlfriend, serpents in frog suits, hide behind the bushes laughing and finally intrude upon his privacy. The tent collapses, wrapping the inept Hudson in swaddling clothes.

When Hudson finally learns to "fish," it is not by reading his book of instructions, not by the rules, but by accidents of nature . . . or instinct. (Before he learns, there is a "men in groups" scene at the lodge bar, where Hudson gives the men "tips"—an approximation of the locker room ritual of sexual tall tales.) But when Hudson wins the tournament, he has the confidence (or virility) to tell the truth.

The incident that disturbs most, before which Hudson has finally given her the long-awaited kiss, is when Prentiss says, "That was terrible," and runs off. How eloquently to express her desperate resistance at being overwhelmed; her sense of inadequacy at the kiss she has dreamed about and longed for and for which, when it comes, she is totally unprepared.

Hawks's conception of woman, as a creature both equal and threatening to man, can be seen as adolescent and anthropomorphic but never idealizing or domesticating. He doesn't penetrate the secrets of a woman's heart and her unique dilemma the way so-called woman's directors do. But at the same time he never excludes them from the action, never even implicitly suggests that woman occupies a fixed place in society—or that she is man's subordinate. Instinctively, he strikes a very modern note in the image of a couple united not by the attraction of opposites, but in the unanimity of similarities. The male-female polarity is reconciled by the struggle to assert oneself in life, in the crazy American scene, in which man and woman can be—as much as man and man—natural allies. [Molly Haskell, 1/21/71]

Marketa Lazarová (1967)

Dir. Frantisek Vlácil; Scr. Frantisek Pavlicek and Frantisek Vlácil
162 min.

With just a handful of films to prove it, Frantisek Vlácil was the Czech New Wave's formalist, postexpressionist wrecking ball. In the modest window between Moscow's Twentieth Congress in 1956 and the tanks of 1968, Forman, Passer, and Menzel made Bohemia safe for the Oscars, Juraj Jakubisko pursued his orgiastic apocalypses, and Jan Nemec crystallized the Kafkaesque suffocation of extra-Soviet life. But briefly, Vlácil was the idiosyncrat and the image master.

Vlácil is known for having pursued what he termed "pure film," and his best movies display a lackadaisical attitude toward narrative clarity and a hypnotic plastic originality. He spent some five years adapting Vladislav Vancura's complex novel *Marketa Lazarová*. Recently voted the greatest Czech film of all time, this crazed musk ox of a movie (1967), a nightmare epic about warring medieval tribes, brands you with images of one-of-a-kind pagan muscularity. The least that could be said is that it's the most convincing film about the Middle Ages made anywhere. Lyrically eliding bloody hunks of plot, and dropping us down into the historical current at seemingly indiscriminate intervals, Vlácil achieves a rampaging forward momentum—never has an impenetrably plotted movie been so riveting. [Michael Atkinson, 6/5/02]

McCabe & Mrs. Miller (1971)

Dir. Robert Altman; Scr. Robert Altman and Brian McKay
120 min.

I happen to admire Robert Altman's *McCabe & Mrs. Miller*, even though many people whose opinions I respect don't like the movie and many people whose opinions I suspect do. Furthermore, the main anti-argument (pretentiousness) strikes a more responsive chord in my critical temperament than does the main pro-argument (realism). *McCabe & Mrs. Miller* is photographed through a test-pattern haze of pea soup, and much of the dialogue is thrown away so hard it bounces. The star turns of Warren Beatty and Julie Christie trip and fall over the most cluttered mise-en-scène since the days of DeMille's jungle salons for slinky Swanson.

No matter. *McCabe & Mrs. Miller* confirms the impression of striking originality that goes beyond the Beetle Bailey mechanics of *MASH* to the more controlled horror and absurdism of *That Cold Day in the Park* and *Brewster McCloud*. It is true that a large part of Altman's originality is more peculiar than effective, particularly the squashed jokes with the predictably deadpan reaction shots as if the joke had not been heard, or if heard, not understood, or if understood, not appreciated, or if appreciated, not acknowledged. By the time every character and every situation is run through this wringer of nonreaction, the audience may begin to yawn with American Antoniennui.

Nonetheless, *McCabe* succeeds almost in spite of itself, with a rousing finale that is less symbolic summation than poetic evocation of the fierce aloneness in American life. I can't remember when I have been so moved by something that has left me so uneasy to the marrow of my aesthetic. Unlike so many of his contemporaries, Altman tends to lose battles and win wars. Indeed, of how many other films can you say that the whole is better than its parts? Beatty's reluctant hero and Christie's matter-of-fact five-dollar whore are nudged from bumptious farce through black comedy all the way to solitary tragedy imbedded in the communal indifference with which Altman identifies America.

However, Altman neither celebrates nor scolds this communal indifference but instead accepts it as one of the conditions of existence. In this way, his stock company never degenerates into a chorus line but remains an anarchic agglomeration of lumpy loners. Lumpy but never too stony. There is give and take and need, as when McCabe rushes upstairs to Mrs. Miller, now suddenly the last great love of his scheming life, and is told casually that she is occupied with a customer, and he stops awkwardly in his tracks, weighs the news with studied calmness on his swaying shoulders, all the while disguising the lover's face with the businessman's mask, but without bitterness or malice or wounded pride in any way diminishing the love he feels for a woman as open as he.

I disagree with those detractors of *McCabe* who argue that Altman imposes an antiestablishment aura on the climatic gunfight. In my view, Altman transforms what might have been parochial politics by shifting keys between the satire and the violence. I also disagree, however, with those defenders of *McCabe* who see Altman's achievement as the final nail in the coffin of the Western genre. Quite the contrary. The best moments in *McCabe* owe their majestic splendor to the moral integrity and psychological implacability of the Western genre. Ultimately, *McCabe & Mrs. Miller* shapes up as a half-baked masterpiece with a kind of gutsy grandeur. It's personal as all get out, and I thought that's what everyone had been screaming for all these years. [Andrew Sarris, 7/8/71]

The Merchant of Four Seasons (1972)

Dir./Scr. Rainer Werner Fassbinder

88 min.

Rainer Werner Fassbinder's *The Merchant of Four Seasons* may be the most exquisite achievement in cinema to reach these shores from Germany since the Golden Age of Murnau, Lang, Pabst, et al. in the years Before Hitler.

Fassbinder deftly balances style with humanity in such a way that *The Merchant of Four Seasons* manages to break the heart without betraying the mind. Fassbinder's achievement is aided in no small measure by the extraordinary presences and performances of Hans

Hirschmüller as the hapless victim, Hanna Schygulla as his beautiful and dilettantishly compassionate sister, and Irm Hermann as his sensually ungainly wife.

We are not too far into *The Merchant of Four Seasons* before we feel the reverberations of *Wozzeck* and *Mother Courage,* but Fassbinder strikes a very distinctive tone of his own on the tin drum of despair. From a certain angle, the produce-peddling protagonist can be viewed as an especially mediocre specimen of Everyman. He has been rejected by the Great Love of His Life and settles for the second-best with a sullen woman who is embarrassingly taller than he is. His previous service with the Foreign Legion had been a disillusioning debacle, and his family has virtually disowned him as a social disgrace. He is a growlingly inarticulate clod of a creature with a constant buzzing in his brain from which he can never escape. He has been discharged from the police force for consorting with a prostitute in the station, and he has transformed this transgression into a tavern anecdote in a futile attempt to understand its significance in his life. But everything in his life is out of synch and out of proportion. He lives by a different clock and on a different scale from everyone else. He earns and he yearns, but only drink can ease his suffering.

For once, the distancing devices of rack focus and artificial color schemes serve to express the chasm between what a character feels and what he is able to communicate to others. Fassbinder does not stop with Rosebud as a psychological spring; he presents the full flowering of the rose in all its tawdry triviality as an objective fact and in all its sublime stature as a subjective fantasy. The death and funeral of Hans is one of the great passages in modern cinema, and the intimation of his great and lost love one of the modern cinema's most lyrical ironies. Earlier, Hans approaches a state of spiritual communion with his sister, but a lapse of concentration on her part sends him scurrying back to the chilling sanctuary of his own introverted psyche, and he is thus doomed forever to emotional isolation. The spine-tingling irrevocability of this sequence constitutes a dramatic spectacle of the highest order and establishes Fassbinder as one of the most forceful filmmakers of the 1970s, a man for both the coterie and the crowd. And if one needed any additional motivation to see *Merchant of Four Seasons,* there is Hanna Schygulla, with the eyes and lips and womanly wiles to lead one to hell itself. [Andrew Sarris, 11/22/73]

Meshes of the Afternoon (1943)

Dir. Maya Deren and Alexander Hammid; Scr. Maya Deren
18 min.

A pioneer working in a virtual vacuum, Maya Deren invented the two genres—psychodrama and dance-film—that most characterize American personal cinema from World War II through the late 1950s. So many of Deren's devices have grown shopworn in other hands that it takes an active imagination to recognize just how innovative her work really was.

Of the six films Deren completed, her three psychodramas are the most substantial. *Meshes of the Afternoon* (1943) was the first and, after *Un Chien Andalou*, the most widely seen avant-garde film ever made. Like that film, Deren's has the logic of a dream; but while Buñuel and Dalí used an irrational narrative to mimic the general structure of the unconscious mind, Deren attempted to depict the specific internal world of her film's protagonist, played by herself. In fact, *Meshes* seems less related to European surrealism than to the Freudian flashbacks and the sinister living rooms that typify Hollywood wartime noir films. Located in some hilly L.A. suburb, the house where Deren's erotic violent fantasy was filmed might be around the corner from Barbara Stanwyck's place in *Double Indemnity*.

The film's haunting power is derived not so much from its symbolism as from a brilliant use of matched cuts, elliptical editing, and slow-motion to reorder time and space. Many of its effects have yet to be bettered. The vision was Deren's, but the skill of its execution was due in part to the expertise of Alexander Hammid, the Czech filmmaker who was then her husband. One needed only to compare the film to the kitsch-arama dream sequence concocted by Dalí two years later for *Spellbound* to see how effectively Deren and Hammid could work with little more than home-movie means. [J. Hoberman, 5/15/78]

The Mother and the Whore (1973)

Dir./Scr. Jean Eustache
210 min.

Jean Eustache's *The Mother and the Whore* is a searing, painful, revealing, egotistical, irritating, often beautiful document that captures, in orgies of sexual gorging and verbal disgorging, the clash between Left Bank libertinism and an astonishingly deep conservatism—deep because it is mystical, rather than political, and is based on matters of life and death, rather than on left and right.

The Mother and the Whore lasts three and a half hours. Thus, by conventional measures of Eustache's work, or what we know of it, he has made the equivalent of two two-hour films. But the length of each grows organically out of the life passage it describes. I would be inclined to agree that a half-hour-plus was adequate to the wistful tale of a small-town adolescent (played by Jean-Pierre Léaud) scrounging for dates and money at Christmastime, while seven times that is barely enough for the transitional period from the late twenties into the thirties, again focusing on Léaud, when the process of seeking and "being free" is likely to congeal, quite suddenly, into something altogether less open and appealing. Léaud's performance is ultimate, in the true sense of the word. He brings up to and out of date the womanizing, theorizing alter ego of the New Wave, under the guidance of a director who, though nurtured on their films, is technically not one of them—but who is probably closer to the Léaud persona than to either Godard or Truffaut.

While they were writing film criticism, then making films and fantasizing la vie de bohème, Eustache, from the evidence of his films and their infrequency, was living it. He demonstrates a well-developed movie consciousness, but he seems to have gone to them because it was on the screen that the French literature of the 1960s was being written.

Eustache's Left Bank drifters—Léaud as the deadbeat intellectual, the "interpreter" of life; Bernadette Lafont as the mistress who supports him; Françoise Lebrun as the compulsively promiscuous nurse he takes up with—are a triangle of dropouts from the bourgeoisie who are past the point of making a point of it. They are one generation beyond the conscious rebels of Godard's and Truffaut's films, just as Eustache's style, patient, permissive, is post–New Wave without being a reaction against it. His fade-ins and long stretches of inactivity serve to emphasize by comparison just how dialectical the cutting of Godard is and how ideological the longeurs of Rivette. Eustache's decisions—the blending of black and white into the twilight in which his characters live, time stretched into a continuum—represent a director's closest approximations of the business of living that has preceded and will succeed (even supersede) the film.

Criticism is almost superfluous to this seamless stretch of life that has been filtered, perhaps just once, through a coarse sieve of understanding, so that it remains in nuggets rather than in granules that have been pulverized and reconstructed by analysis. In the onslaught of verbiage—strings of untranslatable and, to French ears, offensive argot—Eustache owes more to Céline, the father of the scatological memoir, than to any filmmaker. And yet with Eustache, there is a conflict, a pull toward an underlying moral orthodoxy that gives the film its special tension. Characters are free to try sexual combinations divisible by three, but at the same time they are compelled to talk, and in so doing reveal just how far they are from following the lead of the body into a nonpossessive polymorphous paradise.

Even as they slip in and out of each other's bed's and lives—Léaud living off Lafont and alternately apostrophizing and ignoring her, gravitating to the professionally thick-skinned Lebrun and enjoying the odor of death that clings to her—they are prey to archaic instincts and emotions. Lafont, earthy, ripe, the "mother," tries to commit suicide in a fit of jealousy; Lebrun, in a scabrous monologue near the end of the film, denounces fucking with the same passion with which Molly Bloom embraced it, concluding that it can be redeemed only by love and procreation. Léaud, no friend to the emancipated woman, must preserve his own unity by dividing his women into virgin and whore—categories that they substantiate, ironically, by changing roles in the end.

Although the Léaud character (as Eustache's surrogate) is the constant, the organizing intelligence and moral raisonneur of the film, it is the two women who emerge as its greatest assets—distinctive and vivid and memorable. And yet they owe their magnificence to their interpreter. Their richness comes, with that liability characteristic of

European cinema, from their being the dramatic center of a man's life, rather than being the designer-dramatists of their own.

The Mother and the Whore is a film to be lived through, from the dregs of surfeit and ennui to the morning-after resolution, when the pregnant Lebrun is vomiting in her nurse's quarters, and Léaud agrees to marry her. I really don't know how to take the ending—the reconciliation, to me, feels hollow and weary, a vow made under the hangover spell of self-loathing rather than from a free and clear conscience. As a retreat into tradition, it seems more destitute and nihilistic in its very decisiveness than does the open-ended confusion of so many contemporary films. [Molly Haskell, 4/4/74]

Mulholland Drive (2001)

Dir./Scr. David Lynch
147 min.

Mulholland Drive parts the veil on a totally cracked, utterly convincing world with David Lynch its brooding demiurge. A Denny's-like restaurant on Sunset Boulevard fronts the abyss. "I had a dream about this place," a smug young creative type explains to someone who might be his agent, even as his nightmare begins to unfold. Crazy!

Fashioned from the ruins of a two-hour TV pilot rejected by ABC in 1999, Lynch's erotic thriller careens from one violent non sequitur to another. The movie boldly teeters on the brink of self-parody, reveling in its own excess and resisting narrative logic. This voluptuous phantasmagoria is certainly Lynch's strongest movie since *Blue Velvet* and maybe *Eraserhead*. The very things that failed him in the bad-boy rockabilly debacle of *Lost Highway*—the atmosphere of free-floating menace, the pointless transmigration of souls, the provocatively dropped plot stitches, the gimcrack alternate universes—are here brilliantly rehabilitated.

What was it that Dennis Hopper called Dean Stockwell in *Blue Velvet*—one suave motherfucker? From the absurd midnight automobile accident on the Los Angeles road that opens the movie and gives it its title, *Mulholland Drive* makes perfect (irrational) sense. Lynch's

Mulholland Drive, 2001; written and directed by David Lynch

outlandish noir feels familiar, and yet it's continually surprising, as when a bungled assassination turns into a Rube Goldberg mechanism involving two additional victims, a vacuum cleaner, and a smoke detector, or a scene begins with an abrupt eruption of pink and turquoise and a studio rendition of the Connie Stevens chestnut "Sixteen Reasons (Why I Love You)."

The narrative, such as it is, commences when a lush brunette of mystery soon to be known as Rita (Laura Elena Harring) dodges a bullet, staggers out of her crashed car, and descends from the Hollywood Hills into the jewel-like city below to find refuge in an empty apartment. She's suffering from amnesia, which makes her the perfect foil for the flat's caretaker, Betty (Naomi Watts), who arrives the next morning—blond, perky, and inanely optimistic—from the Ontario town of Deep River (named perhaps for the sinister dive where Isabella Rossellini made her home in *Blue Velvet*). Betty is innocently avid to become a star; Rita is forced by circumstance to impersonate one. Their first meeting is a mini Hitchcock film, with the dazed brunette assigning herself a name from a handy *Gilda* poster.

Where did Rita's suitcase full of money come from? What is the significance of the blue key in her pocket? There's a definite Nancy Drew quality as the naively trusting and ever enthusiastic Betty takes it upon herself to solve the enigma of Rita's identity: "It'll be just like in the movies. We'll pretend to be someone else." Although Betty is initially a mass of cornball clichés, possibly modeled on Eva Marie Saint or Lynch himself, it unexpectedly develops that she really can act. (So too Naomi Watts.) Betty's audition at Paramount, a sensational performance in a tryout worthy of Ed Wood, presents the possibility that everything she has done and will do is calculated for effect. "You look like someone else," Betty exclaims when Rita gets a makeover to more closely resemble . . . her. Thanks in part to that new blond wig, the women get together in a scene that is not only exceptionally steamy and tender but contains what is surely the greatest amnesiac sex joke ever written.

Whatever *Mulholland Drive* was originally, it has become a poisonous valentine to Hollywood. (This is the most carefully crafted L.A. period film since *Chinatown*—except that the period is ours.) The locations are quietly fabulous; there's a museum quality to the musty deco apartment where Betty and Rita live under the watchful eye of a showbiz landlady (Ann Miller). The cloyingly lit nocturnal landscape and splashy glamour compositions seem pure essence of 1958, as do Betty's ingenue poses. The ominously rumbling city is malign and seductive; the movie industry—or, should we say, dream factory—is an obscure conspiracy. In a secondary narrative, an inexpressive, self-important young director (Justin Theroux) is compelled to endure a production meeting from hell wherein a shadowy cabal seizes control of his movie—but only so that the presence of a single unknown actress can be dictated by an irony-resistant bogeyman called the Cowboy (Monty Montgomery, the producer of Lynch's *Wild at Heart*, among other credits).

Alarming as the Cowboy is, *Mulholland Drive*'s most frighteningly self-reflexive scene comes when Betty and Rita attend a 2 A.M. performance—part séance, part underground art ritual—in a decrepit, near-deserted old movie palace called Club Silencio. The mystery being celebrated is that of sound-image synchronization, which is to say cinema, and the illusion throws Betty into convulsions. At the show's climax, Rebekah Del Rio sings an a cappella Spanish-language version of "Crying." She collapses onstage, but the song continues—

just like the movie. For its remaining three-quarters of an hour, *Mulholland Drive* turns as perverse and withholding in its narrative as anything in Buñuel. Similarly surreal is the gusto with which Lynch orchestrates his particular fetishes. In *Mulholland Drive*, the filmmaker has the conviction to push self-indulgence past the point of no return.

Curiouser and curiouser. From the moment Betty and Rita leave the club, the narrative begins to fissure. *Mulholland Drive* flows from one situation to the next, one scene seeping into another like the decomposing corpse I've neglected to mention that's at the story's center. Characters dissolve. Settings deteriorate. Situations break down and reconstitute themselves, sometimes as fantasy, sometimes as a movie—which is to say, much of what has previously happened, happens again, only differently. Love is now a performance. Rita reverts to femme fatality. The parental demons return.

Betty's dream becomes a nightmare—or perhaps the previous story was itself only a dream. Not that it matters. *Mulholland Drive* is thrilling and ludicrous. The movie feels entirely instinctual. The rest is silencio. [J. Hoberman, 10/3/01]

Naked (1993)

Dir./Scr. Mike Leigh
131 min.

Mike Leigh once offered a good biblical word for his movies: *lamentations*. They lamented, he said, "how difficult life is." His brave new film, *Naked*, the most biblical of all, could also be called a laceration. It's painted in bruise colors, especially black and blue.

Why is it called *Naked*? Because it's about a man, Johnny (David Thewlis), stripped to his flayed skin. Because it's about Homo sapiens dangling at the end of the evolutionary vine. Because the stupid body lies at the core of the difficult sex thing. Because exposure can be cathartic. You will think of more reasons.

Naked opens with a rape. At least, it looks like one. Given what we later see of Johnny's modus operandi, it's probably consensual sex turned nasty. Whatever, she breaks away, yelling, and Johnny bolts in the opposite direction, steals a car, and drives it to London. There he looks up an old girlfriend from Manchester, Louise (Lesley Sharp), who isn't home, but her depressive, black-clad, marble-mouth housemate, Sophie (Katrin Cartlidge), invites him in for tea. When Johnny kisses Sophie, he bites her mouth hard and pulls her hair. By the time Louise comes home from work, Sophie's deep in love. She can't keep her hands off Johnny, and hands on him drive him mad.

One thing Leigh has the temerity to present is a terrible sexual dynamic: men hurting women and women relishing the hurt. The badly bruised women in *Naked* are stuck on men who mistreat them—with their unwarranted loving kindness causing the men to kick free. But in the end, women show a toughness and a resilience, a greater tensile strength than do men, who, for all their brutality, are more pitiful; they're unable to connect. Probably this gender standoff is most pithily represented by two scruffy Scots—Neanderthal man and his mate—bellowing each other's names ("Maggie!" "Archie!") into the winter night.

But to talk about the film this way obscures the naked heart of *Naked*, Johnny's brilliant, nonstop yammering into and at the void. For

Naked, 1993; written and directed by Mike Leigh

all its acidity, Johnny's near monologue forms a bravura lyric diatribe, his Mancunian cadences transmuting into music. A present-day prophet, Johnny is no Baptist; there's no messiah to advance. He's more Old Testament doomsayer come to argue that the human experiment has failed. "The end of the world is nigh, Bri; the game is *up*." The spiritually obsessed Brian (Peter Wight) is a night watchman who invites Johnny into the empty space he guards. (Aren't we all protecting the equivalent of empty space?) With a little persuasion, everyone invites Johnny in. Only in one case is he ordered out (that he goes is a kind of miracle). Usually, it's Johnny who's compelled to split. Disillusioned, he wants more rigorous standards. To him, everyone seems a victim of sentimental thinking.

Leigh's meditation on the human condition is studded with references to the species' evolution. Read the details: a joke about the missing link, diagrams of the human skeleton, tribal carvings from Africa, and Aboriginal boomerangs, a stuffed reptile, a shark's jawbone, a veritable "jungle" of plants, Gleick's *Chaos*, replicas of Greek sculptures, a poster for "Attila," as well as references to Nostradamus, Ezekiel, Deuteronomy, and the Book of Revelation. When a poster hanger sticks up a sign reading "Therapy?" (over "Megadeth") and then pastes "Cancelled" over it, it's a political, maybe a cosmic, joke. No treatment, man, the case is terminal.

This is a brilliant, radical work from Leigh, who's delivered quite radical works in the past. It's also so abrasive that some viewers are likely to be revolted. If Fine Line seems brave to be bringing out such a film during this jolly holiday season, it strikes me as a perfectly religious offering. O come all ye faithful, *Naked* is joyful and triumphant. [Georgia Brown, 12/21/93]

Night and Fog in Japan (1960)

Dir. Nagisa Oshima; Scr. Toshirô Ishido and Nagisa Oshima
107 min.

Night and Fog in Japan, made by Nagisa Oshima in 1960, is the least compromising commercial film one can imagine. As formally radical as it is politically uncool, for its twenty-eight-year-old director the film was a virtual act of self-destruction. With sublime aesthetic opportunism, Oshima exploited the success of his early youth films, a crisis of confidence within the Japanese film industry, and the most intense period of political unrest in postwar Japanese history to uncork a fiercely stylized, ferociously left-wing harangue on the deficiencies of the Japanese left.

A complicated story of youthful fanaticism and class resentments, sexual jealousies and generational conflict, *Night and Fog* jumps back and forth from the early 1950s to 1960, spiraling around key incidents of political betrayal. The wedding of a journalist who had been a Stalinoid student militant during the Korean War to a young student radical for the 1960 AMPO (Japan-American Security Treaty) struggle becomes a bitterly acrimonious trial. With mad, drunken, ideological compulsion, his friends and hers begin to claw at each other's generations as well as their own. (If *The Sun's Burial* is Oshima's *Los Olvidados*, *Night and Fog*—which, flashbacks aside, takes place in and around a single garden pavilion—is his *Exterminating Angel*.)

Made directly after *Cruel Story of Youth* and *The Sun's Burial*, two ambiguous celebrations of teen punkery run wild, *Night and Fog* is another movie about the arrogance of youth. Here, however, the intellectuals have center stage and—in its totally unsparing view of student activism—*Night and Fog* is a harbinger of such New Left analyses as Godard's *La Chinoise* or Jancsó's *The Confrontation*. Japanese critic Tadao Sato called it "one of the most beautiful films about youth in the history of Japanese movies." But beauty in this case is a function of both Oshima's formal control and his brutal honesty.

Ironic, nihilistic, and megalomaniacal by turns, Oshima's young radicals are universal types. The pompous jargon-spouting leader with his collection of Shostakovich—"the greatest socialist, he's even popular in America"—and bogus calls for unity is maddeningly oblivious of the privileges his family's wealth confers on him; the sardonic intellectuals are reduced to backbiting and sour banter; the ineffectual faculty adviser ("He's nice but stupid") is unable to take a stand even when his young charges flagrantly break the law by holding an alleged "spy" prisoner in a dorm closet. ("Hey, spy," the militants taunt this pathetic character, "you're taking up our precious study time!")

The issue of the spy, his roughing up and escape, and the suicide that may or may not have been a result of the incident is the central episode in *Night and Fog*. It's a mistake, however, to see the film as a *Rashomon* or an Agatha Christie novel whose narrative secrets will either be schematized or revealed. Guilt here is universal and free-floating, absorbed from one heedless generation to the next. "What a bunch of Stalin zombies you are!" the unshaven Ota, a comrade of the bride, explodes in exasperation after a succession of painful confessions. "Call this a wedding? It's a funeral!"

Night and Fog—the title is an allusion to Alain Resnais's famous short about the Nazi death camps—has a ferocity born of experience. Oshima came of age with the general strike of 1947 and, like his Stalinist protagonists, was a leader of the Communist Party–founded Zengakuren (All-Japan Student League) during the Korean War. It was a period in which the Japanese Communist Party embarked on a disastrous course of domestic terrorism and preparation for armed revolutionary struggle. Its main achievement was triggering a right-wing reaction in the form of the Subversive Activities Prevention Bill. Both Oshima and his coscenarist Toshirô Ishido participated in the ensuing so-called Molotov Cocktail struggle of 1952, and, in large measure, *Night and Fog* is their corrosive self-portrait.

Oshima's politics hindered his career, but his first films appeared amid the largest mass movement in Japanese history, the 1959–1960 struggle against the renewal of the Japanese-American security pact. With students demonstrating daily in the streets during the spring of 1960, the Japanese government was obliged to cancel President Eisenhower's state visit. But that was the movement's greatest victory. The security pact was passed over their snake-dancing bodies. In light of this failure, Oshima made *Night and Fog* with the utmost urgency. The film was released in October 1960 and yanked from distribution three days after its theatrical premiere. The assassination of the Socialist Party leader by a right-wing student was evidently used by the Shochiku studio as an excuse.

What's truly amazing is not that Shochiku suppressed *Night and Fog* but that the studio allowed it to be made at all. Not only is this a film of continual, impassioned talking—with a blandly exhortatory youth anthem segueing from one foggy nighttime flashback to the next (the title is absolutely literal; Oshima permitted no daylight after *The Sun's Burial*)—but it's also a long-take tour de force fashioned out of a mere forty-three setups. (There are virtually no reverse angles; the first scene is a deftly choreographed six- or seven-minute shot that maps out the ideological terrain of the entire wedding party.) With its restless tracking camera—moving from face to face or sweeping over a gaudy stretch of rainy, banner-strewn pavement—and well-exploited widescreen format, *Night and Fog* unfurls like a scroll. The dominant tone is midnight-blue illuminated by the flash of orange bonfires, set off by bloody bandages.

Juxtaposing 1952 and the present through the use of dramatic blackouts, evoking demonstrations and ghosts through blatantly theatrical stylizations, *Night and Fog* demands real concentration. And yet, even as Oshima's superb stock-company actors use body language to underscore their ideological positions, it's a film whose emotional power transcends its immediate historical framework. *Night and Fog in Japan* doesn't cozy up to you like *The Big Chill*, but it's some kind of great movie. For anyone who served time in the turbulent streets or smoky college cafeterias of the 1960s or the 1930s, the chill here is a cold shock of recognition. [J. Hoberman, 2/15/85]

Night of the Living Dead (1968)

Dir. George A. Romero; Scr. John A. Russo and George A. Romero

96 min.

Night of the Living Dead (directed by George A. Romero and seen occasionally on 42nd Street) is crude, derivative, and one of the best horror films ever produced. Made for $125,000 in the environs of Pittsburgh by a local company and exploiting what must be members of an amateur thesping society, it involves the audience in such straightforward and simple acts of cruelty that one wonders why no clear-eyed horror filmmaker was able to perform so effectively before.

The gluey, bottomless horror of the film oozes from an amalgam of studiedly derivative elements. The plot—people with clashing personalities trapped together in a shabby country house by the ambulatory, flesh-eating corpses lurching outside—is secured in the gruesome psychology of those EC Comics banned in the 1950s: two of the characters, the good-looking, stylish, good-natured young couple, are confirmed in our sympathy only to be roasted alive and devoured with gusto by the ghouls, while the darkie, the grubby survival-fit persona of the comics, is the only one to last out the night of horrors. The final twist is that even he is killed, except by everyday monsters. His natural enemies, Pittsburgh cops and rednecks (the credits acknowledge the assistance of the local police department), out early shooting ghouls in the brain, shoot him without trying to find out whether he's alive or a living dead.

Studded throughout the comic book dread and brought to its service are many situational motifs from Hitchcock movies and several bits of well-integrated Hitchcock technique. The Hitchcock aspects are shorn of their evasive, level-hopping, metaphysic-implying obfuscations and work simply to increase dread. In the chirping-stabbing in the shower, Hitchcock abstractly presented a bottomless chamber in which reverberated knifed frigidity, the sounds of catatonia violated. When *Night of the Living Dead* has the mother lie inert under the trowel effectively wielded by her little daughter-turned-ghoul, her shrieking inertia happens simply because, at this point, things are so demonstrably bad, life is no longer desirable.

Hitchcock's technique, too, is simplified effectively. The classical reaction shots of Tippi Hedren holding her head in three different directions in response to the gasoline explosions in *The Birds* were blunted by her unpleasant and complicated face. The same manner of studied reaction shot in *Night of the Living Dead* uses the less problematic face of the black actor and receives the awful substance of the preceding shot like an outfielder's mitt poised at a graceful angle. Other Hitchcock techniques—the frame's mysteriously unfilled areas, the ability to depict a body's fall as important without showy effects—succeed to crudely accomplished and spontaneous effect, and catapult, instead of complicate, events.

Night of the Living Dead, as a matter of fact, appears to have been made in a state of frenzy. The camera's erratic and seemingly instinctive striving to reveal the characters' dilemma anew in shot after shot produces the feeling of the best montage: of each shot's transcending its predecessor. Furthermore, the manic overacting—especially by the eerily homely, flat-voiced young couple who are separated in the graveyard by a ghoul at the beginning—is wed correctly to the cruelty. The actors' frenzies (of panicked flailing running, arduous pushing, fiendish clutching) are of an enthusiasm rarely seen in films but here look simply like reasonable responses to the circumstances.

The plot, too, is unrestrained and incorrigibly kills all the characters in what, near the end, becomes an avalanche of atrocities. These fervently acted out, unpremeditated cruelties in the midst of situations already at an intolerable level resemble the comic building in silent movies, and *Night of the Living Dead*, by its daring crudeness and while scaring the pants off the audience, rediscovers the silent art of storytelling. [Richard McGuinness, 12/25/69]

Still scary after all these years, George Romero's raw, unrelenting first feature—a film in which fresh corpses rise from their graves to kill and eat the living (roughly the same premise as *Plan 9 from Outer Space*)—was discovered by horror buffs on 42nd Street and went on to become one of the most popular "midnight movies" of the early 1970s. The film is ultra low-budget, but cheapness works in its favor: Romero's vérité-style, hand-held camera, contrasty black-and-white film stock, and rural-nowhere locations have a news report immediacy, underscored by his adroit use of radio and television broadcasts to further the plot.

The film's tension is considerably heightened by the incessant bickering between the protagonists as they hole up in a ghoul-besieged farmhouse. Indeed, *Night* is leavened only by a certain grim humor, increasingly evident on repeated viewings. "I think we're either gonna have to move mother out here or move the grave to Pittsburgh," a brother whines to his sister as they grudgingly leave a wreath on their father's tomb, moments before the first ghoul lurches into the picture. Pointedly, the ghouls constitute an almost comic cross-section of middle-American types. For *Night of the Living Dead* is to the Vietnam war as *Invasion of the Body Snatchers* and *Invaders from Mars* are to the Cold War—a brilliant, open-ended metaphor for topical anxieties. The evident distrust with which many of the characters regard the film's black hero, the images of family members feasting on each other's flesh, the climactic scene of redneck vigilantes shooting do... nary" citizens are apt reflections of 1968's social hysteria.

Appropriately, *Night*'s cult popularity peaked during the perio... when the trauma of Vietnam was being most actively repressed. The film is not only a horror classic, but a remarkable vision of the late 1960s—it offers the most literal possible image of America devouring itself. [J. Hoberman, 1/13/82]

Los Olvidados (1950)

Dir. Luis Buñuel; Scr. Luis Alcoriza and Luis Buñuel
80 min.

A great, great movie, as well as a personal favorite, *Los Olvidados* (The Forgotten Ones) is the means by which exiled Luis Buñuel reestablished his international reputation. This low-budget account of Mexico City street kids, inspired by actual cases, as well as by Buñuel's impressions of his new country, is a masterpiece of social surrealism and the founding work of Third World barrio horror. *Los Olvidados* is strong enough to make a hardened communist cry or drive a (true) Christian to despair. The title is in part ironic. Once seen, this movie can never be forgotten.

In no way "ennobled" by their struggle to survive, Buñuel's children are predators who band together to rob the crippled and the blind. *Los Olvidados* is set in a world where one child is abandoned by his father and another has to steal food from his mother. The weak prey on the weaker, dogs dress as people, and people die like dogs. Buñuel, who anticipated this cruel universe with his 1932 antidocumentary *Land without Bread*, may have been only slightly exaggerating when he recalled that patriotic Mexicans stormed from the movie calling for his expulsion.

Appearing in 1951 at Cannes, where André Bazin wrote that it "lashes the mind like a red-hot iron and leaves one's conscience no opportunity for rest," *Los Olvidados* mugged the then dominant neorealist tradition from which it ostensibly sprang. (As a critique of naturalism and an assault against audience pieties, *Los Olvidados* had the same relationship to neorealism as Buñuel's 1929 *Un Chien Andalou* had to the French avant-garde. And as in *Un Chien Andalou*, the presence of professional actors subtly confounds expectations.) The movie provides no basis for reformist optimism, although, in his brilliant dream sequence, Buñuel attributes a Freudian unconscious to the wretched of the earth. This is his humanism. [J. Hoberman, 1/26/05]

Once Upon a Time in the West (1968)

Dir. Sergio Leone; Scr. Sergio Leone and Sergio Donati
165 min.

Once Upon a Time in the West begins with a gunfight at a train station shot as a low-angle panorama of Western wasteland psychology and ends after another shootout near a railroad in construction with a last shot of a high-angle panorama of Western expansionist history. With authenticated American actors like Henry Fonda, Jason Robards, Charles Bronson, Jack Elam, and Woody Strode, *Once Upon a Time in the West* is Sergio Leone's most American Western, but it is still dominantly and paradoxically European in spirit, at one and the same time Christian and Marxist, despairing and exultant, nihilistic and regenerative.

In the very beginning, Strode, shortly before he is to be gunned down, feels some drops of water falling on his forehead as he is framed in close-up on the frescolike wide screen. He places his Stetson on his head so that it will receive the water between its camel-like humps, and then he shortly thereafter drinks the water from the Stetson in a gesture so ceremonial as to make the hat seem like a holy chalice. After this portentous, implacable technique, Leone leaves no way out for his characters. It is kill or be killed. Nonetheless, *Once Upon a Time in the West* unfolds across the screen in time and in space with all the mellowness and majesty of such great Westerns as *The Searchers*, *Rio Bravo*, and *Seven Men from Now*. Especially enjoyable is Ennio Morricone's extraordinarily melodious score, but at its most melodious it never extends beyond the emotional range of Leone's editing of eagle-eyed expressions interspersed with a circular orchestration of screen space.

We have been told that Italians and other "furriners" should not meddle in a distinctively American art form. But actually Leone is no further away from the legends of the American West than the Florentine Renaissance painters were from the Crucifixion, and if film is even partly a visual medium, Leone's vision is as valid as anyone else's. Indeed, Leone has succeeded in making what is essentially a silent movie with aphoristic titles for dialogue. All the dialogue could be eliminated from the movie, and we would still have been shown all that it is essential to know about the obsessive concerns of the characters. We would come to understand Claudia Cardinale's role as the bearer of water, life, and continuity to the civilization of the New West. We would see that around the edges of the Bronson-Fonda confrontation is the fashionable leftist flourish of the Latino revenging himself on the Anglo, but only around the edges.

At the core of the confrontation is not the politics of a revisionist genre, but the mythology of a poetic parable, and how fitting it is that the aging prairie liberalism of Fonda's features should be foredoomed by a revenge plot of awesomely Freudian dimensions. Even so, Leone takes no chances with his archetypes. Fonda's hubris cannot be curbed merely for past excesses. In the course of the movie itself, he and his long-coated henchmen must be shown exterminating an entire family down to a small child as an expression of big business at work overcoming obstacles at whatever cost to moral values. And we must see again and again (without any dialogue) the dreamlike reenactment of the traumatic experience of Charles Bronson's revenge-seeker with the harmonica so that all the violence and all the close-ups may finally fit into a harmonic pattern of the feelings of loss we can never forget or even endure until we have transformed them into the poetry of fables and fantasies. The Western is above all fable and fantasy, as the desire for revenge is childish and fruitless. Leone has understood fully that in setting out with his hero to learn to kill, he has learned instead that he has come this way only to learn how to die.

The gunfights themselves partake of Leone's penchant for the circular staging of the corrida. At one point Bronson actually extends one foot forward as if to execute an intricate maneuver with a cape, but this is the West, and history comes out of the barrel of a gun, a dynamic truth Leone emphasizes with his intercutting of locomotives thrusting out of cavernous gun barrels. *Once Upon a Time in the West* is perhaps the exception to the rule that the best films come out of nationally nuanced cinemas without cross-dubbing and international financing. But it is so glorious an exception that the rule can never seem quite so rigid again. [Andrew Sarris, 8/6/70]

Out of the Past (1947)

Dir. Jacques Tourneur; Scr. Daniel Mainwaring
97 min.

Jacques Tourneur's quietist *Out of the Past* represents the film noir high end—as compared to the pulpy inventions of Edgar G. Ulmer's low-end *Detour*. It's distinguished by Tourneur's masterful, eerie control of surfaces (dialogue recorded at a customarily low level while visuals glide forward with otherworldly grace), as well as a jokey, hard-boiled argot ("Well, I really hadn't ought").

The movie isn't so much keyed to Robert Mitchum's hunky somnambulism as it is in full accord with it. Dick Powell was originally to appear and Bogart desperately wanted the part, but Tourneur lucked out with Mitchum, whose weary remove was more on his wavelength. The plot is rife with double-crossing machinations perpetrated on Mitchum's Jeff by a decidedly ungangsterish Kirk Douglas and perhaps the most stunning femme fatale in movies, sultry, full-lipped Jane Greer. Once Greer's Kathie walks into the Mexican cantina where Mitchum has tracked her (after she's pumped Douglas full of holes and made off with his forty thousand dollars), all bets are off for Jeff—and the audience.

Out of the Past lays to rest the notion that noir was strictly a matter of rain-soaked streets and shafts of light flooding through venetian blinds, since its most striking sequences take place in a lake region under California sunshine, shot with unsurpassed delicacy by Nicholas Musuraca. A genuine directorial triumph, *Out of the Past* has one of the bleakest endings of any Hollywood film of the period: tune out Roy Webb's syrupy musical assault and you'll experience Tourneur's subtle and haunting delicacy in full flower. [Kent Jones, 3/4/97]

Pather Panchali (1955)

See The Apu Trilogy

Peking Opera Blues (1986)

Dir. Tsui Hark; Scr. To Kwok Wai
104 min

The power-pop triumph of the past few years, *Peking Opera Blues* lures you in with its pounding, crazy beat. The very first image is a close-up of an elaborately made-up Chinese opera performer staring down the camera and howling with laughter. His stylized gaiety is infectious; it dares the viewer to remain aloof. This action comedy by Hong Kong director Tsui Hark is a breathlessly choreographed jape that's almost irresistible.

Like much recent HK fare, *Peking Opera Blues* is a period piece that reflects the Crown Colony's anxiety vis-à-vis reunification with the People's Republic. Tsui has described the movie as a satire on the Chinese "ignorance of democracy," but it seems equally a fantasy about the breakdown of an established social order. Set in 1913, two years after the fall of the last emperor, the film is the sort of tangled narrative thicket in which unscrupulous warlords engage in sinister conspiracies, while adventurous gold diggers search for hidden jewels amid frequent bouts of stylized make-believe. As the title suggests, theater rules: Tsui's cubistic backstage is a vortex of entertainment, greed, and intrigue wherein three attractive heroines—a comic gold digger, a would-be actress, and a general's daughter, who, for no particular reason (and not very convincingly), has disguised herself as a boy—join forces to pursue their separate agendas. Typically, the aspiring actress is the most "sincere" character.

Peking Opera Blues is a glitzy, ironic pajama party in which the stars almost never stop role-playing, their antics punctuated by all manner of reversals, sight gags, and subversively gender-bending pratfalls. (Women were not permitted to appear in the Peking Opera, something addressed here with a vengeance.) The whole movie has a knowing quality that hovers over, and ultimately supersedes, the perfunctory plot. With its kick fights and chases egged on by the gongs and the clicks of James Wong's keening, twanging score, the film is a continual coming attraction for itself—the action as accelerated in Tsui's bang-bang editing as it is amplified by his performers' exaggerated reactions, continual hide-and-seek, and frequent disguises. (The most frequently asked question: "How come you are here?")

In its insouciant, breakneck pace, *Peking Opera Blues* owes something to the *Indiana Jones* films, but it's less overweening and more deliberately flimsy (not to mention wholly immune from ethnocentric Indy-imperialism). The mode is self-aware rather than self-conscious. As blatantly two-dimensional as the movie is, it engages the entire spectrum of popular amusement East and West. When Tsui travesties a traditional opera by having a pair of (disguised) characters turn up onstage in identical costumes, he combines the consternation of two of the most celebrated Marx Brothers routines. But at the same time that *Peking Opera Blues* parodies its source, it derives the most spectacular acrobatic stunts organically, from the rich soil of the opera's form.

Tsui suggests a comic Eisenstein. It's not just his machine-gun editing, but his use of typage, his analysis of circus attractions, his fascination with signs, and his interest in political upheaval that link him to the Soviet master. If Tsui belongs to the Internationale of commercial entertainment, it may be because the era of revolutionary heroism is long since over. Like Eisenstein's, Tsui's movies seem to flow from some preideological wellspring. For all its pow, *Peking Opera Blues* has an unexpected backbeat of melancholy and loss—it's the Boat Person's *Battleship Potemkin*. [J. Hoberman, 1/31/89]

Persona (1966)

Dir./Scr. Ingmar Bergman
83 min.

Ingmar Bergman's *Persona* seems to bewitch audiences even when it bewilders them. The perennial puzzle of What It All Means is quite properly subordinated to the beauty and intensity with which faces, beings, personae confront each other on the screen. The feeling spectator can supply his own psychic fantasies to fill Bergman's blank spaces. Identity, Communication, Alienation, even Schizophrenia: these are not so much the director's subjects as they are his spectacles. Two characters, a nurse and an actress; two actresses, Bibi Andersson and Liv Ullmann. Tensions, conflicts, ambiguities, confessions, intimations, and, as always, impending violence. Take it as it comes, and don't worry about the puzzle. When pieces to a puzzle are lost forever, the puzzle ceases to be a mystery and becomes instead a permanent incompleteness.

Certified Bergman-watchers may be awed by the Pirandellian pyrotechnics fashioned with arc lights, loops, and leaders, but students of Stan Brakhage are more likely to yawn. Brakhage has spent (wasted?) his whole life taking the medium apart. By contrast, Bergman has turned out twenty-seven feature films without even beginning to suggest an instinctive affinity to the medium. His stylistic flourishes have always been strained, derivative, archly symbolic, or obtusely obscure. Some reviewers have indicated that more than one viewing is necessary to understand *Persona* fully. I doubt it. A hundred viewings will not bring what is off the screen onto the screen. A thousand will not unlock Bergman's mind. What Bergman chooses not to tell must remain unsaid.

The Bergmaniac can canvas the artist's career for such cross-references as the animated cartoon unrealistically projected (*Illicit Interlude*), the surfside sonority of dialogue on a beach (*The Seventh Seal*), the magic lantern mystique of childhood (*The Magician*), the emphasis on the role of costumes (*The Naked Night*). But why bother? If Bergman is not yet beyond interpretation, he is certainly against it. As compared to *Brink of Life* and *Wild Strawberries*, *Persona* is devious in its intransigence, perverse in its denial of pleasure. Bergman has taken his place with the modern deities of the cinema—Antonioni, Fellini, Godard, Resnais. Paradoxically, his greatest talent is as a classicist, a writer of dramas and a director of actors. Nonetheless, he remains obsessed by technique for its own sake. I wonder if there is a director of his rank who worries so much about the cinematic form he will devise to express himself.

All in all, Bergman's stature is incontestable. His vogue began at a time when audiences were rejecting facile equations of art and politics. The collapse of liberal optimism and Marxist aesthetics opened the door to the dourest Swede since Strindberg. Bergman had no politics to speak of—or to film of—simply because Sweden itself lacked significant political tensions. The angst of alienation came more naturally in a country that was not suffering from overpopulation. Aldous Huxley once observed that the Lake Poets would not have taken such a benign view of nature if they had grown up in Equatorial Africa. Similarly, Bergman's metaphysical concerns might not have been as asocial if race riots exploded now and then in Stockholm. Bergman's American admirers on the art-house circuit were nonetheless ripe for Bergman not only because his concerns were more relevant to the angst of sheer affluence, but because he seemed immune to the corruptions of mass taste. His small crew in Sweden was an eloquent rebuke to the massive apparatus of Hollywood films.

Ingmar Bergman remains essentially an artist in an ivory tower in an isolated country. Still, he manages to invest the faces of his players with an expressive excitement and their characters with a demonic energy none of his technically more accomplished colleagues in Sweden can approach. The Bibi Andersson of *Persona* towers over the Bibi Andersson of *My Sister, My Love*, and therein lies the mystery and magic of Bergman's art. [Andrew Sarris, 3/23/67]

Pickpocket (1959)

Dir./Scr. Robert Bresson

75 min.

Pickpocket is the fifth of six films Robert Bresson has directed since 1943 and only the fourth to be released in America. You may not like Bresson, but you have to respect him. Or, as one of his most fervent admirers explained to me several years ago, Bresson is simply too good for people.

There is something unearthly about his art, an art of austerity so bleak as to make Carl Dreyer look like a sinful sybarite. Yet Bresson is a Catholic and Dreyer a Protestant; one expects Catholic art to be richer in the juices of life—but not Bresson's.

Pickpocket concerns a pickpocket who finally finds grace and redemption in the love of a fallen woman. Why has Bresson's protagonist chosen his vocation? For the money? Because of "psychological" compulsion? Not really, and not on those terms. Bresson once remarked that he had always been intrigued by hands, because they expressed better than anything else the full range of a man's character, achievements, and potentialities. Consequently, the very subject of the pickpocket takes on a metaphorical significance for Bresson.

We are a long way from the sociological tract and the case history. Bresson's pickpocket drifts through the streets of a curiously ascetic Paris as if he were sleepwalking through a dreamlike allegory. The acting of Martin LaSalle is drained of all the expressions and emotions that might have particularized his personality. What Bresson has done to his players throughout his career is at once impressive and hateful. Indeed, if the world were ruled by actors, Bresson would be burned at the stake as a destroyer of souls. This is all a part of Bresson's purity and integrity as an artist. He gives nothing to actors or to audiences, either, because he serves a cruel Deity faithfully or because his own point of view has become insufferably God-like.

Where Bresson cannot be faulted is his technique. The famous pickpocketing ballet that erupts in a drowsy railroad station and that evokes the normally hidden universe of grace and dexterity is one of the most sublimely realized technical exercises in the history of cinema. Even if one cannot accept Bresson's vision of life, and I cannot, the technical expression of this vision deserves the attention of every serious moviegoer. *Pickpocket* is a great film even for nonbelievers. [Andrew Sarris, 5/23/63]

Do this job long enough and you learn to accept certain realities. Some people will laugh at *Written on the Wind* and cry over *Sleepless in Seattle*—instead of vice versa. There are reviewers who find Godard boring and think Lukas Moodysson is a genius. And although it is tiresome to hear two-buck chuck extolled as Château Lafite Rothschild, you realize that hey, this is America—everyone's got an opinion, and if it weren't for bad taste, many folks would have no taste at all. But I reach the edge of my tolerance in the case of Robert Bresson.

Bluntly put, to not get Bresson is to not get the idea of motion pictures—it's to have missed that train the Lumière brothers filmed arriving at Lyon station 110 years ago. The late French filmmaker made thirteen features over the course of his forty-year career; each is a drama of faith so uncompromising as to border on the absurd. Bresson's actors do not act, they simply are; his favorite effect is the close-up. His movies may be cerebral, but their effect is primarily emotional—or physiological. They naturally induce a state of heightened awareness. Some might call it "grace."

Pickpocket was shot during the summer of 1959—the same season as Godard's *Breathless*. Like *Breathless*, *Pickpocket* is the story of a petty criminal, and even more than Godard's first feature, it is designed to confound audience expectations. The opening title, "This film is not a thriller," has the effect of Magritte's famous surrealist painting *Ceci N'est Pas une Pipe*.

Pickpocket was inspired by Dostoyevsky's *Crime and Punishment*, but all incidental anecdote and psychology have been stripped away. Employing few establishing shots and little camera movement, Bresson distills narrative down to a particular essence of looks, gestures, and precisely placed audio effects. ("The noises must become music," he wrote in his notebooks.) His mise-en-scène is as understated as his montage is aggressive—creating performances out of reaction shots, using sound to signify offscreen events. Bresson refers to this method as cinematography, opposing it to "the terrible habit of theater."

Indeed, *Pickpocket* might be described as a solemn carnival of souls. There's something almost medieval about it. The city is inhabited by angels—fallen and otherwise. In the movie's most elaborate scene, the antihero and his cohorts create an assembly line of theft at the Gare de Lyon. These unstoppable blank-faced thieves descend like a plague upon the world. Ultimately inexplicable, this concentrated, elliptical, economical movie is an experience that never loses its strangeness. [J. Hoberman, 10/5/05]

Pierrot le Fou (1965)

Dir./Scr. Jean-Luc Godard

110 min.

Pierrot le Fou is the first Godard film I have ever had to stand on line to see, and thus another coterie taste has been engulfed by the crowd.

But I wonder what the crowds make of Godard now that he has become popular as well as fashionable. In 1966, when *Pierrot le Fou* graced the New York Film Festival along with *Masculine Feminine*, Godard's films never had much of a first run. The pattern was always the same. Each new film would be assailed by his detractors as his biggest mess yet, and even his friends would look a little uncomfortable. A year later, the same film would look like a modern masterpiece, and two years later, like the last full-bodied flowering of classicism.

Pierrot le Fou, however, was something very different, the last local stop for Godard's express train of history. If I prefer *Pierrot le Fou* to, say, *Weekend*, it is because I find the end of an affair an infinitely more interesting subject than the beginning of a revolution, and *Pierrot* is nothing if not a lament for a lost love. Time has sweetened the song as it has soured the singer. Why? The main reason is Jean-Paul Belmondo. He gives Pierrot more charm, dignity, and resignation than Godard himself alone is capable of, and the jokes that worked in *Breathless*, those churlish jests that haven't worked since, work once more.

Without Belmondo's too-many-drinks-and-cigarettes-the-night-before-this-morning face to serve as ballast, Godard's giddiness becomes too flighty for the gravity required of any effective humor. Belmondo's appeal, like Bogart's, lies not in the actor's insolence, but in the weary gallantry the actor's insolence never quite conceals. Also, Belmondo, again like Bogart, testifies with his face to a life lived to the hilt.

Godard's very unique sensibility spills over every frame of the film from the first illustrations of the Velázquez aesthetic—white tennis tunics against pink flesh, Paris as a night landscape against the blue-green Seine, Belmondo gazing at the sensuous stream of colors on a bookstall—to the last shot of the sea that reconciles the doomed lovers after death to the recited lines from Rimbaud: "Elle est retrouvée./ Quoi? - L'Éternité./C'est la mer allée/Avec le soleil."

Pierrot le Fou is a film of fireworks and water, of explosion and immersion, the metaphorical expression of passion being cooled by existence, the visual equivalent of feelings being chilled by words. The influence of Renoir, Jean even more than Auguste, is everywhere, even in Belmondo's hilarious imitation of Michel Simon, but especially in the pervasive wetness of *Pierrot le Fou*, itself at least partly an ode to liquid pastoral à la Lautréamont in *Weekend*. It is, of course, no accident that Anna Karina's alter ego is an Auguste Renoir print plastered on the screen in Godard's peculiar montage-collage style that seems less peculiar with each increasingly fragmented year. Even the "inside" cinematic jokes—Sam Fuller in person describing the cinema as a battleground of emotions, the umpteenth joke about Nicholas Ray's *Johnny Guitar*, a reverent reference to Jean Renoir's *La Chienne*—seem to slide into the stream of sensibility without any bumps.

Audiences may still be jarred somewhat by the violent clash between blood-red melodrama and sky-blue contemplation, by the contradictory rhetoric of musicals and metaphysics and by the director's lingering affection for what he considers to be dying genres, but that is precisely what I love about *Pierrot le Fou*. Belmondo and Karina and Coutard and Antoine Duhamel (music) translate Godard's most tentative ideas into sensuous spectacle so that what is actually on the screen is usually more interesting than anything that can be said about it. Interestingly enough, none of the topical satire has dated in the slightest, not Godard's first tentative comments about Vietnam or his relatively gentle gibes at car culture or even a breathtakingly romantic defense of the love-struck moon against the calculating Cold War onslaughts of American and Russian astronauts.

There is not the slightest intimation of sexual intercourse in *Pierrot le Fou*, and yet, time and again, I felt the chilling sublimation of love into art and then the warming translation of art back into love. Nevertheless, I'd hate to imagine *Pierrot le Fou* without Belmondo, if only because Belmondo magnifies Godard's soul on the screen, much as Mastroianni magnified Fellini's *8½* and Chaplin the inspired actor always magnified Chaplin the ignoble self-pitier. The bleary-eyed Belmondo undoubtedly looks the way Godard felt when Godard was making *Pierrot le Fou*, and the resultant unity of feature and feelings is beautiful to behold. [Andrew Sarris, 1/23/69]

Basically Godard's version of a location thriller, *Pierrot le Fou* is shot, widescreen, in primary colors, mainly in the south of France. It looks sensational, as does Anna Karina, who, as she captivates and abandons Jean-Paul Belmondo, is herself the movie's documentary subject. The insouciant grace of Karina's spontaneous outbursts is paralleled by the film's: culturally, *Pierrot le Fou* is all over the map, juxtaposing Sam

Fuller and Garcîa Lorca, Vietnam and Auguste Renoir. Possibly no Godard film has ever been more hostile to Americans and more devoted to their cars.

Pierrot is hardly free of Godard's romantic misogyny, but it radiates the joy of cinema. "Let's go back to our gangster movie," Karina tells Belmondo after an idyll on the beach. Chantal Akerman says this is the movie that inspired her to becomes a filmmaker, and I hardly think she's alone. I first saw *Pierrot le Fou* when I was seventeen, having sneaked into a press screening at the New York Film Festival, and was convinced it was better than *Duck Soup*, maybe the greatest movie ever made. It probably is, for a seventeen-year-old—two hours, as we used to say, of Technicolor Marx Brothers projected on the wall. [J. Hoberman, 10/19/89]

Pink Flamingos (1972)

Dir./Scr. John Waters
108 min

There recently have been two glaring changes in the mood of moviegoing that has prevailed for, say, the last ten years. The shift from the mood necrophiliac, wherein we sat in miserable silence staring at films mangled by bad programming, reminded gloomily of the continuing existence of the filmmaker as being somehow in the way between his films and the mausoleums and archives, and the shift in the press away from a certain kind of review that hopefully can no longer be written. The kind of review a periodical used to send the toughest hatchet-dyke on its staff out to write about a certain kind of film—so uncommercial it's ultimately commercial, thereby threatening the business foundation of the Brassiere World. This is not meant to imply any disloyalty toward lesbians . . . only toward the kind, female *or* male, who in a fuchsia wool suit, a silver breastplate, a stylish hat tilted over the eye, combat boots, and a brassiere, busts into the theater and takes notes for the kind of review she knows in her purple heart she is making a living by writing. You know—the kind of review that quickly boils the movie down to a checklist of the oily moments, glossily smirks over the sex novelties, and points the fairy finger. Two notable such devil-dykes literally exist in the movie pages of the *Voice* who, except for the additional curiosity that they are males, are spear-carrying members of the hoof 'n' mouth lesbian legion. These are: Jonas Mekas, who as Golden Brassiere Publicity Mummy fed all the baby filmmakers (the kind she prefers) (and lately the video-babes) useless tidbits of information, then blurbed them in print and sponged off the baby-vomit of art, while taking the opportunity to slip the museum price tag of death around the neck of each. The brassiere sister of Mekas in this glandular activity, of course, Andrew Sarris, tireless laundry lesbian of all the dry-cleaning style nuances of big-time landlord cinema authority respect that could occur to a cattle-tranquilizer-bemused Major Hoople brain in her column "Formulas in Focus."

I have a more morbid interest in these matters, since, besides having been fair fingered by them, I have been processed into the Sarris column as an example of the abuse of permissiveness, and processed and recycled into the Mekas column as confirmation of all the bean-baggery it has continued over the last ten years; since my film, *Flaming Creatures*, designed—like John Waters's *Pink Flamingos*—as a comedy, had riotously laughing audiences at its first screening, right up to the time the media lesbians began to witch their spicy, orchid hothouse and turned my film into a sex issue of the *Cocktail World*, giving rise to the speculation, understandable in their case, that a real brassiere-dyke may not be able, professionally or otherwise, to recognize a difference whatsoever between comedy and sex. So besides the exhaustion of that particular formula for movie reviews, they are further prevented from doing the usual number on *Pink Flamingos* because of a nausea factor that Waters seems uncannily to have built into the film, the excesses of which would be too revolting when described in portfolio lesbian style—and that includes the Breeze of Death style of Mekas and the secret media-maid peter patter of Sarris.

"They can eat shit"—in the words of the dialogue of one of the best scenes in *Pink Flamingos*, the speech in the opening, which is marked by a moronic quality that you know at any moment could erupt into filth. This moment is deliciously held back for a few seconds until the "you can eat shit" line spews irresistibly from the lips of one of the film's two spectacular leading ladies. From that moment on, the dialogue becomes a gilded torrent of filth, the colors become more and more garish as the story unfolds of a clash, which results in a trailer-burning, between two families, each in the thrall of a superbitch who opposes the other on the issue of which of them is the world's filthiest woman. This issue, hardly resolved by the trailer burning, is at last settled by the one known as Divine, a queen (whose family trailer it was) who sticks her fingers into a fresh pile of her dog's shit on the sidewalk and licks it off in the film's closing moments.

Queer? I think such antics seem virile and wholesome when compared with the unmanly activities of her publicity dykes of Atlantis seemingly bursting with film chatter who really are only pyorrheal piranhas. Anyway, the world needs its queers—who else would upholster your black velvet urinal flaps on your mausoleum theater seats?

Aren't movies a little too important to us to permit their meanings to be endlessly obscured by professional attention bandits who, if they ever had anything to say, must have said it better long ago? Maybe if everyone wrote their own reviews, we could get information instead of stomach rumblings and the dried-up brassiere-gals of Mu could be put out to pasture where they might find something besides public logorrhea marathons to occupy their flaccid plush-warmers when they sway, hoisted by their own brassiere straps, in their stalls at night. After all, no one demands such a sacrifice. [Jack Smith, 7/19/73]

Platform (2000)

Dir./Scr. Jia Zhangke
154 min.

One of the richest films of the past decade, Jia Zhangke's superbly detached *Platform* spans the 1980s, filtering the period through the mutation of the propaganda-performing Fenyang Peasant Culture Group into the equally cheesy All Star Rock and Breakdance Electronic Band.

Jia has a strong visual style (scrupulous compositions based on long fixed-camera ensemble takes) and a powerful set of thematic concerns (the spiritual confusion of contemporary China, caught between the outmoded materialism of the Maoist era and its market-driven successor), as well as a vivid sense of place (dusty, inland Shanxi province). Following on his 1997 debut, *Xiao Wu*, the semidocumentary story of a supremely diffident Fenyang pickpocket who fails to adapt to China's new liberal economy, *Platform* puts Jia at the forefront of current Chinese cinema.

Elliptical yet concrete, *Platform* is a laconic tale of lackadaisical love and even more haphazard entertainment, as played out in a series of unheated factory halls and outdoor courtyards. The environment is at once dreary and exotic, prisonlike and vast. The group tours throughout the Chinese interior; the Great Wall, casually used as a place to rehearse or tryst, is a recurring visual motif. Geographic markers are matched by the precise fashion changes in hairstyle and dress that Jia uses to indicate the passage of time. *Platform*—which takes its title from a Chinese hit rock song of the 1980s—is pop art as history. Paeans to Chairman Mao are supplanted by Taiwanese rock anthems ("Gen-Gen-Genghis Khan"); communal screenings of the 1950s Hindi musical *Awaara* give way to "marital aid" sex education videos; braids become perms; suddenly, one notices color TV.

Platform, 2000; written and directed by Jia Zhangke

With its objective, almost clinical viewpoint and lovingly chosen, generally bleak locations, *Platform* looks like a documentary. But, perhaps influenced by Hou Hsiao-hsien's *The Puppetmaster*, Jia finds many subtle ways to transform the world into a stage. The play of the proscenium against the filmmaker's clear Bazinian taste for unmediated reality is fascinating. When one character is poised to disappear forever from the narrative, Jia allows her the privileged moment of a solo dance number performed in the privacy of her room.

Jia also uses a distanced camera placement for maximum context. There's a quietly magnificent, deeply melancholy shot of the hapless Electronic Band, listlessly pelted with garbage by one of its first audiences, performing by the side of a highway on the banks of the Yangtze, boats full of Panasonics floating past. The penultimate image, held long enough for the full weight of quotidian despair to infect the audience, is the epitome of the film's odyssey from kindergarten collectivity to failed privatization. [J. Hoberman, 3/2/01]

Playtime (1967)

Dir. Jacques Tati; Scr. Jacques Lagrange and Jacques Tati
119 min.

Playtime is unquestionably one of the most important films of the last decade, and yet it is probably for the best that it comes too late. We are surely better equipped today than in 1967 to understand a film such as *Playtime*, a film incredibly avant-garde, now that so much of the modern cinema has passed before our eyes and been partially digested.

Playtime was more than three years in the making. Anyone seeing the film might wonder why. And the answer begins to reveal the dimensions of deception behind an apparent simplicity: all those buildings, Virginia, are sets! When Tati found it difficult to close down Orly airport or the offices of British Petroleum for a month or two so that he could shoot his film there, he went out and built a city of his own. One million, eight-hundred thousand cubic feet of concrete, 43,000 square feet of plastic, 33,000 of framework, 13,000 of glass: a studio larger than three and a half acres.

What did it cost? To Tati, such a question is a gaucherie comparable to asking your hostess what she paid for your pastry. And as irrelevant. It's not worth going to see *Playtime* for the sets for the excellent reason that Tati has done everything to make sure you never begin to suspect his buildings are on wheels.

Playtime rigorously exploits all the elements of the medium. Sound, color, the big screen: all of these are essential to Tati's purpose. (The picture was originally in 70 millimeter, though not in full scope ratio.) While in former Tati films the M. Hulot character was the center of attention, here he is only one, equal, among many. Whereas Keaton was pursued by five hundred cops and the motion was unidimensional, Tati will put a hundred people in a shot, each mobilized in a different action. Of great importance is the "dialogue" between the people in a shot and the objects around them and, of course, the decor within which they are immersed. There is never simply one gag in a moment; there are many, far more, in fact, than one can catch in three or four viewings.

Tati eschews a dialectic on montage such as exists in the classic comedy. There are no reaction shots, no creating of the comic situation through analysis into different fragments, no underlining of a joke through its isolation. The procedures of the long take and the large screen are essential to accommodate the immense detail of *Playtime*, but the film derives from Tati's conception of a new comic style rather than the reverse.

Everything is not given to you analytically and univocally as in the classic cinema of montage; instead, it requires the viewer's imagination to supply the missing deductions of meaning. "With *Playtime*," said Tati, "I wanted to get people to participate a bit more, not do all the work for them. All the risks I took are in this direction. If it's always necessary to put the dots on the i's, it's not even worth the bother to live anymore; you're just a big battalion."

The infinite multiplicity of the points of interest in *Playtime*, the seeming inexhaustibility of its contents in viewing after viewing, comes not by chance but by calculation. Tati works like a mathematician; there probably has never been in the whole history of movies a script (five hundred pages) so detailed and precise, every button in place before a frame was shot. Typically, Tati's color was plotted into the decor itself, and a glance at any shot will reveal how the gradations of attention would disappear if the film were viewed in black and white.

Likewise, Tati has employed sound in a manner unrivaled for its complexity and importance. I suppose one would have to sit through *Playtime* blindfolded to appreciate this, and as I have not done so, it's convenient to recall Bazin on *Les Vacances de M. Hulot*: "It is the sound which gives to the universe of *M. Hulot* its breadth, its moral side. Ask yourself whence comes that great sadness at the end of the film, that immoderate disenchantment, and you shall perhaps discover that it is from the silence. All throughout the film the cries of the children at play inevitably accompany the views of the beach, and their silence for the first time signifies the end of vacation."

The humor, of course, derives from the fact that nothing really happens just as it is supposed to. All the wondrous gadgets eventually don't work; all the marvelous ordering of society simply makes a grand confusion. The milieu of the modern city is inescapable. It is, Tati tells us twenty-four times a second (as Godard would say), not only saner but probably no less realistic as well, to laugh when the world doesn't work the way we've planned.

Or else to go out and construct our own world, our own city, the way Tati did, and call it *Playtime*. And in that world, it is surely not the least most wonderful thing that the hilarious discombobulation goes right on happening even when we (or M. Hulot) are paying no attention to it at all. [T. A. Gallagher, 8/2/73]

The Portrait of a Lady (1996)

Dir. Jane Campion; Scr. Laura Jones
142 min.

As *Raging Bull* is to Martin Scorsese, *Portrait of a Lady* is to Jane Campion. Masterworks by filmmakers at the top of their game, each is a study in masochism as the internalization of social currents and riptides one navigates in claiming a sexual identity. To put it crudely, where Scorsese's boxer punishes himself for his failure to achieve an idealized masculinity, Campion's "lady" thwarts her own desire to escape the bonds of femininity by marrying a two-bit sadist who has contempt not only for her aspirations but for her very sex. And though her prison is a Roman mansion, she, like the boxer, is reduced literally to banging her head against its walls.

In Campion's scrupulous adaptation of Henry James's nineteenth-century novel, the orphaned American Isabel Archer (Nicole Kidman) travels abroad to find herself. Bright but unsophisticated, stubborn, beautiful, and terrified of her own erotic impulses, Isabel speedily bestows herself—and the inheritance that might have substantiated her illusion of free will—on the least worthy of suitors, the decadent art collector Gilbert Osmond (John Malkovich).

Like the novel, the film is split into two parts. The first part closes with Isabel's engagement to Osmond. The second part opens after a three-year ellipsis. The honeymoon is long over. We learn, after the fact, that Isabel has married Osmond and has borne a son who died in infancy. Campion, who feverishly depicts the sexual hungers and humiliations that James largely kept under wraps, follows his discretion vis-à-vis the details of the wedding night, the pregnancy, and the loss of the child who might have provided some raison d'être for what Isabel now realizes is a terrible marriage. The self-knowledge that eluded her during her brief heady moment of independence has smacked her in the face. It's not love that proffers "the clearest of mirrors" but hate. Isabel finds herself only when that very self is all but eviscerated by Osmond's will.

From the novel, Campion takes not only this intricate narrative web but its structuring pictorial oppositions: light and shadow, summer and winter, interior and exterior. Early on, Isabel describes her search for knowledge as a "light that has to dawn." Campion makes us aware of that light in every shot, using it as the great portrait painters do: to illuminate both flesh and inner life. Unlike most period films, *Portrait of a Lady* doesn't rely on the conventions of studio lighting. It's as if Campion (abetted by her marvelous cinematographer Stuart Dryburgh) reimagined the nineteenth century—its dank drawing rooms and verdant landscapes—in terms of natural light.

But Campion's aesthetic is more expressionistic than James's was, even in his most gothic fictions. Campion's oblique framings, her disruptive, vertiginous camera movement, her abrupt shifts of position are lifted from the language of horror films. Campion's camera telegraphs Isabel's feelings directly to our solar plexus. The camera moves; we catch our breath.

Nowhere is this more stunning than in Osmond's first seduction of Isabel, in a moldy mausoleum with only skulls to bear witness to their perverse tryst. It's not the triumph of Eros but of Thanatos, the sickly love-death that promises to obliterate an all-too-troublesome ego. While Isabel stands frozen between fight and flight, Osmond seems to come at her from every angle, mesmerizing her with the spiraling pattern of her own striped parasol, which he twirls like some B-movie hypnotist. Shocked by the intensity of her erotic response to his coolly practiced touch—it's fear that turns her on—Isabel seizes on Osmond's devious protestation of love as a cover for her own shame.

Portrait of a Lady is a cautionary tale for the contemporary young women shown in the film's peculiar prologue—women who, coming of age a century after Isabel, are still marked by the same confusions about sex, power, and romance. While Campion does not suggest a solution to this dilemma, she refuses to nail the doors of Isabel's prison as securely as does James. Her Isabel may have stopped dead in her tracks, frozen in panic. But at least she's not packed on a train bound for Osmond's waiting arms.

Kidman, who doesn't shrink from making Isabel every bit as irritating as she is in the novel, is remarkable both for the range of her performance (her transformation from an impulsive, earnest adolescent to a wary sophisticate) and for the cacophony of emotions she brings to every moment. The barely audible "oh" that escapes her lips when she's cornered is, in every sense, inspired. [Amy Taubin, 12/31/96]

The Power of Kangwon Province (1998)

Dir./Scr. Hong Sang-soo
110 min.

The brightest filmmaker to emerge from South Korean cinema's recent boom years, Hong Sang-soo has been making a career of reinventing the notion of the "reverse angle." No, not the editorial exchange of shots of characters engaged in conversation across a breakfast table or bang-banging it out over the tops of tumbleweeds. Hong has a much more metaphysical and broadly spaced sense of give and take.

Hong came fully into his own with the masterful *The Power of Kangwon Province*, in which a young professor and his younger former student-lover make separate desultory pilgrimages to the titular vacation spot—a woodsy mountain range filled with shady paths, lonely waterfalls, and threatening cliffs—over the course of the same sad weekend, yet never catch so much as a glimpse of one another. Back in Seoul, the miserable lovers reunite, but the force of the film isn't so much in their final clinch as in all the strange details that characterize their weekend away: a fish mysteriously flopping about on a remote mountain trail far from any stream, an ill-fated minor character who floats past both protagonists like a noonday ghost, the sobs of a lovelorn policeman, hanging from a balcony, too drunk to fall or fly.

Gorgeously photographed and filled with startlingly fresh performances (*Kangwon*'s Oh Yun-hong, a sylph with the shape of a sea fluke and eyelids like swollen cotton sops, is a standout), Hong's films are also peppered with sly bits of cinephilia. But while the director's modern mannerisms and multiple film-fest awards clearly tickle international critics, his films are every bit as Korea-specific as anything by culture-curator and *Chunhyang* director Im Kwon-taek. Brilliantly bifurcated and deeply suspicious of reunifications of any sort, Hong's films aren't just mounting portraits of broken lovers; they're exploring the most difficult regions of his politically and geographically fractured nation's historically broken heart. [Chuck Stephens, 10/29/03]

Primer (2004)

Dir./Scr. Shane Carruth
77 min.

A repeat-viewing brain twister to file alongside millennial puzzle films like *Mulholland Drive* and *Memento*, Shane Carruth's *Primer* unites physics and metaphysics in an ingenious guerrilla reinvention of cinematic science fiction. Its analog-egghead approach may be the fresh-

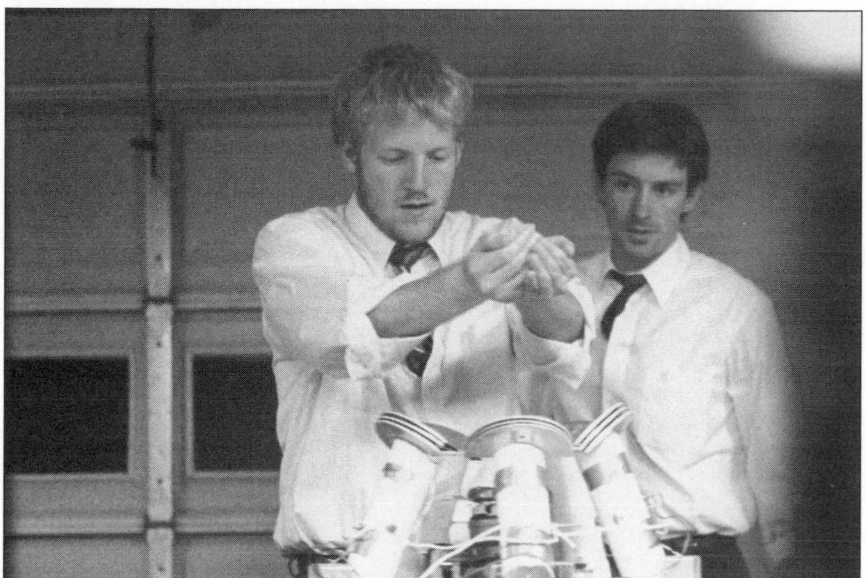

Primer, 2004; written and directed by Shane Carruth

est thing the genre has seen since *2001*. Less H. G. Wells than J. G. Ballard, Carruth's prodigious no-budget debut is also the nerdiest and most plausible time-warp fantasy that movies have ever dreamed up.

In a garage deep in the Dallas suburbs, four guys in corporate-drag white shirt and tie tinker away on a variety of science projects, hoping eventually to win financial reprieve from their day jobs. Aaron (Carruth) and Abe (a superbly antsy David Sullivan) break away from their pals to work covertly on a—well, it's hard to say *what* exactly, but they call it "the box," and it seems to involve an old catalytic converter and refrigerator copper tubing. Put a Weeble in it, and fungal proteins breed at an accelerated rate. Put a watch in it, and really inexplicable things start to happen. Before long, Abe and Aaron are talking about building a box big enough to get into . . .

At once clinical and lyrical, practically compactor-pressed at a mere seventy-seven minutes, *Primer* exists in a haze of naturalistic confusion. Fitting for a film about the limits of knowledge, it doubles as an experiment in narrative inference. Scenes begin and end in medias res. Meaning is elided, occluded, or embedded in texture and ambience. The overlapping dialogue, a rush of lab-speak gobbledygook that at times resolves into a sort of techie poetry, suggests David Foster Wallace rewriting David Mamet.

Carruth daringly sustains the disquieting opacity for a full half-hour before—semi-spoiler alert—it finally becomes clear that Aaron and Abe have invented a time machine and intend to use it daily. They crawl into coffinlike crates every afternoon, and six hours later, because the boxes reverse the flow of time for their occupants, it's twelve hours earlier. Thanks in part to its lulling, voice-over-enhanced delirium, *Primer* evokes *La Jetée*, the mother of all time-travel loops. But Carruth gives his fantastical scenario a seductively prosaic veneer. The machine is rudimentary by sci-fi standards, and the film assumes, as given, the paradoxes bound to bedevil any attempt at chrono-manipulation. The protagonists casually remark on the toll of thirty-six-hour days, tossing off lines like "I haven't eaten since later this afternoon." As physical impossibilities arise, so do ethical impasses. Living each day twice, Abe and Aaron exploit their prescience for stock market gains, but the prospect of absolute impunity soon brings to mind more grandiose abuses. Complicating matters, a double is spawned each time the machine is utilized—and that's before we hear about the secret machine that one of them has been harboring or contemplate the possibility of putting a time machine inside a time machine.

Shot for a purported seven thousand dollars in Super 16, *Primer* is both a deadpan satire and a heartening embodiment of DIY enterprise (designed to attract repeat customers, it's an unbeatable business model—a second go-round clears up many, but by no means all, of its mysteries). Carruth, an engineer with no previous film experience, shot only one take of every scene; his parents handled craft services, and the cast double-dutied as crew.

Visual ideas keep pace with the onslaught of hard science. Grainy and overexposed, the film looks like it's been irradiated. There's no shortage of memorable images: a shower of hole-punch confetti, the harshly lit corridors of a storage facility, the windowed panels of a garage door shot to resemble a filmstrip. The polymath director, who shares cinematography credit and composed the atmospheric score, has devised a syntax to reflect the slippage inherent in his premise. Sound and image are often subtly out of sync. A narrator obfuscates point of view, switching from past to future conditional tense.

The final third—a what-the-fuck snarl of recursive cycles and causal short circuitry—is where *Primer* essentially turns into an experimental film. Earlier scenes recur, sinister side effects emerge (the time travelers—or their doubles?—suffer bleeding ears and wobbly handwriting), and there are the tiniest shreds of plot to pick out if you're so inclined: a reverse-engineered act of heroism, a run-in with a potential funder who may have discovered their invention. The fissured disorientation powerfully conveys an infinite unraveling—a sense that nothing less than space-time as we know it is spinning off its axis. [Dennis Lim, 10/6/04]

Psycho (1960)

Dir. Alfred Hitchcock; Scr. Joseph Stefano
109 min.

For many years American and British critics have been mourning the "old" Alfred Hitchcock who used to make neat, unpretentious British thrillers before he was corrupted by Hollywood's garish technical facility. "Oh, for the days of *The 39 Steps*, *The Man Who Knew Too Much*, and *The Lady Vanishes*!" Meanwhile in Paris, the wild young men of *Cahiers du Cinéma*, particularly Claude Chabrol, were proclaiming the gospel that Hitchcock's later American movies stamped him as one of the screen's major artists.

A close inspection of *Psycho* indicates not only that the French have been right all along, but that Hitchcock is the most daring avant-garde filmmaker in America today. Besides making previous horror films look like variations of *Pollyanna*, *Psycho* is overlaid with a richly symbolic commentary on the modern world as a public swamp in which human feelings and passions are flushed down the drain. What once seemed like impurities in his cut-and-chase technique now give *Psycho* and the rest of Hollywood Hitchcock a personal flavor and an intellectual penetration that his British classics lack.

For one thing, Hitchcock no longer cheats his endings. Where the mystery of *Diabolique*, for example, is explained in the most popular after-all-this-is-just-a-movie-and-we've-been-taken manner, the solution of *Psycho* is more ghoulish than the antecedent horror, which includes the grisliest murder scenes ever filmed. Although Hitchcock continually teases his conglomerate audience, he never fails to deliver on his most ominous portents. Such divergent American institutions as motherhood and motels will never seem quite the same again, and only Hitchcock could give a soft-spoken state trooper the visually sinister overtone of a dehumanized machine patrolling a conformist society.

Psycho should be seen at least three times by any discerning filmgoer, the first time for the sheer terror of the experience, and on this occasion, I fully agree with Hitchcock that only a congenital spoilsport would reveal the plot; the second time for the macabre comedy inherent in the conception of the film; and the third for all the hidden meanings and symbols lurking beneath the surface of the first American movie since *Touch of Evil* to stand in the same rank as the great European films. [Andrew Sarris, 8/11/60]

Pulp Fiction (1994)

Dir./Scr. Quentin Tarantino

154 min.

More than anything else, Quentin Tarantino is a spinner of tall tales—the superbly garrulous, living embodiment of the movie enthusiast's hey-wouldn't-it-be-great-if . . . aesthetic.

Pulp Fiction is a movie of interlocking stories set in an imaginary demimonde and held together by languorous fades, humorous ellipses, and nonstop conversation. The comic structure is largely based on a series of two-handers: Tim Roth playing verbal footsie with Amanda Plummer, a goofily stoned John Travolta escorting the haughty Uma Thurman, world-weary Bruce Willis coming home to kittenish (and ultimately tiresome) Maria de Medeiros, *Die Hard* Willis battling volcanic Ving Rhames, rattled Travolta debating the wired, superbad Samuel L. Jackson.

Tarantino has an unerring command of slang and, in lieu of visual ambience, invents an aural one. Every character has a rap or a riff, if not a full-fledged theory of life. No wonder actors love Tarantino. Not only does he write hilarious, convoluted dialogue, but he permits them to posture through every scene as an extended one-on-one gabfest confrontation. Call the mode "Talk Talk Bang Bang." The language is as calculatedly brutal as the action—full of baroque racial, xenophobic invective, as well as continual profanity.

Tarantino's America is a wondrously wild and crazy place. "They robbed a bank with a telephone," says one character in amazement—especially as he, and nearly everyone else in the cast, is packing heat. Violence erupts out of nowhere—or rather, it erupts out of some kind of "innocent" fun. A fetishistic close-up of fixing, shooting, and booting smack leads, by the by, to a bloody, drooling OD, hysterical panic, and finally, the most successfully horrific comedy sequence in the movie. Tarantino is too fascinated by the nuance of situation to be a master of suspense, but *Pulp Fiction* is predicated upon his gift for abruptly raising the stakes. A couple talk themselves into robbing the joint where they're having breakfast—chitchat giving way to lunatic frenzy. Two professional killers riff on European taste in American fast food en route to a wildly theatrical hit. Toying with one victim, the gunman offhandedly shoots a second, then apologizes to the survivor: "I'm sorry—did I break your concentration?"

Despite its title, *Pulp Fiction* has less to do with the hard-boiled detective stories published sixty years ago in *Black Mask* magazine than with the déclassé action movies of the early 1970s. The movie resonates with echoes of biker and doper flicks, vigilante sagas like *Dirty Harry* and *Walking Tall*, the genres *Variety* dubbed spaghetti Westerns, chopsocky, and, especially, blaxploitation, as well as the contemporary art-splatter of Hollywood auteurs Peckinpah, Scorsese, and De Palma—movies that were not only violent but steeped in moral confusion. More generally, the title suggests Tarantino's spongelike capacity to absorb whatever he sees. The 1970s are always a touchstone, but *Pulp Fiction* lifts bits of business from *Kiss Me Deadly* and *Psycho* and Jean-Luc Godard, the inventor of movie postmodernism who has spawned yet another disciple.

In *Reservoir Dogs*, Tarantino's fanciful creatures asserted their reality by analyzing Madonna or musing upon the TV series *Get Christie Love*. *Pulp Fiction* is an even more naturalized hall of mirrors. Thurman wears Anna Karina's wig-hat; Willis does Ralph Meeker doing Brando. Jackson's Fu Manchu mustache, fierce mutton chops, and oiled 'fro make him pure essence of 1974. (All he lacks is the lime green leisure suit.) Travolta's character is *Welcome Back, Kotter*'s Vinnie Barbarino grown up into a hit man called Vincent Vega—as in star. "We're gonna be like three little Fonzies here," Jackson soothes the participants of one Mexican standoff by way of saying Be Cool.

Pulp Fiction's most elaborate set piece endearingly sends up Tarantino's own mind-set, inventing a made-for-57th Street theme-restaurant populated by 1950s icons. "It's like a wax museum with a pulse," Travolta smirks—as if he weren't sitting in his own personal Hall of Fame, particularly once Thurman maneuvers him into a Twist contest that quickly turns into a *Bandstand* extravaganza of tiptoe swiveling, lasso moves, and synchronized shoulder strokes.

Never mind that Tarantino lifted *Pulp Fiction*'s riff on Ezekiel 25:17 from an old kung fu movie or Jackson's redemption from *Kung Fu*, he is some kind of miracle worker. Reminiscing (with Dennis Hopper, no less) in the current *Grand Street*, the filmmaker recalls, with some bemusement, the powers of persuasion he honed during his years behind a video store counter: "I remember—this is really weird—I created a following for Eric Rohmer in Manhattan Beach and the South Bay area." That was talk talk without the bang bang. [J. Hoberman, 10/11/94]

Punishment Park (1971)

Dir./Scr. Peter Watkins

88 min.

Peter Watkins's *Punishment Park*, his first American film, is a science-fiction nightmare in the form of a documentary. In the near future, while the war in Indochina continues to expand, a rapid escalation of political repression in the United States results in massive arrests. Youths are offered amnesty from lengthy prison terms only if they succeed in crossing a fifty-mile stretch of desert on foot within three days, and the film cross-cuts relentlessly from one group suffering this ordeal to the angry tribunals that precede this torture. The rigorous way in which Watkins has worked this out is extraordinarily believable, and it is impossible to emerge from his ninety minutes of psychodrama unbruised. The considerable gut reactions Watkins's films provoke may partially explain the extent to which they are despised and ignored. No other filmmaker I can think of, with the possible exception of Samuel Fuller, expresses his "liberalism" in such hysterical paroxysms of hate, but the spectator's difficulty in identifying even with the hero-victims of Watkins's "punishments" is precisely what continues to make them so disquieting and lethal. [Jonathan Rosenbaum, 6/17/71]

A key film in the unimpeachable cry-in-the-wilderness corpus of Peter Watkins, *Punishment Park* (1971) is an act of howling political righteousness, a dystopian critique intended for the peace-movement years but possibly even more relevant today. The premise is so simple, it leaves singe marks: Watkins begins with the very real McCarran Act, which grants Ashcroftian summary-judgment powers to the president in times of potential "insurrection." The Nixon-'Nam years were those times, and so the film follows two groups of arrested protesters as they're led to the Western desert, interrogated by a tribunal, and then sent running, with national guardsmen and riot police following on the hunt.

Shot like most of Watkins's films as a fake documentary, the movie might be the most radioactive portrait of American divisiveness and oppression ever made. The impassioned cast was largely unprofessional and, in fact, largely conformed to their radical-victim/reactionary-monocrat roles; often, it's less a narrative than a democracy-in-crisis street fight. The on-the-fly shoot became so fraught with conviction that at one point Watkins worried that real bullets were being surreptitiously used. Of course, *Punishment Park*, like most of Watkins's other work, was barely given a commercial run in this country and has been effectively suppressed ever since. [Michael Atkinson, 12/7/05]

The Puppetmaster (1993)

Dir. Hou Hsiao-hsien; Scr. Wu Nien-jen and Chu T'ien-wen
142 min.

The Puppetmaster, the latest film by Taiwanese genius Hou Hsiao-hsien, is a multidecade tale along the lines of *Farewell My Concubine* about performers or prostitutes coping, as best they can, with the political upheavals of the twentieth century. But it is also sui generis—neither documentary nor fiction. The suggestive Chinese title translating as *Drama, Dream, Life*, it dramatizes the early life of eighty-four-year-old Li Tien-lu, Taiwan's most famous puppeteer, an official "national treasure" as well as an actor in Hou's last three films.

Hou calls Li "a living encyclopedia of Chinese tradition," and *The Puppetmaster* is a comparable anthology of narrative ploys. A half-dozen stage performances—usually shown head-on, some in a single long take—alternate with an ongoing family melodrama that unfolds in a series of domestic settings as adroitly framed, sensuously illuminated, and powerfully discreet as a Vermeer interior. (The Cherry Gardens brothel is represented as one more kitchen table.) *The Puppetmaster* is periodically enlivened by Li's distinctive voice-over, and the "narrativity" of any given tale is emphasized with the image of wiry old Li telling it. As the protagonist is simultaneously godlet and puppet, his story is both life and its representation. The action fades in on a meal at which the family discusses their plans for another meal—namely, the party to celebrate Li's birthday. His confused genealogy parallels Taiwan's complex historical situation.

The Puppetmaster is distanced and presentational. Rarely using close-ups, Hou frequently shoots an entire scene from a single point of view. When he cuts, it's often to a slightly longer shot—a tendency that further situates his characters in a particular socio-historical-geographical space. Hou has compared his elliptical structure to Godard's *Breathless* and "ancient Chinese theater," with traditional Chinese painting providing the inspiration for his economical use of detail and synecdoche. (The outbreak of World War II is represented by the sound of air raid sirens; the end of Japanese occupation by a cacophony of firecrackers.)

Beginning a scene in the midst of unexplained high emotions, holding a shot several beats longer than expected, *The Puppetmaster* offers a startlingly advanced use of editing, a dozen new ways to structure a scene. Li's description of his mother's death is accompanied by a complex alternation of presence and absence, audio as well as visual. For all the emphasis on real time, a single cut can span a dozen years even as the voice-over loops over and around the various staged scenes, knotting a story line so unobtrusively complicated, it makes a time traveler like Alain Resnais seem all thumbs.

Ignore the blurbs, forget what the hypemeisters tell you, a movie of this magnitude doesn't appear in New York every week. *Farewell My Concubine* suggests the second coming of Irving Thalberg; *The Puppetmaster* is more like a rebirth of the cinema itself. [J. Hoberman, 10/12/93]

Real Life (1979)

Dir. Albert Brooks; Scr. Albert Brooks, Monica Johnson, and Harry Shearer
99 min.

In Albert Brooks's first and funniest feature, *Real Life* (1979), Brooks plays "Albert Brooks," a supremely self-absorbed filmmaker who, assisted by a crew with helmet-cams, sets out to immortalize the "ordinary life" of a Phoenix veterinarian (Charles Grodin) and his family. Obnoxiously abrasive and manipulative, he's comparable to Rupert Pupkin. After trashing the hall of mirrors in which he finds himself, Brooks whines that "the audience craves fake—reality sucks." Nevertheless, according to the actual Brooks, "85 percent of the reviews for *Real Life* thought it was literal. Someone wrote, 'Why did Paramount Pictures let this man do an experiment like that?'" They must have heard Brooks's killer rendition of "Something's Gotta Give," performed for the citizens of the suburb where his film is set: "When an old immovable object such as you meets a young, honest guy like myself . . ." [J. Hoberman, 4/12/05]

Rear Window (1954)

Dir. Alfred Hitchcock; Scr. John Michael Hayes
112 min

James Stewart has been in town basking in the deserved glory of Alfred Hitchcock's *Rear Window*. I caught Stewart at a press conference conducted by Richard Roud at Avery Fisher Hall. Most of the questions were respectful—the only even faintly discordant notes were struck when one interrogator raised the subject of Donald Spoto's alleged discovery of a "dark side" to Hitch, and another propounded the theory that Hitchcock's worst films had been made when the portly film director was on a diet. Stewart squelched the latter line of speculation with a one-liner to the effect that Hitchcock didn't know the meaning of the word "diet." As to Spoto's revelations, Stewart said simply and graciously that he had never been aware of Hitch's "dark side" and doubted that Hitch could have hid it so successfully if it had actually existed.

With Hitchcock, the works themselves provide the strongest rebuttals. Does that mean that the poor wretch who brought up Hitchcock's weight deserved to be squelched? Not really. Who else but a fat, virtually immobile Buddha-like movie director would have recognized the enormous cinematic potentialities of the Cornell Woolrich story? Feminists have complained that women have traditionally been enslaved by having their destiny determined by their anatomy. Nonetheless, one's anatomy does have a great deal to do with one's destiny, which is to say that one of the problems of "selling" Hitchcock has had to do with his conspicuous girth. Indeed, Vernon Young, one of the more dyspeptic of the Hitchknockians, once concluded one of his turgid transatlantic diatribes against the director by referring to him as the "fat boy."

Spoto shocked many people not by uncovering any mortal sins or even lurid deviations in Hitchcock's life, but, rather, by imputing to this jovial jokester of pop folklore some hitherto unsuspected sexual impulses vis-à-vis his beautiful leading ladies. It was apparently little more than a fumbled pass here, a drunken advance there. One unfortunate consequence of the book is that Hitchcock's venal failings have been magnified out of context.

There is something undeniably unsettling about *Rear Window* from an ethical standpoint. Robin Wood tried valiantly to reconcile Hitchcock's work with the moral imperatives of the Lewis-Lawrence tradition and finally renounced the effort under the pseudonym of George Kaplan, the name of the imaginary character in *North by Northwest*. Rohmer and Chabrol and, to a lesser extent, Truffaut invoked Hitchcock's Jesuitical upbringing as a key to his Catholic morality. Truffaut came closer to understanding the humor in Hitchcock than his French compatriots did, but he, too, had trouble following Hitch through every twist and turn. When one compares *Rear Window* with the original Cornell Woolrich short story, one is struck first by how much the film owes to the story, and then by how seemingly minor modifications alter the entire universe in which the action transpires. The first change is in locale, from Woolrich's undisclosed Midwestern city with a "Lakeside Park" to New York's Greenwich Village. The view from the rear window has been expanded and two women characters have been introduced: Grace Kelly as the narrator-voyeur's fashion-model girlfriend and Thelma Ritter as the wise-cracking nurse from the insurance company.

Woolrich's ending is a bit on the facile, trashy, gun-happy side, as opposed to Hitchcock's more sustained confrontation. Woolrich's situations are more involving and more ingenious than his characters are. He leaves room for directorial amplification and movement. There is nothing in Woolrich that would have suggested an opportunity for Hitch to indulge in the most delicious ironies of sexual attraction, which is to say that Grace Kelly's Lisa is never so desirable to James Stewart's seemingly impotent photographer as when she is in danger of being strangled by Raymond Burr's cornered husband, and the photographer is unable, as all moviegoers are unable, to do anything but watch. Though, as John Belton has noted, the mannerisms of the bedeviled husband have been slyly copied from those of David O. Selznick, Hitchcock clearly identifies with much of the guilt and the pathos of the husband. That *Rear Window* can be profitably misunderstood and underinterpreted is a tribute to the grace and the deviousness of Hitchcock and his scenarist John Michael Hayes in diverting attention from the moral sickness lurking in the darkness. Neorevisionists such as David Thomson and Raymond Durgnat, and even Wood himself, have pounced on this sickness as a reason to diminish Hitchcock's stature. I would agree that the sickness is there, but it was in the nature of Hitchcock's genius to surmount this sickness with wit and humor and the most beautifully articulated feeling of which the motion picture medium was capable. [Andrew Sarris, 10/18/83]

Reds (1981)

Dir. Warren Beatty; Scr. Warren Beatty and Trevor Griffiths
194 min.

Reds is more a love story than a revolutionary chronicle, and as it happens, I prefer love stories to revolutionary chronicles. But *Reds* is not another *Doctor Zhivago*. Nor is Beatty's Reed of Russia the charismatic equivalent of Peter O'Toole's Lawrence of Arabia. Indeed, *Reds* is not at all the kind of movie in which the spectacle engulfs the characters. For a movie that runs for three and a quarter hours without intermission and reportedly cost 33.5 million greenbacks, there is a surprising lack of grandiose crowd scenes and garishly cluttered scenery. Where, then, did all the money go? Probably into the time-consuming fastidiousness of Beatty's brand of historical chamber drama. With the possible exception of George Plimpton's buffoonish caricature of a *Paris Review*–type editor, no performance strikes a jarringly false note. No scene goes on too long. No rhetorical passage sounds pompous.

The very title of the movie reflects Beatty's shrewdness in disguising humanist sentimentality as ideological audacity. You call us Reds, Freaks, Monsters, but do we not bleed, are we not human? "Reds" may be the epithet hurled at John Reed and Louise Bryant, but their epitaph was spoken by one of the film's many real-life "witnesses": "They were a couple." And so they were, and that is what *Reds* is mostly about.

Beatty claims our most serious attention by seeming to go diametrically against the grain by playing one of our earliest homegrown communists—at a time when the radicals of the right are flexing their muscles in Washington. The only recent movie to which *Reds* can be linked politically is *Ragtime*, and that, at least, was adapted from a best-seller. There is no "book" behind *Reds*, only fifteen years of research by Beatty and about five by his co-scenarist Trevor Griffiths. Much of this scholarship was devoted to the left-bohemian coterie of Reed, Bryant, Eugene O'Neill, Max Eastman, Floyd Dell, and Emma Goldman ensconced just before World War I in good old Greenwich Village.

What is most interesting about *Reds* is Beatty's strenuous efforts to manufacture a legend out of comparatively nonlegendary material.

John Reed himself has been almost completely forgotten, and Louise Bryant even more so. Since it is a bit early to speculate on why Beatty has identified himself so closely with John Reed, it can be said this time that *Reds* achieves the most enjoyably sustained level of bull-session camaraderie I can remember in an American movie. The stirring impact of ideological clamor is augmented by overlapping dialogue and the asynchronicity of sound and image. The crackle-snap editing of Dede Allen and Craig McKay can be detected as a crucial component of the film's strategy. For all its length, therefore, *Reds* never sags. Vittorio Storaro's cinematography is never given the opportunities of *Apocalypse Now* and the Bertolucci carnivals of color. The red flags, for example, are never rendered with the brightness of an emotional explosion but rather as frayed signs of an idea born more from the mind than the heart.

Reds never turns sour on the aspirations of its characters. What happens instead is that the John Reed of Warren Beatty, the Louise Bryant of Diane Keaton, and, above all, the wondrously romantic Eugene O'Neill of Jack Nicholson upstage the radical chic of their time and even the Russian Revolution with a prophetically poignant meditation on the problems of men and women trying at long last in human history to live and love as equals or, in the political parlance of their movement, as comrades. Yes, Beatty and Keaton and Nicholson proclaim to all who will hear, there can be a great, enduring passion shared by "modern" characters who write and think and talk and act on the stage of history. One need not go back to past centuries and more exotic cultures. Here finally are people who can recognize turning points in their lives. There is something infinitely touching, for example, in Keaton's suddenly looking up at Beatty in a Moscow hovel and thanking him for giving her the journalistic break of her life. Later, when Nicholson's O'Neill sneers at Louise's worshipful mention of Russia and then dismisses her Russophilia as the latest version of Roman Catholicism, the dramatic aptness of the conversation is uncanny.

Whether he intended to or not, Beatty stole a march on *Ragtime* with his daring deployment of a Greek chorus composed of such real-life "witnesses" as Roger Baldwin, Henry Miller, Adela Rogers St. John, Hamilton Fish, Rebecca West, Will Durant, George Seldes, Arthur Mayer, and two dozen more, none of whom are identified by captions. Recognized or unrecognized, the various witnesses provided an indispensable authentication of Beatty's nervy voyage into a risky past. [Andrew Sarris, 12/2/81]

Reminiscences of a Journey to Lithuania (1972)

Dir. Jonas Mekas
82 min.

Jonas Mekas's *Reminiscences of a Journey to Lithuania*, a film dedicated "to all the displaced people in the world," has itself become the object of some displacement. Screened jointly with Adolfas Mekas and Pola Chapelle's *Going Home* at the New York Film Festival, defined in the program as a non-narrative film and by its author as a home movie, it has become a casual victim of "convenient" programming and somewhat deceptive labels. Whatever "non-narrative" and "home movie" mean, they are less than helpful in describing the achievement of what must be called Jonas Mekas's testament. If they must be used, let it be understood that *Reminiscences* is a home movie about homelessness, a non-narrative film with one of the most beautifully constructed and articulated narrative lines in autobiographical cinema.

Reminiscences exhibits a continual fight against nostalgia, despite an underlining effort to reconcile years and distances and to address the state of displacement and dispossession through the disciplines of its structure. It is frequently said that whatever happens in a movie occurs in the present tense, but unless the film is silent or shot with direct, synchronized sound, the "present moments" it records are different slices of time overlapped—generally, the sights of one present, the sounds of another. *Reminiscences*, juxtaposing past footage with spoken reflections from a later date, is a film of many presents and many pasts, and much of its moving resonance comes from the ways in which different times complement, evoke, explain, define, and reinforce one another.

Each of the three sections supplies a different definition of "home." The first shows Jonas's early years in America, mainly 1950 to 1953 in the sorrowful streets of Brooklyn, shot with his first Bolex. ("We loved you, New World . . . but you did . . . lousy . . . things to us," he says on the soundtrack, and the everyday street images seep into the ellipses and the pauses, telling us more than streets or words could say alone.) "One Hundred Glimpses of Lithuania, August 1971," a journey back to his family and native village, composes the second and longest part, and here we feel even more the desperate pull between sound and image: an unleashed camera rushing about to take everything in as though to repossess it, a continual movement of pans, exposure changes, and cuts; against this a somber narration conveying loss, distance, stasis: "You led sad and hard lives, the women of my childhood." Part three, shot later the same month, details a visit to a Hamburg suburb—the site of a slave camp where he and Adolfas spent a year during the war ("When we asked around, nobody knew that a labor camp was there—only the grass remembered")—and then a trip to Vienna, where he once planned to attend school (a dream shattered by the war) and where he now luxuriates in the company of friends and the richness of Vienna's past. But even the temporary comfort of Vienna is disrupted by change: the film ends with the burning of a fruit market, perhaps destroyed (the narration speculates) to make way for a modern replacement.

Clearly, the protagonist of *Reminiscences* is not the Jonas Mekas whom we see on the screen. Nor is it quite the Jonas Mekas whom readers of the *Voice* have come to know—the Pied Piper of avant-garde cinema with the profile of Pan and the charming intimidation of a poet-salesman. No, it is the accented voice with its imperfect English, its deliberate pauses, its tragic seriousness and depth that is coming to terms with the rest of what we see and hear; a disembodied consciousness seeking to fix it all at last, spurred by necessity into an unnatural eloquence. This Mekas can be glimpsed intermittently in the notebook format of *Diaries, Notes and Sketches*, in the attempt to find Walden Pond in Central Park, peace at a friend's wedding, a lost childhood in the glories of a circus. But the "diaries" show only blossoms that have sprung from displacement—still blossoming, still very much "work-in-progress." *Reminiscences*, a finished work, gives us blossoms, too, but it also gives us more of what the earlier work—and what the "American experience"—seems to suppress and inhibit: it gives us roots. [Jonathan Rosenbaum, 11/2/72]

Rose Hobart (1936)

Dir. Joseph Cornell
19 min.

Rose Hobart premiered in 1937 at the Julien Levy gallery, then the main surrealist venue in New York, as part of an evening of "Goofy Newsreels." No riot ensued, although Salvador Dalí reportedly made a violent scene and jealously accused Cornell of plagiarizing his thoughts. Dalí's behavior was atrocious but understandable, for *Rose Hobart* ranks with *Un Chien Andalou* as a surrealist masterpiece—and in some respects, it is a more profoundly radical work, introducing notions of "distance" and "materiality" hitherto absent from cinema, as well as bringing key surrealist ideas to their logical conclusion.

Cornell was never an official surrealist, but rather a sort of "naive" American cousin. This movement served him as both the catalyst and the initial audience for his own sweeter, more eccentric vision. With its abrupt mixture of reverie and melodrama, and haunting images of evening clothes in the jungle, *Rose Hobart* (which recycles footage from the 1931 jungle adventure *East of Borneo*) is actually less suggestive of Buñuel and Dalí than of the popular precursors surrealists loved: Feuillade, Rousseau, and Verne. However, one of the tenets of surrealism was that commercial movies (and particularly juvenile trash like *East of Borneo*) had a dreamlike latent content that could be precipitated by deranging or bypassing the manifest content of their narratives. André Breton called this procedure "synthetic criticism," but until *Rose Hobart* it had never occurred to anyone to practice synthetic criticism of the film-stuff itself.

Rose Hobart proved to be a work that opened, rather than closed, aesthetic possibilities. In the late 1950s, Cornell lent a print of it to Ken Jacobs, a filmmaker then in his employ, and Jacobs, much excited, showed the movie to his associate Jack Smith. In a general sense, both artists were extremely sensitive to Cornell's use of superficial rawness in the service of formal sophistication. But a measure of *Rose Hobart*'s richness is that its influence can be seen in two of the 1960s' most brilliant films, Smith's 1963 *Flaming Creatures* and Jacobs's 1969 *Tom, Tom, the Piper's Son*. In a spirit similar to the Cornell film, *Flaming*

Creatures presented exotic Hollywood-style imagery (and "found" musical accompaniment) without narrative restraint, while *Tom, Tom, the Piper's Son* followed Cornell's lead in using a preexistent film as the ready-made material for a new one. [J. Hoberman, 10/26/80]

Rosetta

Dir./Scr. Luc and Jean-Pierre Dardenne
95 min.

Rosetta's stylized rough-and-tumble vérité is established from the onset, as its teenage protagonist slams through a factory, fighting ineffectually and violently to keep the job from which, for reasons never specified, she's just been fired. The handheld camera is kept disorientingly close to Rosetta (Emilie Dequenne) and will remain so for nearly every minute of this pummeling, jagged, and extremely well-edited film. This is the second feature by the Belgian brothers Luc and Jean-Pierre Dardenne, after their terrific illegal-immigrant drama *La Promesse*; like that 1997 release, it puts twenty years of social-documentary experience in the service of a powerfully single-minded metaphor.

Living in a trailer park with an alcoholic mother who mends old clothes for her to peddle, Rosetta is a furiously sullen bundle of energy. She's not quite pretty but too fresh-faced to be dowdy, often expressionless but also impulsive ("You only drink and fuck," she screams at her mother as the prelude to one of several scuffles). Most significantly, Rosetta lives in a state of existential dread. The woodland swamp that borders the trailer camp exemplifies the "rut" into which she fears she might fall. In her quest to forestall this fate by finding work, she is befriended by a young guy who operates a waffle stand. He treats her to a dinner of beer and fried bread, plays a tape of him practicing the drums, and tries to teach her to dance—at which point Rosetta doubles over in the stress-related stomach pain that plagues her throughout this fiercely compelling movie.

Devoid of music, elliptical in its narrative, *Rosetta* has not been universally admired. That it stormed out of nowhere to win the Palme d'Or at Cannes, while David Lynch's heartwarming *Straight Story* was overlooked, seems to have struck some Americans as a conspiracy orchestrated by the Evil Empire from beyond the grave. Others directed their animus against the Dardennes' unglamorous heroine. Rosetta is neither likable nor ennobled by struggle. She is, rather, some form of brute life force. Cunning as an animal, she scrambles, hides, and hoards. The movie makes a spectacle of her repeated dodging and ducking across the highway into the woods. Laid off by a baker (Olivier Gourmet, the father in *La Promesse*), she goes into a rage—clinging to a heavy sack of flour as though it were her life raft. Most appallingly, she betrays the only character who has shown her sympathy.

Rosetta was shot in the same drab neighborhoods as *La Promesse*, but one could easily imagine the movie transposed to the United States—although I wonder if a career-conscious American indie would care to present so needy and (relatively) unattractive a protagonist or plot a trajectory of such sustained anxiety. Is Rosetta an abstract construct? The Dardennes have signaled their modernist ambitions by comparing her to the hero of Kafka's *Castle*. But their movie's ugly-duckling heroine, her repeated routines and spiritual anguish, as well as the harsh clarity of the ending, suggest a Marxist remake of Bresson's *Mouchette*.

Rosetta strives for a material state of grace. Her will to survive is identical to her overwhelming desire to find a "real" job in this world. During the brief period when she operates a waffle stand—the camera, as usual, fixed on her every moment—she becomes almost human. It's a small miracle; work is a pleasure. [J. Hoberman, 11/3/99]

The Rules of the Game (1939)

Dir. Jean Renoir; Scr. Jean Renoir and Carl Koch
110 min.

The masterpiece of the personal, "plotless" cinema is Jean Renoir's *The Rules of the Game*. And it is in *The Rules of the Game* that we see the superiority of Renoir over Bergman. Cinema versus theater. Whereas Bergman sustains his scenes through the dramatic climaxes, the theatrical stuff, Renoir avoids any such dramatizations. There is no Aristotle in Renoir. Renoir's people look like people and, again, are

The Rules of the Game, 1939; directed by Jean Renoir; written by Jean Renoir and Carl Koch

confused like people, and vague, and unclear. They are moved not by the plot, not by theatrical dramatic climaxes, but by something that one could even call the stream of life itself, by their own irrationality, their sporadic, unpredictable behavior. Bergman's people do not have a choice because of the laws of life itself. Bergman's hero is the contrived nineteenth-century hero; Renoir's hero is the unanimous hero of the twentieth century. And it is not through the conclusions of the plot (the fake wisdom of pompous men) that we learn anything from Renoir; it is not who killed whom that is important; it is not through the hidden or open symbolism of the lines, situations, or compositions that Renoir's truth comes to us, but through the details, characterizations, reactions, relationships, movements of his people, the mise-en-scène. Gradually, as the film progresses, plotless as it is, the whole nerve system of the prewar French aristocracy is revealed to us, sickening as it is. And that is the secret of the art of Buñuel and Renoir; occasionally they are able to enter and communicate from the inner regions, from where they see everything in the right human perspective. Very few mortals do. [Jonas Mekas, 1/26/61]

Safe (1995)

Dir./Scr. Todd Haynes
119 min.

Like all of Todd Haynes's work, *Safe* doesn't make concessions to conventional expectations. It could be that people are put off by the ostensible subject, environmental illness—technically, multiple chemical sensitivity—or, as the movie puts it, a flat-out allergic reaction "to the twentieth century." One still and luminous California evening, stepping out of the family Mercedes into the family garage, Carol White (Julianne Moore) sneezes. "Bless you," replies her husband, Gregg (Xander Berkeley). God bless Carol White. By the end of *Safe*, the life of this San Fernando Valley housewife has been changed utterly.

When we meet Carol, she's so pale and impeccable, she looks more like a doll than a living being. In her sterile mansion, she stands in the wings like a showroom mannequin. Her tiny, babyish voice sounds robotic—as if the doll has batteries and a string to pull. Everything about Carol is self-denying. Having sex with her husband, she appears both bored and vaguely distressed. (Marital sex here looks patently ridiculous.) An aerobics class at the local health club provides a rare glimpse of messy color and movement. Unlike the other ladies, however, Carol is so cool she doesn't sweat (a detail that ties into Haynes's longstanding fascination with bodily secretions).

It's no wonder that Carol recoils at the delivery and the installation of an ominous black couch ("We ordered *teal*," she insists). At night, she can't sleep and wanders her garden like a haunted maiden, or matron, out of Munch. In the daytime, she goes about her errands. At the hairdresser's, on a rare impulse, Carol decides to get a perm. Afterward, looking at herself in the mirror (even if he hadn't studied Lacan, Haynes would love mirrors), she squeals: from her nose flows a perfect rivulet of deep magenta.

Comedy or horror? Some viewers, critics among them, have a hard time catching Haynes's tone, much less his point of view. Some call him cold and academic. I find Haynes to be one of the most emotional and deeply compassionate of filmmakers—so emotional, intuitive, and empathic that his movies, *Superstar: The Karen Carpenter Story*, *Poison*, and the short *Dottie Gets Spanked*, seem poised on the verge of nervous breakdown. He seems unable *not* to deal with perilously fraught, intimate materials.

The first time I saw *Safe*, I was smitten but mystified. Everything about the visual world grabbed me: the shimmering, hyperreal colors, the hilariously weird architecture and cold yet sensuous light, Carol's brooding nights in the Garden of Evil—or is it Good? The ominous, hyped sound: Carol gulping milk, hovering copters, background voices like garbled transmissions from outer space. *Safe* makes you hold your breath. One reviewer from Sundance called it "suffocating." He didn't mean the word as a compliment, although it could be.

Like Freud's patients, Carol is just waiting to be diagnosed as a hysteric. "Nervous disorder" is written all over her. On the other hand, she is suffering from an objective illness, and so she'll get violated many times, in many ways, by those who treat her. Once she moves to Wrenwood, a New Age "healing" colony outside Albuquerque, she's at the mercy (odd word) of creepy, silky-toned gurus who preach that the ill are responsible for their illness, that right-thinking and pure lifestyle can make them well. Quackery aside, illness, as it often is, is a blessing in that it forcibly removes her from an impoverished, unlived life.

In case you're unaware, multiple chemical sensitivity is an authentic illness—"recognized as a legitimate disability by 10 United States Government agencies" and "protected by the Americans with Disabilities Act," so the film's production notes inform us. It's also an illness tailor-made for Haynes, whose ongoing subject is stigma. His films tend to focus on afflicted souls, too sensitive to live in this world. Carol has much in common with the anorexic Karen Carpenter of Haynes's 1987 *Superstar*—the forty-three-minute underground mock-doc made with Barbie dolls. In the 1991 *Poison*, characters in each of the film's three "tales of punishment" die in escape attempts, last-ditch flights to far-better worlds.

Eschewing an ending out of TV's "disease movies," Haynes leaves his heroine without wings to fly. At the end, confronting menacing red splotches on her face, Carol is so pathetic and deluded, I think Haynes means her to be more beautiful than ever. [Georgia Brown, 6/27/95]

Salesman (1969)

Dir. Albert Maysles, David Maysles, and Charlotte Zwerin
85 min.

I have been delaying writing anything about the Maysleses' *Salesman*. I consider I shouldn't waste any of my space on films that are widely enough discussed in the "regular" press—even if I like the film. *Salesman* opened in a large commercial theater and is doing an average business; it doesn't need my help. If it needs—then it's too bad. Somehow, during the last few years, I don't seem to feel much pity for films or filmmakers who fail commercially. If they want to play the commercial exhibition game, they should be prepared to take bravely all the consequences. The house is not doing too well? Well, why did you want that big house in the first place? You want to reach more people? Oh, how pompous! You'll say, you can't get your money back unless you play it in a big house? So, you do something and then you want something back from it for yourself? How petty. Can you imagine a composer who spends three years on a symphony and then he doesn't let it out into the world because they aren't paying him for all those three years, in cash? God, how corrupt we are.

Oh, what's the use. The summer is here, it's too hot, and too smoggy, and they won't let Mailer clean out the air, people are so stupid, they prefer to sit in their own muck until they die. So I am pretty depressed. And I don't want to write about *Salesman* because the movie is so grim, and I just spoke with David (or was it Al) Maysles and he said he hasn't seen my review yet. *Salesman* is a very well-made film, but God, it's so grim, so boring. And that's why I am not writing about it: I can't figure out why this good movie is so boring. Every shot is good, but when they are spliced together, next to each other, the whole thing looks like a big pancake, without any sense of structure. Second, following the good old naturalistic tradition, Maysles concentrated only on certain grim, gloomy, sick aspects of their protagonists and their activities. After seeing the film, one is ready to condemn their profession, and them as people, and even the Bible itself. Which is silly. Because we know that these people in reality are neither that grim nor that corrupt. In any case, they are less to blame than the system that makes them do what they do.

And here is one of my problems. There are films and novels that are complete, total works. Dreiser's *An American Tragedy* is such a work. It presents both the facts and the interpretations of the facts, the commentary. And then there are films and books that are only half-works. They present their cases perfectly and in a concentrated manner—*Salesman* is such a work—but they abstain from (or are not capable of) any interpretations, commentaries. In such cases, it's up to the critics, to the columnists, and to any intelligent member of the society to provide interpretations. As it is now, the meanings are there, but they are dormant. Which is okay. But God, why it has to be so boring! That I can't answer. Why must truth be so boring? And myself, being a farmer, whenever I am facing anything that is so grim and boring, no matter how "serious" and "good" it is, I become very suspicious. There must be something wrong, or paranoiac, or sickly contorted about a boring truth; it cannot be a healthy truth, it has no sense of humor. [Jonas Mekas, 6/12/69]

Sans Soleil (1983)

Dir./Scr. Chris Marker

100 min.

An eccentric rumination on downtown Tokyo, Chris Marker's *Sans Soleil* is philosophical journalism. Emerging from the compost of newsreels and travelogues, *Sans Soleil* is rooted in the least pretentious, most debased documentary forms. But it's as though Walter Benjamin or Jorge Luis Borges had scripted *The Sky Above, the Mud Below*.

The mysterious Marker (best known here for his sci-fi slide show *La Jetée*) appears on the continuum of French cineastes somewhere between Alain Resnais (a one-time collaborator) and Jean Rouch (with whom he is credited for "inventing" cinema vérité). Having made films in and about Africa, Finland, China, Japan, Siberia, Korea, Israel, and Cuba, the sixty-three-year old Marker is at once an explorer-filmmaker in the mode of Werner Herzog or the pioneers chronicled in Kevin Brownlow's *The War, the West, and the Wilderness* and the hippest film correspondent of the European left since Joris Ivens.

Sans Soleil has the feel of a testament. It purports to be the footage of a peripatetic cameraman, accompanied by voice-over readings of his letters to the muse. Within this factoid fictional framework, the film plunges headlong into themes of memory and death by proposing itself as the Japanese bridge between a casual shot of three Icelandic children frolicking through a summer field and shots of the same town several years later buried up to its church steeple in molten lava.

At one hundred minutes, *Sans Soleil* is too dense to easily assimilate on a single viewing, but, as Marker's surrogate says on Japanese TV, "Not understanding adds to the pleasure." Taking its somber title from a Mussorgsky song-cycle, the film's structure is lyrically free-associational. *Sans Soleil*'s images are often superb—its Tokyo comic book futuropolis more startling than *Blade Runner*'s—but it's the flow of language that binds together the film's disparate vignettes. Unlike most documentary filmmakers, Marker foregrounds his subjectivity by persistently identifying photography with consciousness. Whether dissecting an exchange of glances between the camera and a woman in a market in Guinea-Bissau (and locating her look in precisely one frame of film) or desultorily restaging *Vertigo* in its original locations, Marker—or rather, his alter ego—is continually speculating on the nature of representation.

Bracketed by life and death in Iceland, Marker's basic juxtaposition of the world's most successful industrial society with the impoverished site of an exemplary Third World liberation struggle is not only to show "the two extreme poles of survival." The montage is as existential as it is political. Japan and Guinea-Bissau are revealed here as two non-Western cultures predicated on worldviews that are profoundly animist. The Japanese are shown to build temples to cats, create singing simulacra of JFK, hold ritual cremations of broken dolls; the camera turns the living people of Guinea-Bissau into moving shadows. Humans, animals, objects—everything in *Sans Soleil* is explicitly possessed of a soul.

In one of the film's most beautiful sequences, bits of the ferociously popular, robot-ridden sci-fi animation *Galaxy 999* begin to insinuate themselves into a leisurely observation of dozing commuters as if to wish them sweet dreams. It's instructive to compare this treatment of urban life to that found in *Koyaanisqatsi*. Nothing in *Sans Soleil* is ever less than compassionate: simple-minded notions of the dehumanized or the unnatural seem not to exist. *Sans Soleil* is suffused with a romantic nostalgia for the present, yet Marker's view of the future is not entirely pessimistic. If, in the film, Pac-Man suggests a metaphor for the species, synthesized video is used to represent one more refinement in the development of consciousness.

Indeed, sometimes Marker's admiration for the citizens of Tokyo—their derelicts and TV sets—verges on the angelic. The exhibition of some priceless jujus from the Vatican at a Tokyo department store prompts the speculation that within a few years, the Japanese "will produce a less expensive and more efficient version of Catholicism." I'm afraid the Koreans will beat them to it with Sun Myung Moon. [J. Hoberman, 11/1/83]

Sansho the Bailiff (1954)

Dir. Kenji Mizoguchi; Scr. Fuji Yahiro and Yoshikata Yoda
120 min.

Based on a melodramatic novel by the popular nineteenth-century writer Mori Ogai, Kenji Mizoguchi's *Sansho the Bailiff* is actually set in the medieval Japan of one thousand years ago, a time and place much like any other, of awakening human consciousness and consequent social chaos. The class system is breaking down, rank holds sway by brute force rather than by moral authority, and the mute masses are restless. Set against the background is the tragic history of a single family torn apart in the tide of history, sacrificing itself for the sake of a higher order. Unlike Ozu, Mizoguchi will never settle for a lesser level of community when a greater may be attained, and nothing will undermine his ultimate commitment.

A Dubeck-like provincial governor defends the rights of his subjects against a harsh decree of military conscription, choosing to follow the dictates of conscience rather than those of custom, affirming the ethic of mercy over the law of the jungle. As a result, he is separated from his wife and two children, deprived of rank, and sent into exile. Seventeen years later, his son, by whim of fate granted the same position (the film is virtually a parody of social mobility as its principal characters are carried arbitrarily up and down the class scale), frees the slaves in his domain, voluntarily exiles himself, and is reunited with his now blind and crippled mother on a desolate beach by the sea. It is the same eternal sea to which Godard turned for the closing metaphor of *Contempt* in elegiac tribute to the epic odysseys of Mizoguchi and Homer, to vanished kingdoms where men and women walked the earth like gods.

Thus the plot of *Sansho the Bailiff* opens and closes with a similarly quixotic gesture, while a father and a sister now dead seem to live on through the deeds of their son and brother. By an action performed within time, time is vanquished. Mortality, personal loss, and social waste are absorbed into a cyclical destruction and regeneration of order. Everything seems to happen more than once in the film, and repetition assumes the quality of ritual.

If a false dichotomy has been imagined by some critics between the aestheticism and the realism in Mizoguchi's work, it is simply because he knows how to look at the whole range of human experience, from the most exquisite to the most base, with the same calm regard and utter comprehension, discovering in the real world those graceful forms sufficient (and necessary) to sustain each incomparable image. Those who would learn the ultimate secrets of *Sansho the Bailiff* are advised to examine a scene in which the hero's sister, like Bresson's Mouchette, finds escape from materiality by entering a watery grave. In this suicidal gesture—religious ceremony and moral lesson—the quest for freedom is reconciled with a submission to nature's immutable laws. The lady vanishes into the lake, leaving behind only a few concentric ripples on its surface—musical spheres emanating from the mind and the heart of an artist who knows, as all great artists know, that truth is merely the surest path to beauty. [Michael McKegney, 12/4/69]

Sátántangó (1994)

Dir./Scr. Béla Tarr
450 min.

Most simply described, Hungarian director Béla Tarr's seven-and-a-half-hour masterpiece *Sátántangó*—adapted from a much esteemed, if still untranslated, novel by László Krasznahorkai—is a bleakly comic allegory of social disintegration on the muddy *puszta*. Set on an entropic collective farm during the last years of Hungarian communism, it's a mordant, characteristically Eastern European tale of hapless peasants and charismatic swindlers.

With fewer shots than the average ninety-minute feature, *Sátántangó* is a double tour de force—for the actors, as the camera circles them in lengthy continuous takes, and for Tarr, who constructs his narrative out of these morose blocks of real time. Krasznahorkai, whose subsequent novel *The Melancholy of Resistance* provided the basis for Tarr's *Werckmeister Harmonies*, is a writer whose long sentences provide a prose analogue to Tarr's mise-en-scène, but *Sátántangó* is in no way literary. Because each cut is an event, the most banal incident can be expanded into something epic. The movie's final shot, in which one character laboriously boards up his window, provides a superbly materialist fade-out.

So far as I know, *Sátántangó* has never been issued on DVD and is, in any case, essentially experiential—meant to be seen in a single viewing. Even so, two hour-long chunks would be remarkable movies in their own right. In one, a fat, drunken doctor spies on his neighbors, taking notes like a character in an Alain Robbe-Grillet novel, then runs out of booze and makes an epic trek through torrential rain to get another bottle. In the other, a ten-year-old girl poisons a cat and then herself. Around halfway through, it becomes apparent that, despite its minimal montage, *Sátántangó* is an exercise in parallel action—much of what happens happens simultaneously. This "devil's dance" is literalized in a remarkable sequence where the collective's repetitive ranting, drunken strutting, and befuddled cavorting are set to the same mind-breaking musical loop.

Despair has never been more voluptuously precise. *Sátántangó* has cast its spell on cineastes as varied as the late Susan Sontag and the rejuvenated Gus Van Sant. If you have a day to devote to it, the same might happen to you. [J. Hoberman, 1/11/06]

Scenes from under Childhood (1970)

Dir. Stan Brakhage
135 min.

Again, there are rumors about putting movies on tape. Any movie. You transfer it from film to tape; you put the tape into a special cassette; you slip the cassette into a special replaying machine, and you watch it on your home screen or on your TV screen. The system has been tested, and it works. The price of an average movie on tape will be the price of an average book. There is a secret bustle in certain places of this town; publishers, record houses, movie companies are trying to tie down films for the near-future "films-on-tape" boom. The gadget is supposed to go on public sale any month now. There is no question that this new system of image dissemination will drastically change a number of conventions, professions, and activities connected with cinema, including the reviewing of films. I think it will be all for the good.

I hope it will come soon, because it should make my job easier. As I have often and sadly stated here, I remain the only chronicler of the non-narrative cinema, and I can't cope with it any longer, too much is happening. The worst part is that most of the movies I'm writing about, nobody can see. The theater won't show them; no business. The tape system would make these films more widely accessible: we won't need theaters to show them. Reviewing films will become like reviewing books: you get your review copy, you look at it, and do your job. You'll know that the reader can always buy it for a buck or two.

I just looked at Stan Brakhage's *Scenes from under Childhood*, Part IV. Brakhage has been feeling very low lately. He is in a "giving-up" mood. Commerce is taking over, he feels. I don't feel that way at all, and I have been at the cannons, too. I know that the civil war of the non-narrative and noncommercial film versus the commercial and narrative film has been clearly won. The existence of non-narrative film forms in addition to narrative film has been established. Particularly one feels this when one leaves New York and visits the universities and small colleges. Stan has this low feeling sometimes, because he lives there alone on the mountain and likes to fight lonely battles. He forgets that he isn't alone, that there is the whole network of filmmakers' cooperatives doing the work, and there is a new breed of film educators across the country and they are doing their job. Slowly but surely.

Where was I? Part IV may be the strongest of the four. The entire cycle (total length of slightly over two hours) is a slowly unfolding biography of the Brakhage family. It is a complex and progressing mosaic, or call it a symphony, of realistic details from daily life, filtered through Brakhage's eye. Details of very simple things around the house, the utensils, the furniture; details of emotions, like tears or outbursts of anger, or joy; details of daily activities, like washing dishes, making bread; details from the very first days of life, and deep into the childhood; details that are real, and details that take the shape of memories and dreams that dissolve and fade in and out.

This fade-in and fade-out of details and memories is one of the constants of the film. Although the film is made of thousands of little pieces, one practically never sees any cuts—they are all submerged into the sea of living, and they keep coming up and sinking again. Another constant is the use of color positive-negative technique through all the parts. The first three parts dealt with early childhood, and everything was more rosy and more pastoral. Emotions were seldom permitted to play any part. Everything remained just images. Part IV uses emotional details, too. But what I really like about it are the details themselves, how they are presented and treated and selected, and the rhythm within which they move. No matter how different my own life was from the one presented in Brakhage's film, detail after detail they reflect in my own memory eye. There is a universality in these images that transcends the personal. As Buddha says, the more personal you are, the more universal you are. What Brakhage has done, in these four parts, he has made a sort of tapestry of our first memories. [Jonas Mekas, 3/5/70]

The Searchers (1956)

Dir. John Ford; Scr. Frank S. Nugent
119 min.

John Ford's *The Searchers* always brings to mind Albany's final words on Lear: "The eldest hath borne most: we that are young/Shall never see so much, nor live so long." Since I can testify that it doesn't take long at all for the youngest to become the oldest, as viewers we pretty much carry around both young and old perspectives. Ford's hero Ethan Edwards (John Wayne) may object to being called Uncle or Sir, "Grandpa or Methuselah," but like Lear he's another jealous elder demanding his due—fealty to the code of fathers, the necessity of blood revenge—and also an incipient, howling babe.

It was enlightening recently when the youngest in my house, the one whose taste and good sense we all rely on, saw *The Searchers* for the first time and upon exiting announced that he couldn't stand Ethan. "I kept wishing he'd get killed." Exactly what Ethan's one-eighth Cherokee, adopted nephew Martin Pawley (Jeffrey Hunter) wishes. "I hope you die!" Martin blurts out—words that show he's his uncle's true son. The bullying Ethan then shoots back those famous words that would soon be recast, lightened up, by a doomed youngster named Buddy Holly: "That'll be the day."

The Searchers is such a lucid text that nearly every one of Frank Nugent's sparse, beautiful, and laconic lines reverberates in memory. A good deal has been written on the film's themes: that doorway between wilderness and garden; marriage and kinship; history; race—the white man's displacement of repressed sexual rage, or general savagery, onto "the other." Like the chase for the white whale, this is another great American hunt. Only here the object is a white girl, and, when found, she sends the rescue party on its way ("These are my people. Go!"). Since when did a woman's choice count when the whole of white civilization, the will of the fathers, says, Come!?

In Ford's magnificent odyssey, an unregenerate Confederate soldier spends what has been variously calculated as five, seven, or ten years tracking down his niece Debbie (Natalie Wood), who's been abducted by a Comanche chief, Scar. (Henry Brandon plays Scar, with Navajos as the rest of the tribe.) What starts as a rescue mission changes course once Ethan views Debbie as "defiled," becoming an all-out effort to kill his last surviving blood kin. Man is keeper of the bloodline, meaning his females' purity; it's such ideas of purity that lead enemies to rape "his" women. Since Ethan's double, Scar, is dedicated to revenging his sons, slain by whites, a revenge cycle is put in motion that could be biblical, Greek, or American.

In ravishing Technicolor, we can now look out from the doorway onto Reconstruction Texas, 1868, from both Eisenhower America of 1956, when the movie was made, and from today—when 125 years have not created the peaceable kingdom Mrs. Jorgensen (Olive Carey) assures us will come. From out of Monument Valley rides a monument. "Ethan?" His brother, Aaron, isn't sure. Aaron's wife, Martha, is; she and Ethan share a past. Inside the homestead, we can confirm our suspicions by looking; we can, as children do, ignore the evidence of our eyes, or, as Ward Bond does, we can tactfully avert our glance. (No doubt, long ago, Martha got tired of waiting.) The marvel is that all of this exposition is unsaid. This is a film about *looking*, as well as looking for.

Recently, a lot of people tripped over themselves distinguishing Eastwood's *Unforgiven* from the classic Western (using words like *revisionism* and *demythologizing*). They may have forgotten that the great elegiac Westerns even in their day were called anti-Westerns and the word *hero* had quotes around it. Here's a chance for them to take another look—and for those who are young and haven't seen this masterpiece to see what they make of John Wayne's terrible, lonely rider. [Georgia Brown, 5/18/93]

Shadows (1958/1959)

Dir./Scr. John Cassavetes

78 min./87 min.

[Editor's note: Jonas Mekas was an early champion of John Cassavetes's Shadows *when it first screened in 1958, but he renounced it after the director recut it the next year. What follows is an exchange between Mekas and Cassavetes, as well as J. Hoberman's reviews of both versions. The original* Shadows, *long thought lost, turned up at the Rotterdam Film Festival in 2004.]*

The same evening there was a screening [in November 1959] of John Cassavetes's second and commercialized version of *Shadows*, which in no way should be confused with the original print, screened a year ago at the Paris Theatre, and about which I will have to say more at a later date, when my unrealistic anger for what has been done to that original simmers down. This should be around the time the original *Shadows* is shown again on January 19 [1960] at the 92nd Street YMCA. [Jonas Mekas, 11/18/59]

Letter to the Editor

Dear Sir:

There would seem to be some discrepancy as to the purpose of trying to better a film. In a recent edition of *The Voice*, Mr. Jonas Mekas, who had for over a year been a staunch supporter of a 16mm film experiment called *Shadows*, blustered forth ridiculous accusations at the second version of the picture, implying that it was done as a commercial concession to would-be distributors.

Perhaps it would be wise to first regard the history of the film, which reaches back over a three-year period. *Shadows* started as a classroom experiment with a view toward fresh approaches to cinematic style. The film was improvised by the actors; it was shot with unbending honesty, care, and disregard for critics. It was made with the conviction of youth challenging the old guard, and everyone who had ever been defeated by expedients of living in an economic world was for the film. Not one actor was paid for his services, nor were the technicians given anything.

We did not know when we started that it would take three years of hard work to finally achieve the best of what we then felt we could accomplish. In the course of three years, the tide of outside enthusiasm dwindled and finally turned into rejection. The *Shadows* people continued, no longer with the hope of injecting the industry with vitality, but only for the sake of their pride in themselves and in the film that they were all devoted to do.

When the first version was finally assembled and ready, it was screened at Paris Theatre before some 2,000 people, in three midnight showings which were free to the audiences that attended. The picture *Shadows*, the original version, was received with mostly hostile eyes; a few, such as Mr. Mekas, felt that it had accomplished a new era in cinematic technique. Mr. Mekas's favor greatly pleased us and made us feel that at least someone had understood our efforts; then when his magazine,

Film Culture, graced *Shadows* with an award for originality, we were overwhelmed.

However the truth of the matter is that the original version of *Shadows* was not accepted by the great majority of thinking people, who had been very much in favor of this kind of picture. The truth as it had to be realized was that the audience failed to empathize with the characters as depicted in the film, and the natural rhythms and style employed in the film, of which we were all so proud, stood surrounded by the thinness of the characters, the lack of all-around design, and the inconsistency within the character development.

The fallacies as we recognized them came as a shock, a shattering admission of our own ineptness. It would have been easy to side with those few who refused to believe that the film was anything but marvelous, for it is one weakness that all human beings are prone to. It would have been easier just to call it a day, to wrap all the criticisms and say that those who didn't understand are idiots, and that we weren't trying to impress anybody.

However, it is my belief that expression of any kind must be understood before it can have any meaning. For me, films can educate, enlighten, entertain, and give people release from their hidden fears, their prejudices. For me, it is imperative that we sustain our integrity as far as it can reach, because given the position of leading and being listened to involves a responsibility that must be responded to. Otherwise, the man lives with the knowledge that he is a fake. Otherwise, it would be impossible, for me personally, to have people think that I am ethical and pure and to know inside me that I am a fraud. It would make me live with the fear of time, the fear that I would waste the only life that I have.

The second version of *Shadows* was attempted with this in mind. Mr. Mekas is right in that he states this version is completely different from the first version. It was made to be better understood, with the understanding that comes from life, not from opinions of others. It in no way was a concession and, in my own opinion, is a film far superior to the first. Some of the music is gone, the poetry of overall expression, but the individual expression, of individual people, is there. The cinematic style which was so prominent in the first gives way to the emotional experiences that the characters encounter. The scenes, in my opinion, are fulfilled; the imagination of youth that sparked the first version came back stronger, clearer, and more determined to enlighten rather than prove.

Perhaps Mr. Mekas is not aware that there is no sale on the picture, and that the money was contributed by various film-lovers. It would be advisable for Mr. Mekas to again look at both versions of *Shadows* without the unfounded prejudices that seems to trouble, and complicate, his thinking on cinema and its purposes.

John Cassavetes
Pacific Palisades, Calif. [12/16/59]

It may seem to some that enough has already been said about John Cassavetes's *Shadows*. After seeing it again at the Film Center, in its original version, and after comparing the exultation of this audience with the perplexity at Cinema 16, I definitely feel that the real case of *Shadows* is only just beginning.

I have no further doubt that whereas the second version of *Shadows* is just another Hollywood film, the first version, however, is the most frontier-breaking American feature film in at least a decade. Rightly understood and properly presented, it could influence and change the tone, the subject matter, and the style of the entire independent American cinema. And it is already beginning to do so.

The crowds of people that were pressing to get into the Film Center (*Pull My Daisy* was screened on the same program) illustrated only too well the short-sightedness of the New York film distributors who blindly stick to their old hats. *Shadows* is still without a distributor. Distributors seem to have no imagination, no courage, no vision, no eyes for the new.

Again, I stress that I am talking about the first version of *Shadows* only. I shall be relentless in stressing this point. For I want to be certain not to be misunderstood. I have been put into a situation, one in which a film critic can get into once in a lifetime (I hope). I have been praising and supporting *Shadows* from the very beginning, writing about it, pulling everybody into it, making enemies because of it (including the director of the film himself)—and here I am, ridiculously betrayed by an "improved" version of that film, with the same title but different footage, different cutting, story, attitude, style, everything: a bad commercial film, with everything that I was praising completely destroyed. So everybody says: What was that critic raving about? Is he blind or something? Therefore I repeat and repeat: it is the first version I was and am still talking about. (Here is the stay-away identification marker: the second version begins with a rock-and-roll session.)

I have no space for a detailed analysis and comparison of the two versions. It is enough to say the difference is radical. The first *Shadows* could be considered as standing at the opposite pole from *Citizen Kane*; it makes as strong an attempt at destroying life and creating art. Which of the two aims is more important, I do not know. Both are equally difficult to achieve. In any case, *Shadows* breaks with the official staged cinema, with made-up faces, with written scripts, with plot continuities. Even its inexperience in editing, sound, and camera work become a part of its style, the roughness that only life (and Alfred Leslie's paintings) have. It doesn't prove anything; it doesn't even want to say anything, but really it tells more than 10 or 110 other recent American films. The tones and rhythms of a new America are caught in *Shadows* for the very first time. Therefore, we may call it the first modern American film.

Shadows has caught more life than Cassavetes himself realizes. Perhaps now he is too close to his work, but I am confident he will change his mind. And the sooner the second version is taken out of circulation, the better. Meanwhile, the bastardized version is being sent to festivals and being pushed officially, while the true film, the first version of *Shadows*, is being treated as a stepchild. It is enough to make one sick and shut up. [Jonas Mekas, 1/27/60]

Arguably the founding work of the American independent cinema, John Cassavetes's 1959 *Shadows* is the prototype for Martin Scorsese's *Mean Streets*, Jim Jarmusch's *Stranger Than Paradise*, Spike Lee's *She's Gotta Have It*, and all their progeny. Cassavetes's first feature was a one-film American new wave; with his aggressive sincerity and swaggering integrity, Cassavetes became the prototype for the American independent director—the Method actor turned filmmaker.

Shadows can be bracketed with *Breathless*, completed the same year, as a low-budget, post-neorealist, pre–cinema vérité Something New. Both are predicated on handheld camera, stolen locations, elliptical editing, and extended bedroom scenes featuring self-conscious performances by twenty-year-old actresses acting like they are characters in a movie. But *Shadows* is more episodic and performer-driven. Using the members of a drama workshop he directed, Cassavetes shot thirty hours of footage based on their improvisations. The Charles Mingus score later added makes the jazz analogue explicit. Indeed, as the movie's principals are black, white, and mulatto, race is crucial to the movie. So is authenticity. Anticipating life in a Warhol movie, Cassavetes's performers struggle to remain in character (in the now) despite miscues, blown lines, and unforeseen improvisations; much of *Shadows*' naturalism derives from applying a workshop sense of invented personalities to everyday life and a corresponding failure of the characters—or is it the actors?—to successfully live up to their images.

Opening commercially in New York in March 1961 (a month after *Breathless*), *Shadows* impressed the *New York Times* as a near documentary "shot without benefit of a screenplay, without a word of dialogue written down, without a commanding director to tell the actors precisely what to do." In fact, the movie had been substantially reshot and re-edited since its first public screening in late 1958. It's appropriate that the restored print is having its premiere at Anthology's Jonas Mekas Theater. Then writing for the *Voice*, Mekas was *Shadows*'s greatest critical champion, at least until Cassavetes revised the movie for narrative coherence a year later. Ray Carney has published a framework for the original version in his BFI *Shadows* monograph. It would be an amazing event if the ur-*Shadows* were ever to reemerge. [J. Hoberman, 6/18/03]

John Cassavetes's *Shadows*, the founding work of the American independent cinema, has always had its own shadow—an ur-version championed in these pages in 1959 by *Voice* critic Jonas Mekas, who subsequently disowned the filmmaker's longer, revised cut. Unseen, supposedly dismantled, and thought lost for more than four decades, an ur-*Shadows* has unexpectedly surfaced.

Turned down by Sundance, where it might logically have been shown, this ur-*Shadows* premiered at the ultra-cinephilic Rotterdam Film Festival. To anyone familiar with the controversy around *Shadows* and its shadow, the seventy-eight-minute ur-film is full of surprises. The known version is not, as Mekas suggested, a virtual remake. Most of *Shadows* is already ur. Nor is the ur-version less narrative. On the contrary: there is radical concentration of activity. The frantic round of parties, performances, and pickups on Manhattan's main stem begs to be diluted. Does the action span 24, 36, 48 hours? Where's the downtime? Other differences: ur-*Shadows* lacks a bedroom scene but boasts a more experimental Mingus score, as well as a few songs whose rights would not have come cheaply.

The reappearance of this extinct creature is due to Ray Carney, a Boston University film scholar who spent years in search of this particular grail. The provenance is still mysterious. Carney, who must utter the word *Cassavetes* more times in a day than most people take a breath, credits the New York City Transit Authority. The movie was apparently left on the subway sometime after its screenings at the 92nd Street Y. Who lost it and how exactly the professor found it remain to be explained. [J. Hoberman, 2/4/04]

Shoah (1985)

Dir. Claude Lanzmann

563 min.

Claude Lanzmann's *Shoah* is not simply the most ambitious film ever attempted on the extermination of the Jews; it's a work that treats the problem of representation so scrupulously, it could have been inspired by the Old Testament injunction against graven images. "The Holocaust is unique in that it creates a circle of flames around itself, a limit which cannot be crossed because a certain absolute horror cannot be transmitted," Lanzmann wrote in a 1979 essay, ostensibly about the mini-series *Holocaust*. "Pretending to cross that line is a grave transgression."

Shoah, which takes its title from the Hebrew word for "annihilation," doesn't cross that line, it defines it. For much of its nine and a half hours, the film seems formless and repetitive. Moving back and forth from the general to the specific, circling around certain themes, *Shoah* overwhelms the audience with details. For those who demand linear progression, Lanzmann's method may seem perverse—the film's development is not a temporal one. "The six million Jews did not die in their own time, and that is why any work that today wants to render justice to the Holocaust must take as its first principle the fracturing of chronology," Lanzmann has written. Although *Shoah* is structured by internal corroborations, in the end you have to supply the connections yourself. This film throws you upon your own resources. It compels you to imagine the unimaginable.

Length aside, *Shoah* is notable for the rigor of Lanzmann's method: the eschewing of archival footage and narration in favor of contemporary landscapes and long interviews (shown mainly in real time) with those who, in one form or another, experienced the Holocaust. "The film had to be made from traces of traces of traces," Lanzmann told one interviewer. *Shoah* embodies a powerful and principled restraint. Like Syberberg's *Hitler, a Film from Germany*, it refuses to "reconstruct" the past, thus thwarting a conventional response and directing one to the source of one's own fascination.

In his *Holocaust* piece, Lanzmann approvingly quotes the philosopher Emil Fackenheim: "The European Jews massacred are not just of the past, they are the *presence of an absence*." This is why, while the vast Auschwitz complex has come to epitomize the Nazi death machine, *Shoah* emphasizes Treblinka—a camp built solely to exterminate Jews, a back-country site razed and plowed under by Nazis themselves in an attempt to conceal all physical evidence of 800,000 murders.

The landscapes in *Shoah* are haunted beyond the mind's capacity to take them in. Piney woods and marshy fields cover mass graves, a brackish lake is silted with the ashes of hundreds of thousands of victims. The camera gazes at the overgrown railroad tracks, end of the line site of a ramp where a quarter of a million Jews were unloaded, then hurried along with whips to their doom; it considers the postcard town of Chelmno where, one day after Pearl Harbor, the first Jews were gassed in mobile vans, using engine exhaust. What can be more peaceful than the ruins of Birkenau's snow-covered cremos and gas chamber? Of course, not every vista is so scenic. In one unforgettable camera movement, Lanzmann slowly pans down to the brown winter grass covering the rusty spoons and personal detritus that still constitute the soil of Auschwitz.

What binds these landscapes together are the trains that chug throughout Europe bound for Poland and the east. Lanzmann even managed to find an engineer who drove the Jewish transports. One of the film's recurring images is that of a train crossing the Polish countryside or pulling up in Treblinka station, with this very engineer, now wizened and bony as some medieval Death, looking back toward his invisible freight. In the argument of *Shoah*, these trains underscore the extent of bureaucratic organization needed to commit genocide, the blatant obviousness of the transports, and, finally, the existential terror of the journey.

If landscapes give *Shoah* its weight, interviews provide its drama. Over and against these images of present-day Poland and Germany is the testimony of witnesses ranging from Jewish survivors to Polish onlookers to Nazi commandants. But the film is as filled with silence as with talk. Pauses, hesitations, are often more eloquent than words.

Moreover, words are belied by expressions. Among the most scandalous aspects of *Shoah* are Lanzmann's interviews with the Polish residents of Chelmno and Treblinka. Although there are exceptions, their blandly volunteered memories and perfunctorily offered concern ("It was sad to watch—nothing to be cheery about") are almost more damning than the casual anti-Semitism ("All Poland was in the Jews' hands") the interviewer has little difficulty in provoking. Real malice surfaces only in tales of "fat" foreign Jews "dressed in white shirts" riding to their deaths in passenger cars where "they could drink and walk around" and even play cards. "We'd gesture that they'd be killed," one peasant adds, passing his finger across his throat in demonstration. His buddies assent, as if this macabre signal was itself an act of guerrilla warfare directed at the Germans.

If the sequence induces the unbearable mental image of trains run by drunken crews, packed to overflowing with a dazed, weeping human cargo, careering through a countryside areek with the stench of gas and burning bodies, jeered at by peasants standing by the tracks, this and more are corroborated by the surviving Jews: "Most of the people, not only the majority, but 99 percent of the Polish people when they saw the train going through—we looked really like animals in that wagon, just our eyes looked outside—they were laughing, they had a joy, because they took the Jewish people away."

As for the Nazis, it's hard to know which is worse, the pathetic evasions of the avuncular Franz Grassler, the onetime deputy commissioner of the Warsaw Ghetto, insisting that the Jews knew more about the final solution than did their jailers, or the affable, expansive Franz Suchomel, an SS Unterscharführer at Treblinka, expressing a grotesque camaraderie with the people he was killing. Among other things, *Shoah* precisely details the means by which the Jews were compelled to participate in their own destruction. Meanwhile, the testimony of Suchomel and others, such as the former head of Reich Railways Department 33, demonstrates that genocide—by which the Nazis proposed to have the Jews vanish *without a trace*—posed incredible logistical difficulties. It is here that the language of problem solving takes on a hallucinative unreality. Suchomel allows that at its peak, Treblinka "processed" twelve thousand to fifteen thousand Jews each day ("We had to spend half the night at it"), a trainload of victims going "up the funnel" in two or three hours. Unlike at Auschwitz, prisoners at Treblinka were gassed with engine exhaust. "Auschwitz was a factory!" Suchomel explains. "Treblinka was a primitive but efficient production line of death."

Lanzmann's most detailed interviews are with former members of the Sondercommando—the Jews who were kept alive at Treblinka and Auschwitz to stoke the annihilation machine. "We were the workers in the Treblinka factory, and our lives depended on the whole manufacturing process, that is, the slaughtering process at Treblinka," one explains. Only the naive or the pitiless can call them collaborators. In a sense, the men hyperbolize the dilemma of Jewish survivors in general—it is one of the Holocaust's cruelties that every Jew who survived is somehow tainted. One woman who managed to weather the war hiding in Berlin describes her feelings on the day that the last Jews in the city were rounded up for deportation: "I felt very guilty that I didn't go myself and I tried to escape fate that the others could not escape. There was no more warmth around, no more soul . . . [only] this feeling of being terribly alone. . . . What made us do this? To escape [the] fate that was really our destiny or the destiny of our people." A terrible fate, an absolute isolation are ideas that recur in *Shoah* again and again.

If the Nazis are all too human, the survivors are as mysterious as extraterrestrials. What is one to make of the urbane, ironic Rudolf Vrba smiling as he describes cleaning the bodies out of the gas chamber, or the beseeching eyes of Filip Müller, a survivor of five liquidations of the Auschwitz special detail? Unlike other accounts of the Holocaust, *Shoah* deliberately minimizes acts of individual heroism—to have been a Jew in Hitler's Europe was to have had the most appalling kind of heroism thrust upon you.

People have been asking me, with a guilty curiosity I can well understand, whether *Shoah* really has to be seen. A sense of moral obligation is unavoidably attached to such a film. Who knows if *Shoah* is good for you? There were many times during the screening that I regarded it as a chore, and yet, weeks later, I find myself still mulling over landscapes, facial expressions, vocal inflection—the very stuff of cinema—and even wanting to see it again. If at first *Shoah* seems porous and inflated, this is a film that expands in one's memory, its intricate cross-references and monumental form only gradually becoming apparent. One resists regarding *Shoah* as art—and, as artful as it is, one should.

Shoah transfixes you, it numbs you, and finally—with infinite tenderness and solicitude—it scars you. There are moments in this film when you simply can't bear to look at another human being; it is something you must experience alone. *Shoah* teaches us the meaning of the word *inconsolable*. The film ends in Israel (as it has to) with a member of the Jewish Combat Organization describing his fantasy, while searching the empty ruins of the Warsaw Ghetto, of being "the last Jew." (After he finishes comes a coda of trains rolling implacably on.)

Leaving the theater, you may recall one survivor's account of a secret trip to "Aryan" Warsaw on the eve of the ghetto uprising: "We suddenly emerged into a street in broad daylight, stunned to find ourselves among normal people. [It was as if] we'd come from another planet." The horror of it is, that planet is ours. [J. Hoberman, 10/29/85]

Shock Corridor (1963)

Dir./Scr. Samuel Fuller
101 min.

Samuel Fuller's *Shock Corridor* is about the most interesting entry in the current loony cycle. Far from assuming a responsible tone, Fuller's surface plot bears the earmarks of the transparent trashiness that characterizes the last Hollywood films of Orson Welles (*Touch of Evil*) and Fritz Lang (*Beyond a Reasonable Doubt*). Fuller would have us believe or at least not disbelieve that an ace reporter bucking for the Pulitzer Prize would have himself committed in a mental institution in order to solve a murder. To accomplish this, he persuades his sweetheart, a stripper, to pretend that she is his sister and that he has been molesting her. The girl is opposed to the project because it is morbid, cynical, and senseless. After all, she argues, Shakespeare and Dickens didn't need Freud to create great art. At this point, one has the heady feeling of hearing flowery silent film titles verbalized for the first time. The dialogue is so intense, so compressed, so lacking in all the shadings of wit and verisimilitude, that it is impossible to escape the impression of a primitive artist at work.

Primitive, that is, only in the literary sense. Fuller's camera style is fluid enough to lend visual conviction to his rhetorical characters. Once the hero is committed to the asylum, the movie erupts with a manic force. He is looking for three witnesses to the alleged murder: the first, an ex-veteran brainwashed in Korea and then returned in disgrace to his Southern family; the second, a black student from a Southern university, the victim of a nervous breakdown that left him believing himself a white bigot and a member of the Klan; and the third, a nuclear scientist who has retreated into infancy. The three major hysterias of America—the Cold War in Asia, race relations at home, and the Bomb—are evoked with startling audacity.

Shock Corridor is ultimately an allegory of America today, not so much surreal as subreal in its hallucinatory view of history, which can only be perceived beneath a littered surface of plot intrigue. There are no extras in the film and no establishment of the commonplace that marked the matter-of-fact approach to horror of the late Tod Browning

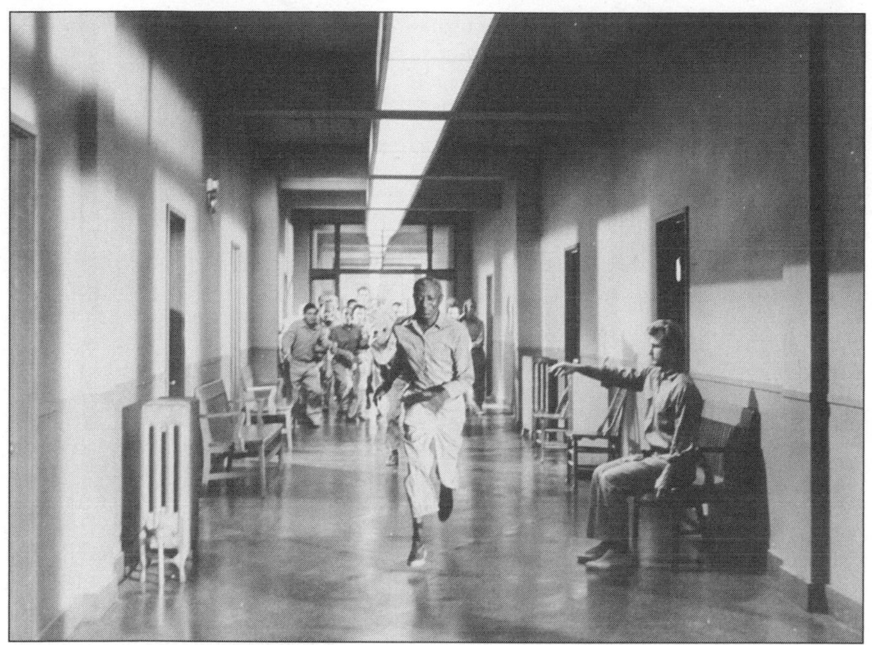

Shock Corridor, 1963; written and directed by Samuel Fuller

and Val Lewton. Nevertheless, *Shock Corridor* emerges as a distinguished addition to that art form in which Hollywood has always excelled: the baroque B-picture. [Andrew Sarris, 9/12/63]

There was a time in America when the sick rivaled the cool. Was it fallout from the Bomb? Criminals were sick, but society was sicker, and jokes about that were the sickest of all.

Jules Feiffer initiated the usage back in 1956, with his *Village Voice* comic strip "Sick, Sick, Sick." Within three years, *Time* was excoriating a new breed of stand-up "sickniks" (including Mort Sahl, Jonathan Winters, Nichols and May, Tom Lehrer, and Lenny Bruce) who made Freudian fun of the nation's sacred cows. The heyday of sick humor coincided with a new, therapeutic attitude in Hollywood: Krin Gabbard and Glen O. Gabbard's *Psychiatry and the Cinema* finds "competent, compassionate, and/or lovable psychiatrists" in at least twenty-two films released between 1957 and 1963. The apex of the trend was 1962. And then came Sam Fuller's *Shock Corridor*.

Insane and inimitable, *Shock Corridor* made literal the idea of a sick society. The protagonist (Peter Breck) is a Pulitzer-obsessed reporter who has himself committed to a mental hospital in order to solve a murder. To get him in, his girlfriend (statuesque Constance Towers) poses as his sister and tells the cops he's been molesting her. What's really bugging her is his insane ambition. "I'm fed up playing Greek chorus to your rehearsed nightmare," Towers cries in wildly empurpled prose. "Hamlet was made for Freud, not you!"

The most excitingly cheap Fuller movie since his 1951 Korean War scoop *The Steel Helmet*, *Shock Corridor* was shot by the great Stanley Cortez in harsh, high-contrast black-and-white interiors—the outside world only present as hallucinations (mostly taken from Fuller's own films). But however hermetic the hospital ward, the conditions are nothing if not topical—the patients subject to doomsday visions, war games, and race riots. A guilt-ridden nuclear physicist has regressed to the age of five. A brainwashed Korean War traitor imagines that he is a heroic Confederate general. The first black to integrate a Southern university now believes himself to be the Grand Dragon of the Ku Klux Klan.

Social pathology merges with individual delusion. Pillowcase over his head, James Best chases a black janitor through the ward, screaming, "Catch that nigger before he marries my daughter!" and, a true schizophrenic, fashions signs directed at himself: "Black Bombs for Black Foreigners! America for Americans!" Best stops the film with the power of his paranoid rants. "They can't breathe our white air and go to school with our white children!" In the extremity of its rhetoric, however, *Shock Corridor* was more factual than prophetic—conceived and shot during the spring 1963 run-up to America's decade-long season of domestic violence.

The nation was still experiencing Cuban Missile Crisis aftershock when Governor George Wallace became a national figure by blocking two black students who were to integrate the University of Alabama. At long last, President Kennedy was compelled to take a public stand against segregation. The same night he made his televised address, a white supremacist killed NAACP leader Medgar Evers in Mississippi.

As Martin Luther King Jr. prepared to march on Washington in support of the civil rights bill, Senator Barry Goldwater expressed concern that anti-integration unrest would spread north and west, while Wallace warned that should the bill pass, Congress would have to withdraw American troops from Berlin to keep order at home. *Shock Corridor* was released two weeks after King's march and four days before the infamous church bombing, Birmingham Sunday. "Sam Fuller apparently is trying to say something significant about certain contemporary American values," *Variety* opined. "The points are sound and have merit. But the melodrama in which he has chosen to house these ideas is so grotesque, so grueling, so shallow and so shoddily sensationalistic that his message is devastated." So is the messenger. The America of 1963 is such that following the logic of *Catch-22* (a sick joke that was the cult novel of 1962), the hero has to be insane to solve the mystery—or even want to. The reporter wins the Pulitzer Prize and is rewarded with a lifetime assignment on shock corridor. Fuller followed up with *The Naked Kiss*, an even more radical diagnosis of the national illness, which effectively rendered him unemployable in Hollywood. [J. Hoberman, 2/17/98]

Star Spangled to Death (1957–2004)

Dir./Scr. Ken Jacobs
402 min.

The ultimate underground movie, *Star Spangled to Death*, Ken Jacobs's epic, bargain-basement assemblage annotates a lyrical junkyard allegory with chunks of mainly 1930s American movies—or is it the other way around?

When Parker Tyler identified the cinematic desire to "provide a documentary showcase for the underdog's spontaneous, uncontrolled fantasy," he was surely thinking of Jacobs's desperately beautiful immersion in childish behavior and political despair. Jacobs began shooting *Star Spangled* in the late 1950s, and the movie has become his life's work. Over the years, he's screened it in various versions—for the 1976 Bicentennial as *Flop*, heavily Reaganized in 1984, and a few years later for his American Museum of Moving Image (AMMI) retro. The movie has always been "too long," but this six-hour, possibly definitive, version, showing at the New York Film Festival, adds even more found footage—including a thirty-minute prologue drawn from a documentary of Osa and Martin Johnson in Africa—while updating sections with references to the war in Iraq.

Jacobs alternates between marshaling evidence and showcasing manic performance. The young Jack Smith appears variously as a sheikh, a matador, a bishop, and an odalisque. Smith is fearless in making a public spectacle of himself. Repeatedly mixing it up with his environment—erupting on the Bowery in gauze-festooned splendor or materializing on St. Marks Place with a paper-bag crown and brandishing a mop—he provides a constant Feuillade effect, introducing wild fantasy into the sooty neorealism of 1950s New York. Jacobs provides him with a foil—an emaciated piece of human wreckage, Jerry Sims, typically seen amid the creepy clutter of his Lower East Side hovel. (In the last chapter, Sims's misery is redeemed—he's permitted to set fire to a campaign poster for the movie's bête noire Nelson Rockefeller.)

Jacobs uses movies throughout—a Warners short made to publicize the NRA; an early, scummy Mickey Mouse cartoon; an excerpt from *Kid Millions* in which Eddie Cantor opens a "free" ice-cream factory—to ground the action in Depression flashbacks. This found material, often layered with added sound, allows Jacobs to brood on human programming, military triumphalism, and—most insistently—American racism. There's a devastating progression from a virtual Nazi-toon version of *Uncle Tom's Cabin* through Al Jolson's infamous "Going to Heaven on a Mule" and an excerpt from Oscar Micheaux's *God's Stepchildren* to Khalid Muhammad's speech in praise of LIRR gunman Colin Ferguson. The Holocaust figures here as well—although Jacobs ultimately apologizes for typecasting the outcast Sims as a suffering ghetto Jew.

Although the movie's collage structure is designed to boggle the mind, individual shots can be breathtaking. Jacobs's dynamic compositions use mirrors, scrims, and random debris in a manner anticipating Smith's *Flaming Creatures*. In the end, the movie turns mournfully self-reflexive. With its intimations of aesthetic utopia amid the rubble of social collapse, this is a tragic meditation on what Jean-Luc Godard called "the film of history." [J. Hoberman, 10/15/03]

Sunrise (1927)

Dir. F. W. Murnau; Scr. Carl Mayer
95 min.

Notes from Academe: While screening F. W. Murnau's *Sunrise* for my Film History class, I paid particular interest to the scene in which Janet Gaynor and George O'Brien as the peasant couple in the city on a kind of second honeymoon pay a visit to a photographer's studio. The photographer is played by an avuncular actor of the period named J. Farrell MacDonald. He is gotten up here in an ill-fitting black wig that makes him look partly *mittel*-European and partly like an old queen trying to cover up his gray hair. Yet his gay mannerisms are very subtle and modulated, almost as if Murnau himself were attempting a quick sketch at a self-portrait.

First, the photographer sneaks a "candid" shot of the two innocent lovers kissing when they think they are unobserved. Then they knock over a small replica of the Venus de Milo and are horrified by the thought that the "head" has been broken off in the fall. The peasant places an orange atop the replica with two eyes poked in, snowman style. The photographer looks at the "composite" statue after the peasant couple has left, is clearly startled at first, but then gradually reconciles himself to this new concept that has presented itself for his inspection.

It is as if Murnau were contemplating the barriers between his own sensibility and that of the simple, innocent, but impulsively passionate characters whom he desperately needed to exorcise his own memories, fears, and regrets. If you do not look quickly and intently, however, you may miss this manifestation of the director's hand. [Andrew Sarris, 2/8/83]

Silent cinema is the art form that died too young. "Not ripe for replacement," aesthetician Rudolf Arnheim wrote in 1930, three years after *The Jazz Singer* broke the sound barrier; silent film "had not lost its fruitfulness, but only its profitability." Indeed, many of the most innovative silent movies were produced in the mode's last days: Dreyer's *The Passion of Joan of Arc*, Sjöström's *The Wind*, Vertov's *The Man with a*

Movie Camera, Dovzhenko's *Earth*, and F. W. Murnau's *Sunrise*.

Friedrich Wilhelm Murnau (1888–1931), a protégé of the great German theatrical impresario Max Reinhardt, was a formidable technician and arguably the supreme cine-aesthete of the 1920s: painter of light, choreographer of camera movement, and maestro of mise-en-scène. Murnau's 1924 visual tour de force, known in the United States as *The Last Laugh*, was one of the first (and few) silent features made without the benefit of intertitles. Following this international success and Murnau's ambitious 1926 *Faust*, movie mogul William Fox brought the "German genius" to Hollywood and gave him the key to the studio.

Sunrise would be the most expensive silent movie Fox ever produced—as well as the most expressionistic. Murnau built a mock German village by a lake and constructed an imaginary metropolis, complete with amusement park, on a tract of empty land just outside the Fox lot. The two locations were connected with a mile-long track on which, in one of the movie's most celebrated sequences, Murnau's estranged protagonists—Janet Gaynor and George O'Brien—ride a streetcar from the heart of the country into the center of town. Other landscapes were also constructed on an interior set.

Carl Mayer's script, a synthesis of American and German movie motifs, is as elemental as Murnau's visuals are complex. (O'Brien and Gaynor are billed as the Man and the Wife; the movie's absurdly universalizing subtitle is "A Song of Two Humans.") Virtuous peasant simplicity is posed against the sinful city, as personified by the flapper with bobbed hair and a smoldering cigarette (Margaret Livingston) who waits for O'Brien by the swamp of depravity and, like a succubus, drains his will with her kiss. The primitive male mind is similarly juxtaposed, with a nod to Theodore Dreiser's *An American Tragedy*, against the diminutive Gaynor's nuanced sensitivity. Emotion is everywhere manifest in the terrain. The glittering maelstrom of city traffic anticipates the vertiginous storm over the lake.

Everything in this fantastic realm is a potential prop, infused with a maximal amount of theatrical magic. Murnau placed an artificial moon over a real marsh and used studio lighting on his back lot to create shadows even in the night scenes. He regularly deployed forced perspective, composed in deep space, lavished close-ups on Gaynor's baby face, and reflected bits of business in store windows, as well as upon the surface of the lake. The camera is almost always in motion, most spectacularly through the vaporous country fields. Murnau's superimpositions and dissolves achieve an almost mystical state of deliquescence. Light not only flows in *Sunrise* but also seems to melt.

Sunrise was shot silent, with very few titles, and was released in late 1927, with a synchronized musical soundtrack. The early reviews were sensational; the grosses were not. Thirty years later, the ultimate cinephile magazine *Cahiers du Cinéma* declared Murnau's first American movie "the single greatest masterwork in the history of cinema." It's an assertion as reckless, romantic, and extravagant as the movie itself. [J. Hoberman, 9/8/04]

Superstar: The Karen Carpenter Story (1987)

Dir. Todd Haynes; Scr. Todd Haynes and Cynthia Schneider

43 min.

Todd Haynes's *Superstar* is a nearly straightforward docudrama on the life of Karen Carpenter. Opening with the discovery of the singer's death from complications from anorexia nervosa, the film flashes back to detail a saga of hit records, White House engagements, family spats, and backstage collapses—as enacted by an ensemble of Barbie dolls.

Thanks to this wonderfully suggestive ploy, Carpenter is at once a hapless toy and a perfect (role) model consumer object, much maligned icon, and fantasy for prepubescent girls. Haynes makes use of elaborate dollhouse sets and crude rear-screen projection, but his most disturbing effect is simply scraping away the Karen doll's plastic flesh to suggest her self-starvation. The film is admirably pragmatic—the "We've Only Just Begun" montage of static wedding cake ornaments and miniature bedrooms is insolently punctuated by a close-up of a single lackadaisically brandished tambourine.

A graduate of the Brown semiotics program, Haynes reads Karen Carpenter as a key 1970s text. She and her brother are taken as a proto Reaganite counteroffensive, opposing the turbulence of 1970 with affirmative, soothing Muzak. ("We've Only Just Begun" ends with bombs dropping on Cambodia.) But more evocative than this perverse nostalgia is the film's treatment of anorexia. Carpenter emerges as a tragic heroine waging a misplaced battle for possession of her image. *Superstar* isn't funny so much as disconcerting—never more so than when making the Carpenters' songs something like poignant. [J. Hoberman, 11/24/87]

Symbiopsychotaxiplasm: Take One (1968)

Dir./Scr. William Greaves
70 min.

Symbiopsychotaxiplasm: Take One may be the ultimate paradigm of self-reflexive cinema, eating Godard's tail for him and one-upping the classic anticartoon *Duck Amuck* by submitting to a cunning entropy and a self-inquiry so relentless the movie never moves from square one. Greaves plays Greaves playing a vague indie filmmaker shooting a film about marital rupture in Central Park. With three mutually interrogating cameras going at all times, the set and the surrounding passersby (including cops) get folded into the meta-vérité mix, which is often prismed out for us as a split-screen triptych. Eventually, the discontented and cerebral crew begin to film themselves complaining about Greaves (and his script) when he's not there, scenes that are sometimes cut up by Greaves later on; in entire chunks of the film, shooting and editing are actions completely at odds with each other. "Stop acting!" someone hollers early on; the magical moment when we see two simultaneous shots get refocused on distractions (a squad car, the actress's legs) is trumped by the sound team's vituperative critique of Greaves's "acting"—on *and* off camera. Intended as one of five films derived from the same pool of 1968 footage, *S:T1* has no end: Its first "sequel," which is numbered 2½ and adds the passage of time to its contemplations, premiered at Sundance this year. Greaves's place in history is unarguable, whether it's then, now, in the future, or all of the above. [Michael Atkinson, 10/26/05]

Taxi Driver (1976)

Dir. Martin Scorsese; Scr. Paul Schrader
113 min.

Taxi Driver is an interesting movie if you forget about any preconceptions you may have on the subject. I don't know what I expected. Girls changing their pantyhose in the back seat? Curbside Kafkas? An itinerary of the five boroughs? Some instant sociology? After all, I live in New York and often take cabs. I have my own ideas and impressions. Perhaps I am too close to the subject. Anyway, *Taxi Driver* made very little sense to me. Robert De Niro's Travis Bickle baffles me. Where does he come from? Who is he supposed to be? He is part Arthur Bremer, part Manson, part Lancelot, part street slob, part cornball, part gun-freak, part Middle America, part alienated Amerika, and all along he is Robert De Niro, an actor whom Scorsese and Coppola and De Palma have rendered in the past as lyrically street-wise and soul-foolish. Hence, there are all kinds of tensions between his past iconography and his incarnation in *Taxi Driver*.

There also seems to be tension between Scorsese's behavioral, improvisational, intuitive rapport with actors and Paul Schrader's metaphorical, metaphysical, massively Bressonian script. I talked with Schrader after I had seen *Taxi Driver*, and he made the link with Robert Bresson's *Pickpocket*, for whose criminal vocation there was neither a psychoanalytical nor a sociological explanation. Do we make different demands on American films, Schrader asked, than we do on foreign films? Of course we do. A Neapolitan pimp or a Parisian pickpocket can serve as metaphors for the human condition, but a Manhattan cab-driver has to conform to some degree of sociological probability and psychological consistency. At the very least, his accent and apparent intelligence quotient can't change from scene to scene. The trouble with De Niro's performance in *Taxi Driver* is that it is all unrelated acting exercises without any unifying context.

Despite De Niro's lack of self-discipline and Peter Boyle's lapses into Son-of-Joe caricature of an ultraconservative cabdriver, Scorsese does manage to score with many of his vignettes. Albert Brooks and Leonard Harris (who says critics can't act?) are real finds as a fidgety campaign worker and a plastic presidential candidate, respectively. And there is a moment of genuinely Scorsesian electricity when De Niro confronts Harvey Keitel's long-haired pimp in a moral reversal of their roles in *Mean Streets*. With the very recently deceased Bernard Herrmann supplying the moody music, Scorsese's opening shots of a taxi emerging ghostlike from a cloud of steam oozing out of the city's lower depths managed to remind me of Alfred Hitchcock's *Vertigo*, Jean-Luc Godard's *Alphaville*, and even a slight mist from Murnau. But I never thought of Bresson on my own simply because Scorsese's players are too histrionic for Bresson's brand of austere stylization.

As in *Alice Doesn't Live Here Anymore*, Scorsese shows a surprising flair for directing women. Cybill Shepherd comes back into her own as the unattainable bitch-goddess of the taxi driver's demented dreams. Top acting honors go to Jodie Foster's breathtakingly goofy teenage hooker, who inspires the film's ultimate bloodbath. Indeed, she takes the Sissy Spacek characterization of *Badlands* one giant step further into a magic realm of imperviousness to evil, and a wildly eccentric timing of line-readings.

There is much to like in *Taxi Driver* if one doesn't mind the disorder in the narrative. I didn't mind the sordidness, the violence, or the mock-ironic ending. What I did mind about the film was its life-denying spirit, its complete lack of curiosity about the possibilities of people. Between Scorsese's celebrated Catholic guilt and Schrader's celebrated Protestant guilt, even a Checker cab would groan under such a burden of self-hatred. You've heard of *Midnight Cowboy*? Well, when you see De Niro and Keitel square off for their final shootout, you'll understand why *Taxi Driver* is being called *Midnight Indian*. That and the exaggerated emphasis of both films on Times Square. After all, how many times can you say cinematically that 42nd Street between Seventh and Eighth is hell? [Andrew Sarris, 2/16/76]

What can be newly said about this savage, many-headed dragon of the American New Wave, a luridly realistic movie about a quiet New York psychopath that became one of the most revered movies of the entire pre-Skywalker century? You either love it or you love it; in any case, Martin Scorsese's history-making scald is truly a phenomenon from another day and age. Which is to say, imagine a like-minded film of this decade killing at the box office and getting nommed for Best Picture.

A retrospective touchstone of the 1970s "cinema of loneliness," *Taxi Driver* is a study in contrasts: New Wave grit versus Bernard Herrmann–scored melodramatic ambience, submergent ur-Method acting entwined within Corman-style plot elements, blood-freezing outsider portraiture mated with an ironically heroic denouement. The resulting fugue had an unmistakably apocalyptic ring to it, even in 1976. Scorsese's infernal visuals were infinitely more articulate about New York than Travis Bickle could ever be, but Robert De Niro's Bickle is no stranger to us—it may be the movie's secret triumph that our intimacy with its underground man was achieved between the lines, with silences and dead stares and abrupt seizures of impulsive destruction.

Or, it was Scorsese's post-Peckinpah insistence on saying, no, real nonmovie violence doesn't ker-blam tastefully and in slow motion, it thwacks, punctures, and bleeds like *this*. Can any of the decade's many social stripteases compare to this lean machine, evoking as it does post-Nixon jaundice in its campaign year distrust and havoc, a post-Vietnam disaffection on an unimaginable scale, and a post-1960s sense of run-away urban pestilence and knotted moral outrage? Bickle remains an authentic everyman, a walking dumb-as-shit smashup of conservative responses, but also a disenfranchised victim of the corporate-imperial combine, an ex-soldier used to meaningless death, lost in the streets of his own empty freedom. There may not be a more essentially American figure haunting the national cinema. [Michael Atkinson, 1/5/05]

That Obscure Object of Desire (1977)

Dir. Luis Buñuel; Scr. Luis Buñuel and Jean-Claude Carrière

102 min.

Luis Buñuel began his movie career by coauthoring the most influential avant-garde movie ever made, the surrealist "incitement to murder" *Un Chien Andalou*, and capped his oeuvre with a masterpiece, *That Obscure Object of Desire*. Such was the consistency of Buñuel's world-view that much of the latter is anticipated by the former.

Pierre Louÿs's 1898 novel *The Woman and the Puppet*, the story of teenage femme fatale Concha Perez and the middle-aged Don Mateo she drives to distraction, had been filmed four times before (most famously by Josef von Sternberg as *The Devil Is a Woman*) when Buñuel tackled it in 1977. Although Buñuel's version is in many ways the most faithful to the novel (including the hilarious scene with Concha's chastity device), it is also the least misogynist. The very title directs attention away from the perfidy of woman toward something else—namely, the fantasy that underlies desire. (The title may sound like a crib from Jacques Lacan, but Buñuel claimed it came from a phrase in the original novel.) Beginning and ending with images of a woman's stained underwear, *That Obscure Object of Desire* is blatantly fetishistic—and also a satire of fetishism. Much of it is related by Don Mateo (Fernando Rey) to a psychoanalytically minded dwarf. That Concha is played by two randomly alternating actresses, Carole Bouquet and Ángela Molina, serves to confound any desire for a coherent narrative—although, according to Buñuel, like the hapless Don Mateo, "many spectators never even noticed."

Beginning with the forcibly sundered couple who attempt to reunite

That Obscure Object of Desire, 1977; directed by Luis Buñuel; written by Luis Buñuel and Jean-Claude Carrière

for much of *L'Age d'Or*, thwarted desire was a Buñuelian theme: the guests cannot leave the dinner party in *The Exterminating Angel*; the would-be diners never manage to feed themselves in *The Discreet Charm of the Bourgeoisie*. *That Obscure Object of Desire* is an even more elaborate exercise in frustration. Fate keeps placing Concha in Mateo's path, and she continually appears to offer herself to him. But an endless series of barriers and delays ensures that he will never have her—only his desire is real. Buñuel's last testament is a comic version of *Vertigo* (or *A.I.*) and perhaps even more profoundly universal: it's the tale of a person madly in love with something that cannot exist. [J. Hoberman, 7/17/01]

There's Something about Mary (1998)

Dir./Scr. Peter Farrelly and Bobby Farrelly
119 min.

There's Something about Mary is less an asteroid sent hurtling toward the audience than a great gobby spitball. Duck if you're squeamish. Proudly lowbrow, hopelessly incorrect, visually strident, and awash in bodily fluids, this third and funniest gross-out yuckfest by Peter and Bobby Farrelly goes a long way in establishing the auteurs of *Dumb and Dumber* and *Kingpin* as the conehead's Coen Brothers.

A romantic comedy, if not exactly the sort that Nora Ephron would concoct, *There's Something about Mary* opens in the filmmakers' native Rhode Island and immediately establishes a typically Farrellian state of mind—Ben Stiller playing a high-school senior afflicted with double braces and tormented by an advanced case of the nerds. Although the Farrellys derive considerable amusement from this prologue—which features the spectacle of thirtysomething actors in outlandish fright wigs reenacting their inarticulate, high-school geekiness—the movie's level of humor is even more regressive, closer to that of a vicious twelve-year-old.

Invited to the prom by the senior-class goddess and eponymous object of desire (Cameron Diaz), Stiller proves completely hapless—unwittingly alienating her excitable stepfather, innocently sending her mentally retarded brother into a frenzy, inadvertently peeping on her toilette, and then, in a paroxysm of embarrassment and the first of the movie's two never-to-be-forgotten bits of business, catching a bit of scrotum in his zipper. Can any amount of Cameron Diaz cheesecake compensate for what is arguably the most excruciatingly visceral castration metaphor in any Hollywood movie since Ronald Reagan had his legs lopped in *King's Row*? Even a cop shows up to gawk.

Thus arrested in his development, Stiller remains fixated on the lissome, unattainable Diaz for the next fifteen years. His simian character is so dorky that even Tostitos corn-chip star Chris Elliott feels entitled to give him coolness tips—and so boring in his romantic obsession that his analyst sneaks out to have lunch as Stiller drones on about the trauma that ruined his date.

Mary's rude assortment of muscular dystrophy, psoriasis, and homophobic jokes might have been scripted by the Garbage Pail Kids for the cast of *South Park*. The material written for Farrelly axiom Lin Shaye—here elaborating her sexualized-hag cameos in their previous films—is approached only by the scene in which Stiller's sleazy rival Matt Dillon is compelled to perform CPR on the Shaye character's terrier. (The gag reflex is a double-edged sword in Farrellyworld.) A satire of inept male behavior predicated on the fear of sexual rejection, *There's Something about Mary* expresses an anxiety so funky that you can practically smell it. The jovially disgusting ribaldry suggests a hetero equivalent to the old Playhouse of the Ridiculous.

There's Something about Mary towers above the usual summer idiocy on its formal qualities alone—the slapstick timing, adroit sight-gag placement, choreographed Abbott-and-Costello misunderstandings. Dillon's stupid huckster not only sports a set of oversized choppers but surprising echoes of Groucho Marx. Not the least of the movie's triumphs is Cameron Diaz. At once eternal foil and holy grail, perfectly oblivious, always credulous, generous in her affection, she's a woman so perfect she even likes to talk football.

Good sport or plastic mannequin, Diaz's Mary is untouched by the stalking, stinking, all-round vulgarity that surrounds her even when it smears . . . never mind. As you are sure to hear around the schoolyard, *There's Something about Mary* has the most startling parody of a money shot—ever. Here, too, the unfailing Diaz radiance brings to mind novelist Fred Chappell's observation in his "Twenty-Six Propositions about Skin Flicks" that "If the whole of history, with its prostitution and unrelenting degradation, has not violated women in their essence, how shall the camera accomplish it?" [J. Hoberman, 7/21/98]

The Thin Blue Line (1988)

Dir./Scr. Errol Morris
103 min.

Film noir, which first cast its shadow in the midst of World War II and flourished for no more than a dozen years, was the nocturnal orchid of Hollywood's garden: the most deliriously aestheticized strain in American popular cinema, characterized by a singularly un-American sense of doom. Not the least impressive aspect of Errol Morris's haunting *The Thin Blue Line* is that without exhibiting a trace of postmodern nostalgia, it's redolent with essence of noir. This brilliantly stylized documentary—which Morris calls "the story of a chance meeting on a road in West Dallas—is as stringently fatalist as Edgar G. Ulmer's *Detour*, as bizarrely artistic as the dream sequences of *Murder, My Sweet*, as convoluted as *Out of the Past*, as tense as the original *D.O.A.*, and as sui generis as Morris's earlier films.

At once oppressive and hypnotic, *The Thin Blue Line* broods over the case of a Dallas policeman, Robert Wood, who—one Saturday night in November 1976—approached a car that was being driven with its headlights off and was shot by the driver five times point blank. Because Wood's partner, Teresa Turko, failed to remember the car's license number or correctly identify its make, the police were stymied until they learned that a Vidor, Texas, teenager named David Harris had been bragging to his skeptical buddies that he was the one who "offed [that] pig in Dallas."

Once the authorities traced the car and the murder weapon to Harris, he fingered Randall Adams, a twenty-eight-year-old factory worker, whom he had picked up hitchhiking on the day of the shooting. According to both Harris and Adams, they'd spent the afternoon driving around drinking and smoking dope, finally winding up at a drive-in movie for a soft-core double bill of *The Student Body* and *Swinging Cheerleaders*. Here at the movies, appropriately enough, their stories diverged. Adams maintained that Harris dropped him off at his motel, where he watched the last half of *The Carol Burnett Show* and the ten o'clock news, then went to sleep; Harris testified that with Adams at the wheel, the pair continued to drive around for a couple of hours, until Adams shot the cop. Despite Harris's extensive criminal record, the jury believed him—Adams, who had no prior run-in with the law, was condemned to death (later commuted to life because of irregularities in the jury selection).

Morris is the great people-collector of the American documentary, and, with *The Thin Blue Line*, he uses the remarkably productive interviewing style he developed with *Gates of Heaven* and *Vernon, Florida* to circle around a single, unrepresentable event—building a case even while presenting mysteries that range from the unexpected affability of cops placed before the camera to the awesome spectacle of an inexorable Destiny. Morris alternates interviews with Adams and Harris, as the two strangers converge in Dallas; he punctuates their discourse with statements by other interested parties and at least a half-dozen scenes that diagram a crime, rather than restage it. The film is a series of iconic talking heads and fragmentary "evidence" underscored by a sinuously implacable Philip Glass drone that raises the anxiety level like the best of Bernard Herrmann.

From the opening credits—where the "blue" of the title is written in scarlet—*The Thin Blue Line* teeters on the edge of comedy. Morris revels in ironic details (Wood's wife had bought him a bulletproof vest for Christmas), lovingly presents sequences from *The Student Body* and *Swinging Cheerleaders* (typically, he picks a scene where some girl declares her innocence), and creates suggestive digressions. That the fractious presiding judge turns out to have been the son of an FBI man involved in the capture of John Dillinger occasions a flurry of excerpts from a venerable crime film, as does the confession by a highly dubious—and ultimately chilling—"surprise witness" that she used to watch *Boston Blackie* on TV and wishes she were a detective herself.

The most elaborate shared fantasy may be the reality of the legal system. Commenting on the Eichmann trial, Harold Rosenberg remarked that in an ontological sense, the accused man in the dock is never the same individual who committed the crime. In this case, Rosenberg's poetic truth seems to have been taken literally. Adams's strident female lawyer suggests that—as Harris was a minor—Dallas County's only interest was in convicting a perp it could fry. Her still-incredulous associate, who gave up his practice after losing Adams's case, remarks that while anyone can find a wrongdoer guilty, it takes a brilliant D.A. to convict an innocent man.

The same may hold true for a filmmaker. *The Thin Blue Line* is not a dispassionate film. (The movie, no less than the case, is a construction—spiraling out from one or two incontrovertible facts.) Both *Gates of Heaven* and *Vernon, Florida* are founded on the disjunction between the universe of belief and the realm of the senses. *The Thin Blue Line* takes this epistemological gap as its subject. What is evidence? How do we know what we see? Repeatedly, Morris closes in on newspaper photographs until the images dissolve in an unreadable sea of Ben-Day dots. *The Thin Blue Line* can be construed as an attempt to create linguistic and visual models for some unknowable reality, to find human equivalents for those majestically indifferent laws that govern the universe. The title comes from the prosecutor's evocation of "the thin blue line of police" that protects the public from anarchy. But as ambiguous as the protection is, that line is more like a twilight zone. [J. Hoberman, 8/30/88]

The Thin Red Line (1998)

Dir./Scr. Terrence Malick
170 min.

The year's most enigmatic studio release, written and directed by one of the most puzzling figures in Hollywood, *The Thin Red Line* projects a sense of wounded diffidence. Terrence Malick's hugely ambitious, austerely hallucinated adaptation of James Jones's 1962 novel—a five-hundred-page account of combat in Guadalcanal—is a metaphysical platoon movie in which battlefield confusion is melded with an Emersonian meditation on the nature of nature.

The first and costliest American victory in World War II's Pacific theater was a six-month assault on Japanese-held Guadalcanal, one of the Solomon Islands east of New Guinea. Malick's movie appears to concern a mop-up operation, late in the struggle, with a battalion of mainly green army recruits landing in relief of the marines who initiated the attack on the stronghold. I say "appears" because although *The Thin Red Line* gives a real—if necessarily idealized—sense of an American army in action, there is a sense in which Malick's movie is not so much about World War II as about a particular existential condition.

Saving Private Ryan opens, in a brutal tour de force that is Steven Spielberg's most visceral filmmaking since *Jaws*, with the GIs landing on Omaha beach. (As a way of conditioning audience response, it's as though Hitchcock began *Psycho* with the shower sequence.) Malick is considerably more contemplative. *The Thin Red Line* starts with a leisurely immersion in a South Pacific paradise as filtered through the consciousness of the pensive Private Witt (Jim Caviezel). It's not too far from Malick's *Days of Heaven*, although the expulsion from this tropical Eden is an hour-plus attempt to storm a Japanese position.

Jones, who saw action and was wounded at Guadalcanal, devoted fully half of his novel to detailing the capture of Hill 209 and so it seems here. Malick orchestrates what could be the longest battle scene in movie history, and one in which shock and hysteria are pervasive. Charging head-on uphill toward an unseen foe, the men drop at random, often from friendly fire. Everybody, with the exception of an almost frighteningly cool captain (John Cusack), is either terrified or crazed.

In essence, this epic battle scene concerns the stripping away of each soldier's self (or its obliteration), and, in the midst of this operation, a philosophical argument breaks out. Colonel Tall (Nick Nolte) screams orders to launch a suicide attack that his subordinate, Captain Staros (Elias Koteas), stuck on a ridge without shelter, refuses to obey. Nor is the debate restricted to strategy or even words. Abetted by Hans Zimmer's brooding score, the entire sequence has the aspect of an extended reverie. Repeatedly, Malick cuts away from the carnage to the image of a young woman—Private Bell (Ben Chaplin) imagining his wife as a battlefield angel—or, even more outrageously, to the light as it changes on the tall grass in the wind.

Guadalcanal, at least as it was portrayed in the 1944 *Guadalcanal Diary* (the key World War II movie released during the war), was the crucible that, more fiery than any urban melting pot, forged the American fighting spirit. *The Thin Red Line* is no less an ensemble film, although its sense of spirit is more expanded. The archetypes are in place—the sensitive mystic (Caviezel) and the cynical sergeant (Sean Penn in a tremendously concentrated performance), the blowhard warrior Colonel Tall and his tender-hearted adversary (Koteas), the efficient good soldier (Cusack) and the fear-crazed survivor (Adrien Brody). But if battle-heightened awareness imbues these soldiers with an undeniable, albeit transitory, übermensch quality, *The Thin Red Line* is scarcely waving the flag. And if the Japanese—most extensively seen as the wounded, freaked-out, praying denizens of an overrun camp—are hardly individuated and never granted the slightest subjectivity, it is clear that Malick himself is consciously striving for what might be termed a "Japanese" quality of stillness and emptiness in the midst of hell.

For all its documentary detail, Jones's novel was born old-fashioned. It was published a year after Joseph Heller's *Catch-22* initiated a vast shift in American attitudes; Allied Artists' quickie movie version was distinguished mainly for having been released on a double bill with Sam Fuller's *The Naked Kiss*. Malick's version—which unavoidably references the great, flawed Vietnam visions of *Apocalypse Now* and (especially) *Platoon*—is, however, anachronistic in a different way. Not exactly timeless and not primarily a narrative, it's a head movie about death and dying.

At two hours and forty-five minutes, *The Thin Red Line* gives ample evidence of suffering all manner of cuts, if not having been simply hacked into its final shape. But this violence only adds to the movie's brave, strange, eroded nobility. As mystical as it is gritty, as despairing as it is detached, Malick's study of men in battle materializes in our midst almost exactly a century after Stephen Crane's *The Red Badge of Courage*—an exercise in nineteenth-century transcendentalism, weirdly serene in the face of horror. [J. Hoberman, 12/23/98]

El Topo (1970)

Dir./Scr. Alejandro Jodorowsky

125 min.

It's midnight mass at the Elgin. Cocteau's *Blood of a Poet* has just ended, and the wait for *El Topo* is a brief grope for comfort before sinking back into fantastic stillness. The audience is young. They applauded Cocteau's sanguine dream as though he were in the theater, but as credits appear on the screen, they settle again into rapt attention. They've come to see the light—and the screen before them is illumined by an abstract landscape of desert and sky—and the ritual begins again.

Alejandro Jodorowsky rides into the picture. He is an actor and he is the director, but he directs the film from the inside: the actor becomes the director. When El Topo rapes a girl, Jodorowsky really rapes her. When El Topo abandons his seven-year-old son, Jodorowsky really abandons his son. Like Artaud, Jodorowsky is an actor in search of real actions who refuses to distinguish between any of the moments of himself. His actions are rituals in the search for enlightenment, in the pursuit of his being—and as a good Catholic, as only a fallen-away Catholic can be, Jodorowsky makes his ritual perform the universe.

Such a proud projection of myth, making one's own life a myth, is certainly out of style in this democratic age. The overpopulated conscience of the art world allows the innovative antihero to flourish, to submerge himself in the mediocrity of the masses and to poke fun, but it cannot tolerate intrusions of the heroic or the dangerous. Thus an artist like Jodorowsky remains in an obscure underground. His art is too violent for the most violent nation in history. The hero is too proud, too self-conscious, and asks too many questions. But it is this very repulsion that *El Topo* elicits, this confusion that it reveals in weak minds, which makes it a work of cinematic cruelty, a weapon of spiritual revolution. Jodorowsky is here to confess; the young audience is here for communion.

El Topo looks like Paladin and, like that dark character, wanders through a mythic landscape to kill men. Blood spurts and gushes, it is smeared over faces, it rouges lips and paints the scenery. The audience has never seen so much blood, even in streets filled with danger and death, and so it is intoxicated, shocked, and thrilled. El Topo is a killer, yet he is a holy man. Like Zarathustra, he wants to overcome all men. He is a seeker who seeks to overcome his masters. And blood is the sacrament by which El Topo soars/falls toward enlightenment.

The episodes of El Topo's progress are parabolic tales performed in concrete poetry. Many of these tales are metaphysical gags in the manner of the Marx Brothers, who often used a Sufi parable to launch their excursions into madness. Their style is often considered frivolous but is one of deliberate anarchy, which Artaud called their "disintegration of the real by poetry." The same sense of humor, rooted at the cruel basis of laughter, is present in *El Topo*. Its humor attacks reality, creating a comedy that provokes laughter in order to overcome horror—a comedy that becomes a cult of salvation.

Of course, *El Topo* was not made for the audience of *Animal Crackers*. Its tone portrays the growth of horror among us. Despite the nostalgic trend in style, this is not the 1930s, and the price of exorcism and the price of initiation have gone up. As was declared in *Weekend*, "It will take more horror to overcome the horror of the bourgeoisie." *El Topo* is dedicated to the metaphysical mechanics of that proposition. [Glenn O'Brien, 3/25/71]

Tribulation 99: Alien Anomalies under America (1992)

Dir./Scr. Craig Baldwin

48 min.

Craig Baldwin's *Tribulation 99: Alien Anomalies under America* has been described, most aptly, by its maker as a "pseudo pseudo-documentary obsessively organized into 99 paranoid rants." This forty-eight-minute masterpiece is at once a sci-fi cheapster, a skewed history of U.S. interventionism in Latin America, a satire of conspiratorial thinking, and an essential piece of current Americana—the missing link between *JFK* and *The Rapture* (and a better movie than either). WARNING, the first of many screen-filling titles announces, THIS FILM

IS NOT FICTION—IT IS THE SHOCKING TRUTH! If this injunction recalls the opening of Edward D. Wood's *Plan 9 from Outer Space*, so do Baldwin's methodology and narrative. *Tribulation* 99's "revisionist eschatology" begins in 1949 with the explosion of the planet Quetzalcoatl. Fleeing their doomed world, the Quetzals relocate at the hollow center of ours; unfortunately, this sanctuary is agitated by underground atomic tests, and the Quetzals vow the destruction of the United States using all manner of futuristic weaponry, as well as humanoid alien automatons as provocateurs.

The joke, of course, is on the notion of "alien" invaders—particularly as the war with the Quetzals is waged successively in Guatemala, Cuba, Chile, Nicaragua, El Salvador, Granada, and Panama. The tone Baldwin adopts is one of a cracked right-winger: Quetzal agent Salvador Allende creates a hole in the ozone over the South Pole in a plan to cause cancer in the "planet's most vulnerable inhabitants: white people"; Granada is taken over by "a rampaging gang of psychic vampires" whose New Jewel Movement is named for "an evil power crystal" and whose leader, an "Atlantean plant," plans to build the largest saucer port in the Caribbean.

Rather than stage this cosmic drama—which ranges from Easter Island to the Bermuda Triangle and involves Howard Hughes, the abominable snowman, Jim Jones, Klaus Barbie, and George Bush, among many others—Baldwin illustrates it with a heady mix of images culled from a variety of newsreels, travelogues, industrials, commercials, *Godzilla* flicks, and movies shot off the tube. (Barry Goldwater is represented by James Bond, Maurice Bishop by Blacula, Manuel Noriega by the Wolfman, Fidel Castro by a mad, bearded prophet from some fleabitten sword-and-sandal epic.)

Baldwin's unrelenting montage is scored by inexorable monster music, punctuated by psychedelic swirls, organized by supermarket tabloid titles ("Earth in Upheaval," "False Prophets Descend among the People"), and mediated by his own rapid-fire voice-over: "In red underwear to escape the evil eye, Noriega flees towards the Hollow Earth through a network of interconnecting caves under the canal, leaving behind a ritual bucket of blood, a maggot-infested cow's tongue, and fifty pounds of highly addictive corn flour." [J. Hoberman, 1/7/92]

Tropical Malady (2004)

Dir./Scr. Apichatpong Weerasethakul
118 min.

World cinema's premier maker of mysterious objects, Apichatpong Weerasethakul is on a one-man mission to change the way we watch movies. Rich and strange, postmodern and prehistoric, his films foster an experience of serene bewilderment and—for the willing viewer—euphoric surrender. They are suffused with a sense of wide-open possibility that sometimes explodes into epiphany—as in 2002's sensual pastoral *Blissfully Yours*, which, a third of the way through, hits the reset button with a long-delayed credit roll.

Tropical Malady boasts an even more severe disjunction. Instructively titled, *Malady* is split down the middle between lovesick daydream and malarial delirium. An idyllic first half, which recounts in fleeting fragments the intensifying attraction between handsome soldier Keng and bashful farm boy Tong, gives way to a nocturnal folk tale that likewise traces an anatomy of desire, but this time with the soldier amid an unearthly menagerie of tiger spirits, phantom cattle, and an aphorism-dispensing baboon.

How do the two halves connect? Which one is real—or realer? Are these pertinent questions? Lulling and pleasurably levitated as it may be, the first section is hardly straightforward or even explicable—right from the uneasy opening scene, in which an army troop cheerfully poses for photos with a dead body.

Incidental mysteries pile up. Some are casually explained, but most linger as gentle bafflements. Like *Blissfully Yours* and Apichatpong's first feature, the exquisite-corpse road movie *Mysterious Object at Noon* (2000), *Tropical Malady* promotes new ways of seeing. These films, at once rapt and dislocated, have the flavor of hallucinated documentary. They compel viewers to look anew at the ordinary, to modulate their passive gaze into a patient, quizzical scrutiny. And what's more, *Tropical Malady* is a film that looks back at you. The characters have a habit of staring into the camera—a gesture that usually signifies complicity, though the effect is vaguely discomfiting here, since we're not sure what we're complicit in.

Tropical Malady, 2004; written and directed by Apichatpong Weerasethakul

Part one of *Tropical Malady* plays almost like a parodic affirmation of Thailand's tourist-board image as the "land of smiles." Everyone radiates faintly concussed grins, and the mood-enhanced vibe is both infectious and a little troubling—one irrationally blinding smile in a men's bathroom just about stops the film dead in its tracks. Keng and Tong's romance may be coy and tentative, but I can't think of another movie that depicts a same-sex relationship with such lovely matter-of-factness—the traveling shot of the boys on a motorbike is pure joy (Apichatpong's characters seem happiest when in motion). They share an easy intimacy that grows increasingly erotic—entwining limbs in a movie theater and, in a startling scene that prefigures the imminent reversion to the animal state, submitting a possibly urine-stained hand to a taste test.

But before getting to coitus, *Tropical Malady* enacts its radical interruptus. The film abruptly halts, fades to black, and is reborn—with a fresh title, *A Spirit's Path*—as a wordless, primordial cat-and-mouse dance/mating ritual between hunter and hunted, complete with intertitles and cave drawings. Keng enters the jungle in search of an unspecified livestock-killing creature, only to confront a tiger ghost that on occasion appears as a face-painted, body-tattooed Tong.

The jungle is infinitely vast and dark, home to restless spirits and elaborately gnarled trees that emit ominous burbling noises; the rustling, chirping, buzzing cacophony suggests a demented white-noise machine. Like fearful, trembling Keng, the viewer is often stranded in blackness (and when your eyes adjust, what you see can be a shock).

The rupture transmigrates the narrative into a mystical realm, but it's unclear whether Keng and Tong have been banished or elevated to this plane of existence. Was their love too intense for the material world? Does the fulfillment of animal hungers require the cover of darkness? The film's mysteries are so cosmic that any attempt to ascribe allegory can seem puny. One offhand early scene may hold the key to the metaphysics. After a brief discussion about the persistence of memory through past and future lives, Keng tells Tong, "When I gave you the Clash tape, I forgot to give you my heart. You can have it today." He rubs his palm on his beloved's back, as if massaging a piece of himself under the skin. This bifurcated film dramatizes what Roland Barthes in *A Lover's Discourse* called "the dream of total union." The soldier, face-to-face with the pursuer that is also the object of desire, heeds the advice of the talking baboon: "Let him devour you and enter his world." And as the lovers merge—in an act of consumption and communion and consummation—so, too, finally, do the film's divided halves. [Dennis Lim, 6/29/05]

Trouble in Paradise (1932)

Dir. Ernst Lubitsch; Scr. Grover Jones and Samson Raphaelson
83 min.

There is no Hollywood movie more insouciantly amoral than Ernst Lubitsch's 1932 *Trouble in Paradise*. Released in the depths of the Great Depression, Lubitsch's urbane comedy concerns a swank pair of thieves, played by Herbert Marshall and Miriam Hopkins, who not only live together in sin but—after successfully fleecing Kay Francis's rich and equally charming widow—taxi off into the sunset utterly unrepentant. The movie's white-on-white deco sets were once the essence of modernity—and so was its worldly attitude. Obviously, *Trouble in Paradise* could not have been produced after the 1934 Production

Code arrived to regulate the fantasy lives of American moviegoers. Hedonism was never more nonchalant. *Trouble in Paradise* has none of the single-entendre tawdriness or salacious Puritanism that gives pre-Code Hollywood its carnival flavor. Style is substance in Lubitsch's instantly recognized masterpiece. "As close to perfection as anything I have ever seen in the movies," the young Dwight Macdonald wrote in a little literary magazine. Indeed, style is morality.

Trouble in Paradise, adroitly adapted by Samson Raphaelson from a Hungarian play inspired by a turn-of-the-century jewel thief, is graced with a shimmering cast, impeccably streamlined in evening clothes and impossibly clinging gowns. Hopkins's self-amused coquettishness embodies the film's sense of mischief even as the superbly slouching Francis provides a sheen of lazy sensuality. Francis has the bewitching bedroom eyes, but the sly, effervescent Hopkins is the scene stealer; she

Trouble in Paradise, 1932; directed by Ernst Lubitsch; written by Grover Jones and Samson Raphaelson

must literally sit on her hands at one point to keep from swiping Francis's jewelry. ("I wouldn't fall for another man if he was the biggest crook on earth," Hopkins fumes upon realizing that Marshall is about to betray her.)

At the apex of the triangle, the stiff yet soigné Marshall, often positioned in the frame to show off his profile (or conceal his prosthetic leg), leans forward to inhale his irresistible costars, both of whom are experts at swooning on divans. Romance in this movie, which opens with a gondolier lip-synching Caruso on a Venetian garbage scow and has comic secondarios Edward Everett Horton and Charles Ruggles sniffing around Francis in doglike devotion, seems markedly olfactory. Francis is the widow of a French perfume magnate while, to judge from its shine, Marshall's pomade was made for aroma-rama. The sets might have been dusted with talcum powder or confectionary sugar; and then, of course, there's the intoxicating smell of money.

This comedy of jewel thieves is itself the prize sparkler of Lubitsch's enterprising career—a ransom that he never quite redeemed. *Trouble in Paradise* combines the visual glitter of Lubitsch's silent films with the verbal wit of his talkies; it leavens 1920s frivolity with a soupçon of 1930s class consciousness. Exceedingly fluid for its day, *Trouble in Paradise* was the director's first nonmusical talking picture; cut to sprightly incidental music and paced by playful spoken rhythms, it dances to its own tune. (Later movies would be heavier, even as they sought to amuse.) Never equaled, *Trouble in Paradise* twinkles like the polestar in the sky above the comedies of Billy Wilder, George Cukor, and (less brightly) Otto Preminger; it anticipates the banter of Hitchcock's *To Catch a Thief* and *North by Northwest*. The ultimate nightmare would be a Vegas-set remake with Hugh Grant, Jennifer Lopez, and Gwyneth Paltrow, written and directed by Nora Ephron.

Trouble in Paradise acknowledges itself as a comic mechanism with the repeated use of clocks to structure its precision-tooled gags. Everything is artifice. The gem-encrusted purse that Marshall pilfers from Francis and then returns for the reward—becoming her private secretary as a result—is only one of several free-floating sexual symbols. Some, like Francis's bed, are not even symbols. Like many of Lubitsch's films, *Trouble in Paradise* riffs on role-playing and mistaken identity. A passion for theater is at the heart of his cinema, and the bed, always empty, is presented as a potential stage throughout. Indeed, as blithe as it is, *Trouble in Paradise* is something of an impossible love story—and not just because of the characters' triumphant self-absorption.

The Venetian prologue, wherein Marshall and Hopkins steal each other's hearts, among other items, is a superb mutual seduction. But it is Francis and Marshall's never consummated affair that occasions the movie's most haunting montage. As dreamy Francis murmurs that she and Marshall will have "weeks," "months," "years" together, Lubitsch frames them in a series of distinct shots—side by side, then reflected in Francis's boudoir mirror, and finally as shadows on her satin sheets. It's a master's touch indeed that renders their desire as both ephemeral and eternal. [J. Hoberman, 6/11/03]

Two or Three Things I Know about Her (1967)

Dir./Scr. Jean-Luc Godard
95 min.

Godard the critic has argued for years that there is no distinction between documentary and nondocumentary cinema: that Nanook waiting for his prey and a Hitchcockian assassin were equally valid as truth, for example; or that Ford's historical re-creations were the beginnings of cinema vérité. In *Two or Three Things*, he shows us an interview with a girl in front of a pinball machine and tells her that "people never speak naturally in films. That's what I'm trying to do with you." And, of course, the interview is staged. He shows us a magazine as it appeared to one girl at "3.37 P.M." and then, "seen 150 frames later," the same object but from the angle of a second girl, and so looking completely different. "So which is truth and what's an object anyhow?" *Two or Three Things* is cinema-truth.

Two or Three Things is hardly a pleonasm. Godard had unbounded enthusiasm for Nicholas Ray's *Bitter Victory* and proudly announced that watching it makes one think, suddenly, "of every other thing, snack bars on the Champs-Elysées, a girl you loved, everything, no matter what, of hatred, of female cowardice, male frivolity, slot machines; for *Bitter Victory* is not the reflection of life, it is life itself made into film." *Two or Three Things* is this sort of film, and if the repeated "yes's" that are all we hear of Anny Duperey's phone conversation in the boutique remind us of *Ulysses*, it's because we've climbed aboard Godard's odyssey, and there are more than two or three things he knows about "her" (Paris and its people: life), but these are only two or three of them.

Godard becomes involved in an argument with a girl over why she will not say, "My sex is between my legs." From being an analysis of the girl, the scene becomes a confession of Godard's frustration when others do not agree with him (for they seldom do).

He demands that we see the way he sees, and his seeing has two objects: the world outside of Godard and the world inside of Godard. Godard, the French intellectual, whose first definition of the cinema has always been "the expression of beaux sentiments": to whom the beauty of discursive thought vies for attention with the beauty of sensory perception. In actual fact, he proves their beauty complementary:

—Scene (& Meditation) in a coffee shop: Godard's camera gawks at the bubbles in a coffee cup as his voice narrates, "I must look around since I'm between Being and Nothingness—the world, my fellow-creature, my brother!" Neither image nor voice would so greatly attract our interest without the other.

—Same scene: "With consciousness everything will fall into place." Some cello music, cut to a long pan of a girl walking around a corner in the Latin Quarter. Gorgeous colors, nature intensified, motion: the mind rushes into it, for an instant trips with it, lost in its beauty.

—A guy working with a stack of books is ordering food and asks for "Today's Surprise." "No surprise today," he is told, and turns toward the camera, his mouth agape in surprise. Godard holds the shot long enough to give us plenty of time to wonder over the logical absurdity of the episode.

—During a 360-degree pan of which she is the center, a girl says, "Sometimes I think I am the world and the world is me. It would

> take books to describe . . . a landscape is like a face," and the camera turns back to confront her.

As an artist, Godard says, he seeks a new world, political and poetic, in which there is a harmony between man and his objects (the world). This is the artist's task—to grasp for ten seconds a meaning for living. What Godard the intellectual vainly yearns to do, Godard the aesthete performs with loving adoration—and much to the delight of Godard the intellectual.

At times he seems to hate language the way only a lover can; a lover, moreover, whose first love is the cinema and whose essays and films challenge literature. Who else but Godard would devote so long and contemplative a sequence to a car being washed (a red car)? And preface it with the battle cry of the cinema, that no words could describe what you're going to see and then fascinate you with just that fact: how much you are seeing, how detailed it is, and how beautiful? But the polemics do not seek solely to justify *abstract* cinema.

"Only a man who is sure of himself can admit defeat," Marina Vlady reads, and then disagrees with it. The author's logic has sprouted wings: there is always the danger of confusing thought with reality. Godard's quest to escape from thought into consciousness has been an almost constant theme. There is a particular satisfaction in this present incarnation, for art is for Godard a form through which one may achieve pure experience, and *Two or Three Things* is an ecstatic experience. [T. A. Gallagher, 5/7/70]

2001: A Space Odyssey (1968)

Dir. Stanley Kubrick; Scr. Stanley Kubrick and Arthur C. Clarke
141 min.

2001: A Space Odyssey is a thoroughly uninteresting failure and the most damning demonstration yet of Stanley Kubrick's inability to tell a story coherently and with a consistent point of view. His film is not a film at all, but merely a pretext for a pictorial spread in *Life* magazine. Kubrick, like Lelouch, is an undeniably competent photographer, but photographers seldom make the best directors. *2001* has little writing or acting to speak of, and makes little sense. The first section of the film begins where *Planet of the Apes* left off at the "Dawn of Man." Kubrick and science-fiction writer Arthur C. Clarke employ a bunch of monkey masks and monkey suits to present a very debatable theory of human evolution in terms of force and acquisitiveness. We then suddenly leap into a routine moon voyage described in great brand-name-plug detail (Bell, Pan-Am, Howard Johnson's, Hilton) with Poverty Row players like William Sylvester and Robert Beatty. A big, black slab figures in each section of the film, but we never find out exactly what it is or what it signifies. The third section, by far the most interesting, features Keir Dullea and Gary Lockwood as two automaton astronauts pitted against a computer that speaks in insidiously wheedling tones. Ironically, the computer seems to have more feelings than the humans do, a curiously pessimistic attitude toward a project of this magnitude in predicting scientific "progress." The ending is a mishmash of psychedelic self-indulgence for the special effects people and an exercise in mystifying abstract fantasy in the open temple of High Art. [Andrew Sarris, 4/11/68]

While we remain in this mood of apocalyptic anguish, I must report that I recently paid another visit to Stanley Kubrick's *2001* while under the influence of a smoked substance that I was assured by my contact was somewhat stronger and more authentic than oregano on a King Sano base. (For myself, I must confess that I soar infinitely higher on vermouth cassis, but enough of this generation gap.) Anyway, unprepared to watch *2001* under what I have always been assured were optimum conditions, and surprisingly (for me), I find myself reversing my original opinion. *2001* is indeed a major work by a major artist. For what it is—and I am still not exactly enchanted by what it is—*2001* is beautifully modulated and controlled to express its director's vision of a world to come seen through the sensibility of a world past. Even the dull, expressionless acting seems perfectly attuned to a setting in which human feelings are diffused by inhuman distances.

However, I don't think that *2001* is exclusively or even especially a head movie (and now I speak with the halting voice of authority). For once, the cuts in the movie helped by making it seem less perversely boring for its own sake. The cuts also emphasized that the greatness of the movie is not in its joints and connections (the literary factor) but in the expressive slowness of its camera movements (the plastic factor) and the distended expansiveness of its environment (the visual factor). I am still dissatisfied by the open-ended abstractness of the allegory, not to mention the relatively conventional sojourn into psychedelia.

Nonetheless, *2001* now works for me as Kubrick's parable of a future world toward which metaphysical dread and mordant amusement tiptoe side by side. Even on the first viewing, I admired all the stuff about HAL literally losing his mind. On second viewing, I was deeply moved by HAL as a metaphor of reason afflicted by the assaults of neurotic doubt. And when his rectangular brain cells were being pulled out one by one, I could almost feel the buzzing in my brain cells as they clung ever more precariously to that psychic cluster I call (quite automatically) *me*. I have never seen the death of a mind rendered more profoundly or poetically than it is rendered by Kubrick in *2001*.

2001 is concerned ultimately not so much with the outer experiences of space as with the inner fears of Kubrick's mind as it contemplates infinity and eternity. As the moon shots should have demonstrated by now, there is absolutely nowhere we can go to escape ourselves. [Andrew Sarris, 5/7/70]

Unforgiven (1992)

Dir. Clint Eastwood; Scr. David Webb Peoples
131 min.

It begins as they often do: in the distance, a lone man silhouetted against the horizon. This time the sky is golden and so is the earth, where the man is digging a grave. The twilight of the Western, of even its revisionist mode, is fading fast. Welcome to cowboy noir.

Like his Brechtian *White Hunter, Black Heart*, Clint Eastwood's *Unforgiven* is a distinctive combination of didacticism and despair. If it's also his most assured work as an actor-director, that's probably because it strikes so close to home. The myth on which he's running a reality check was once his own.

Eastwood's William Munny, the former gunfighter turned hog farmer, could be the "Man with No Name" or the ghostly avenger of *High Plains Drifter* twenty years later. Midway through his life, Munny met a woman who helped him hang up his guns and throw away the bottle. He's made a saint of her, which is easy enough since she's dead of smallpox. Now his hogs are dying, he doesn't know how he's going to feed his kids, his body's brittle, and he's turned his killer anger upon himself.

When a would-be young gun tells him about a thousand-dollar bounty on the heads of two men who've cut up a prostitute, he hesitates, but barely. This gig has some age-old rationales for breaking the first commandment: by avenging the honor of a woman, he'll earn enough to give his family a new start. Munny recruits his only partner, Ned Logan (Morgan Freeman), and the three set out for the town of Big Whiskey.

It's guys like Big Whiskey's Sheriff Little Bill Daggett (Gene Hackman at his least sentimental) that make it hard to support gun-control legislation. An affable sadist, Daggett keeps order by kicking the shit out of anyone packing a weapon without his permission. No sooner has Munny, who's come down with pneumonia riding in the rain, confessed to Logan that he's scared of dying than Daggett's wiping the floor with his face.

Munny takes a significant three days to recover, though not even the pain and humiliation he suffered can resurrect the cold-blooded killer instinct. "It's a terrible thing to kill a man. You take away everything he has and everything he's going to have." With every shot, *Unforgiven* pounds home the lesson that death is not abstract, that the person you gun down has the same subjectivity as you. The film is just enough of a shoot-'em-up to make it a meditation on the practice, not just the theory, of violence.

Unforgiven maps a terrain of psychical depression relieved by bits of absurdist humor that often as not turn vicious at the punchline. Less desultory than it seems, the film gives us the lag time we need to notice our complicity with its emotional confusions and ambivalences.

On the most obvious level, *Unforgiven* is a critique of Hollywood's construction of the myth of the frontier. The cowboy hero, it seems, got his courage from a bottle. History is hyperbole embroidered over lost weekends. Only by falling off the wagon can Munny quiet his superego long enough to give vent to a murderous rage that's eminently justified. "What happens after?" asks the dwarf sheriff in *High Plains Drifter*. "You learn to live with it," answers Clint. But in *Unforgiven*, the cathartic final shootout is already tempered by regret.

Much more interesting is the subtext of sexual difference in David Webb Peoples's lucid script and Eastwood's coolly expressive direction of it. It's not only that an incident of sexual abuse (occasioned by an inexperienced prostitute's laughter at the sight of her puffed-up client's remarkably tiny pecker) and a woman's consequent demand for justice set the plot in motion, it's that *Unforgiven* opens and closes with a question about a woman's desire. Why, asks William Munny's mother-in-law, did my daughter marry a man responsible for the deaths of countless children, women, and men? It's a question asked by "the other" about "the one." And it's the question that the film tries to answer for us, the audience. Why are we married to Clint Eastwood? And for so long? Why is he "the one" whose image we fetishize in widescreen?

Though Eastwood often identifies with women (as in *Tightrope* or *Sudden Impact*), his films are ultimately about the Eastwood persona. I'm crazy about *Unforgiven*, but I focus on it at the expense of a potential film Eastwood allows to surface for only about half a minute. That film is about Strawberry Alice (played by the mercurial Frances Fisher), the prostitute who, like Munny, comes alive with her anger. It's Alice who calls in the bounty hunters to avenge the slashing of her friend. There's an extraordinary moment, after the cowboy is killed in the gully and the rocks start flying through the whorehouse window, in which Alice realizes that her righteous actions will have consequences beyond her control. I want to see a film where Alice, the ancestor of Louise, and maybe of Thelma, too, is "the one" and not "the other." And if someone were to make that film, she or he might do worse than borrow the ending from William Munny. It's as mythic for an outlaw to retire to San Francisco and "prosper in dry goods" as it is to wind up at the bottom of the Grand Canyon. [Amy Taubin, 8/18/92]

Les Vampires (1915)

Dir./Scr. Louis Feuillade
399 min.

Film junkies with a taste for the marvelous will need no urging to declare Thursday a holiday and head for the Museum of Modern Art basement to catch one of the rare local unspoolings of Louis Feuillade's *Les Vampires*. The ten chapters of Feuillade's 1915 serial are about forty minutes each; with intermissions, the show runs over seven hours. From "The Severed Head" through "The Bloody Nuptials," the saga is complete although the print has no intertitles—a mixed blessing that accelerates the action even as Feuillade's fantastically unsynopsizable plot recedes behind his mastery of the visual.

Feuillade, who reached his peak during World War I, is the lone European director whose epic, epochal vision can legitimately be compared to that of D. W. Griffith. But unlike Griffith, Feuillade had no interest in dramatic montage. His films are all delirious mise-en-scène. Feuillade's great innovation was his use of actual, often open-air locations as the backdrop for an unending rondo of sinister doings. It is as though Thomas Pynchon wrote scripts for Roberto Rossellini. *Les Vampires*'s eponymous antiheroes and antiheroines are a criminal gang in outrageous Spiderman drag, specializing in abductions, jewel heists, frauds, and dancing the turkey trot in Montmarte cabarets. With its trap doors and disguises, secret messages and sliding panels, poison rings and hypnotic trances, satanic masterminds and femmes fatales, *Les Vampires* is a spectacle of bourgeois terror; the Vampire gang (whom it is impossible not to root for) were popularly identified with France's pre–World War I anarchist movement.

An anonymous hack in his own time—although he anticipates everyone from Lang and Hitchcock to Beth and Scott B—Feuillade was rediscovered by the French in 1945, when Henri Langlois revived *Les Vampires* and other serials (*Fantomas*, *Judex*, *Tih Minh*) at the French Cinémathèque. *Les Vampires* played the London Film Festival in 1963 and arrived at Lincoln Center two years later, the Camp sensation of the 1965 season duly sanctified by the presence of Andy and Edie. Personally, I think Feuillade is savored best in weekly installments rather than in marathon events, but there's no doubt that as repackaged by Langlois (and later Richard Roud), Feuillade has had considerable aesthetic impact. A kindred mixture of melodramatic artifice and raw nature, served up in movies of mad duration, can be seen in the work of admirers as disparate as Jacques Rivette and Andy Warhol.

Of course, Feuillade has always had his partisans. During the 1920s, the surrealists discovered and claimed his ten old-fashioned serials as they did the photographs of his near-contemporary Eugene Atget. ("It is in *Les Vampires* that one must look for the great reality of this century—beyond fashion, beyond taste," wrote Breton and Aragon.) Walter Benjamin's famous observation on Atget—that he photographed the street as though it were the scene of a crime—can be applied literally to Feuillade. Indeed, there is a sense in which the Vampire gang becomes a metaphor for cinema's inherent duplicity. The Vampires' labyrinthian conspiracies imbue Feuillade's near-documentary presentation of 1915 Paris with an awesome sense of unreality, presaging poet Paul Éluard's dictum "There is another world, but it is in this one." It is for this reason, perhaps, that the most banal elements in Feuillade are ultimately the most haunting. The trees never seem more verdant, the weather more idyllic, the breezes more balmy, the natural world more mysterious than in the convoluted thrillers of Louis Feuillade. [J. Hoberman, 4/19/83]

Vengeance Is Mine (1979)

Dir. Shohei Imamura; Scr. Ataru Bab
140 min.

Alan Poul, the programmer who has helped build the Japan House into a model showcase for a national cinema, has been claiming for years that Shohei Imamura is the major filmmaker presently active in Japan. *Vengeance Is Mine* goes a long way toward proving that point. This 1979 film is a dramatic study in criminal psychology that I can only call awesome.

Vengeance Is Mine is an eclectically horrifying mosaic about a psychopathic criminal named Iwao Enokizu. The film's story is based on police records and a 1976 nonfiction novel by Ryuzo Saki. The plot evolves from an entwined pattern of flashbacks tracing Iwao from his life as a persecuted youth in a family of Catholic fishermen under the prewar military party to his eerie burial, which resists a final exorcism. Imamura maintains a rich sociological and historical context on the Japanese people—some critics describe his forte as anthropological—while remaining disconcertingly clear-eyed in graphically chronicling Iwao's progress as extortionist and mass murderer.

The very title, *Vengeance Is Mine*, begins implicating the viewer in a mystery play that is both compelling and repelling. Iwao is a truly dangerous creature of prey without conscience or remorse, yet he is fully immersed in a stream of humanity. At least half a dozen characters, including father, wife, mistress, and victims—all of whom share sophisticated and emotive interlocking relationships—chip away at Iwao's veneer but come away with only pieces of the mystery.

In some scenes, Imamura is receptive to "found" location moments, as in the camera's pause on a teeming eel fishery or in the ghostly passage of white-robed schoolgirls descending a cable car from a mountain cemetery. In others, shadows obscuring a face and glass panes distorting eyes seem to be charmed moments when nature collaborated with the director's designs. Most frequently, however, the camera starkly isolates an act or angularly searches for the psychological nuance among characters formally arranged within a tight frame. I have never seen such intimate sex acts more naturally rendered or more revealing of the psyches within the body-play. It takes an iron will and a major artistic vision to hurtle through so many rich options and still retain a thematic coherence. *Vengeance Is Mine* demands much—I'd almost call it courage—for the viewer to stay astride this tiger Imamura has released. [Tom Allen, 10/22/79]

Vertigo (1958)

Dir. Alfred Hitchcock/Scr. Alec Coppel and Samuel Taylor
128 min.

The Strange Lady: I believe that he was searching for someone who could no longer exist! Someone whom he knew he could

> only find alive in me, so that he could remake her but not as she desired—for she no longer desired anything!—but as he desired her! Ah—madness—madness—

These lines are from Pirandello's *As You Desire Me*, but they might equally well have been spoken by the disconsolate Judy (Kim Novak) in Alfred Hitchcock's masterpiece *Vertigo*. Though adapted from a mystery novel by Boileau and Narcejac (the authors of *Diabolique*), *Vertigo* is more Pirandellian in its parts and certainly in its uncompromising conclusion than the sentimental film version of the play with Greta Garbo.

A woman re-creates herself in her own, or someone else's, image. In the irradiating conceit of both works, a woman stands beside (or sits facing) the painting of a woman whose likeness she becomes—an extreme, poetic version of what women everywhere do all the time. Upon discovering that their desirability rests in surfaces, they transform themselves into works of art, adjust their essential being to the glazed reflection in a man's eyes.

The appeal of art is similar to the appeal of dreams. The fragmented self is momentarily suspended as, in art, we exchange our identities for another or, in dreams, we temporarily integrate the mismatching pieces of our biographies. The process of identification, which has lately come under attack as a piece of bourgeois manipulation, is really the expression of a primal need. In permitting us a new or revised identity, art and dreams approach—as they retreat from—the kind of insanity that takes permanent refuge in another identity. If dreams stop short of madness, art comes through it and out the other side. Like the ideal transference between psychiatrist and patient, art enables us to live the illusion and simultaneously understand its meaning. If the fundamental theme of all art is the distinction between illusion and reality, its natural subject is woman because while men have been creating beautiful lies, she has been living them.

From the moment when, with feverish precocity or strenuous resistance, she wears her first "heels" or applies her first lipstick, she is remolding her psychic self and delimiting her freedom. And all the subsequent lies and ruses and underhanded devices for gaining power can be traced to that fateful initiation into—call it female eunuchry, the second sex, or (most damagingly) sexual politics.

To return from these soapbox verities to the question of illusion and reality, which will be with us as long as there is any duality at all—sun and moon, body and mind, man and woman. This paradox, dizzying to contemplate, is the crux of much great art and is raised to its most definitive expression in Hitchcock's film. It is what makes watching the film and thinking about it such a vertiginous experience, a descent into a maelstrom of conflicting responses, a dizzying flight through mental space in which you reach out for touchstones like positive and negative, healthy and sick (Hitchcock's vision, after all, is profoundly moral), and at the same time realize the uselessness of all such labels outside a normal frame of reference. Dream or nightmare, the Hitchcock film is the trip the Pirandello should have been, beyond the safety zone of social discourse, through the labyrinthine ambiguities of human behavior. And it is Woman, born with paintbrush and mirror in her hand (and thus already outside the moral convention of truth and deceit) who leads us on this perilous journey. For in questioning man's allegiance to the Ideal, Hitchcock and Pirandello are challenging not just the precepts of morality, but of art. It is art that, in aspiring to beauty, often rejects truth. In remodeling reality, art pays a terrible price—it denies, robs, or kills the thing it "loves," reality.

In *Vertigo,* Jimmy Stewart plays Scottie, a flatfoot—and never was the term so apt. In the opening chase sequence over the rooftops, he discovers that he has vertigo, and as a result of his fear a policeman loses his life. The sequence ends with Stewart hanging onto a gutter-pipe, dangling in space. Since we are never shown or told how Stewart escapes, we are left with the sense, as Robin Wood points out in his brilliant essay, of Stewart suspended throughout the rest of the film.

In the next sequence, we are introduced to Midge (Barbara Bel Geddes), a bespectacled buddy who works as a commercial artist and has always been in love with Scottie, but who, some years before, took the decisive action of breaking off their engagement when she realized his indifference. Scottie, as we see him in the beginning, is the charming clod Hitchcock so astutely recognizes in Stewart. He is literal-minded, philistinish, complacent, and, by the accidental discovery of his vertigo and the loss of his job, utterly adrift. His world has literally and figuratively fallen out from under him; along with his equilibrium, he has lost his security.

When an old school friend proposes that Scottie follow his wife, who has been acting mysteriously and seems inhabited by the exotic spirit of her dead grandmother, Stewart scornfully dismisses the possibility of magic or mysticism. But something in him—desire for escape, romance, the spark of doubt that assails the most literal minds—prompts him to accept the job. It is with one of the oddest and most expressive movements in the Hitchcock oeuvre, one that defines the whole nature of the subsequent quest, that the camera "discovers" Madeleine for us and for Stewart. She is sitting at a table across the restaurant, in a red evening dress; the camera approaches her, and, just as we realize who she is and expect to move closer in on her, the camera stops. We are contained at a tantalizing distance from this divine creature, who then compounds her aura of mystery by coming close to but passing by us, giving us only her profile. She hesitates, as if to taunt us with the idea that in proximity, she is even more inaccessible than at a distance. In Scottie's hypnotic pursuit of Madeleine (which lodges itself in the memory as one long tracking movement), he follows her through the streets of San Francisco to her haunts: the flower show, the Spanish mission, the graveyard, the museum in which she sits (visible to us in profile) gazing at the portrait of Carlotta Valdez.

The first time we see Madeleine's full face is when she awakens in Scottie's bed, after he has rescued her from drowning. Naked and vulnerable, she faces him, presenting the one opportunity of a confrontation. But she is another man's wife; Scottie's scruples prevail against the higher and more dangerous principle of passionate attraction. Eroticism is, indeed, inimical to romantic illusion; if sex is the act that cheats death, it is also the arch enemy of perfection, of purity, of chivalry, even—possibly—of love. Scottie falls madly in love with Madeleine, the Illusion. He wants desperately to cure her. "There's got to be an answer," he says, not realizing that the answer he seeks is absolute—death.

Scottie and Madeleine's embraces are violent and ecstatic, too ecstatic perhaps, too isolated from the rest of the world, too close to the precipice. They evoke, as Wood perceives, the delirium of the romantic cliché. Throughout the film, there is a strong element of cliché, capped most exquisitely in Midge's joke: a reproduction of the portrait of Carlotta Valdez, substituting her own lovely, plain, modern face for the original. Scottie fails, as he must, to see the humor: a brilliant insight on Hitchcock's part into the nature of obsession, whose identifying mark is that it cannot be reached by humor.

Vertigo is not Hitchcock's most popular film, and even for its inveterate admirers it may present problems the first time. The shock of Madeleine's "death" halfway through the film is exceeded by the even more devastating news that she is not dead at all but lives in her genuine identity: a common shopgirl named Judy. This is *more devastating*—we would rather have the porcelain Madeleine dead than alive as this vulgar and intractably real human being. But as it denies conventional expectations, *Vertigo* fulfills metaphysical ones, most completely in the moment that we are taken into Judy's confidence when we don't want to be, explained the truth of the plot we don't want to hear, told that she really does love Scottie, and come to understand that she will do anything to make him love her.

Scottie's efforts to turn Judy into Madeleine constitute the most brilliant and agonizing passage in the entire film, issuing as they do not only from the deluded and arrogant desire of a man wanting to turn a live woman into a dream (a director manipulating an actress?), but from a man who thinks he is a murderer wanting to resurrect his victim and atone for his guilt, and a man who is in love wanting to recapture it. And meeting, as it does, not just the natural resistance of a woman who wants to be (or reclaim) herself, but the partial complicity of a woman who recognizes, in the role she created, some aspiration to beauty in herself. But since the reality of Madeleine now exists only in Scottie's imagination, the burden of bringing it to life, and the possibility of madness, rest with him. He has been given, as he says, a "second chance."

I can think of no other film ending as unsettling as that of *Vertigo*, and the image of Jimmy Stewart, bent slightly forward, arms akimbo, a look of cosmic bewilderment on his face. His vertigo has been cured and a woman has died. In psychoanalytic terms, Scottie has reenacted the drama that gave rise to the trauma and thereby regained his sanity, but at what a price! He has turned a woman back into a dream where she could only wake up or (which is the same thing) die.

But perhaps in a sense she was already dead, and her fall from the bell tower is only the physical confirmation of her soul's descent. Like the Strange Lady, her assumption of a fictional role was a sign of her rejection of her real self. She was already divided in two: Judy, who was tough, no-nonsense, and admitted no fantasy, and Madeleine, who was pure fantasy. But unlike Pirandello's heroine, Judy/Madeleine does not have the insight that would enable her to understand (i.e., integrate) herself. It is to Stewart that insight must come; his spiritual growth is assured, as happens so often, in life, by another person's death. His guilt is no longer personal and absolvable, but eternal and universal: the guilt that is all man's for abjuring reality in favor of illusion, and for which there is no cure. There is only the spiritual development, not of "dispelling illusions" but of recognizing the dark forces and fears that produce them, and of welcoming the insecurity where dreams wrestle with reality. And finally, perhaps, it is in the birth of passion, which Scottie feels for the first time in the pursuit of Madeleine, that death is redeemed.

Or is it the kind of passion, of which the Strange Lady accuses her decadent writer-lover Salter, that feeds on itself:

> Salter: I have wrecked my life for you!
>
> The Strange Lady: For your insane passion—not for me.
>
> [Molly Haskell, 6/10/71]

If you've never seen Alfred Hitchcock's rhapsodic and perverse *Vertigo*, you are invited to stop reading and get on line at the Ziegfeld. And if you have seen *Vertigo* and wonder whether the new 70mm restoration is all that it's been hyped—you don't really have to ask. *Vertigo* is a mystery that only improves with knowledge of its "solution," not to mention projection in its original format on a huge screen.

Indeed, it seems nearly redundant to be promoting the film in these pages. Back in the auteurist heyday of the late 1970s, the *Voice* film section voted *Vertigo* the greatest American movie of all time. (A callow, fifth-string, part-time reviewer, I topped my ballot with the Oscar Micheaux film *God's Stepchildren*, but that's another story.) For more than a few people, *Vertigo* is the ultimate movie—a movie that is, after all, concerned with being hopelessly, obsessively, fetishistically in love with an image. Or, as the *New York Times* reported in June 1958, it is "all about how a dizzy fellow chases after a dizzy dame."

Back in the day, *Vertigo* was received with genial condescension. *Time* called it a typical "Hitchcock-and-bull story." Hitchcock was then heavily involved in television, and although "Hollywood's best-known butterball" (*Time*), he was perceived to be stretched a mite thin. Only *Cahiers du Cinéma* and the mavens who wrote for the Hollywood trade papers took the movie seriously.

Quintessential film modernist though Hitchcock may have been, he was also a dedicated Pop Artist—the master not only of suspense but of self-promotion and gimmickry. (*Vertigo* was promoted with a party on the twenty-ninth floor of an unfinished East 42nd Street skyscraper.) Stars Jimmy Stewart and Kim Novak aside, the movie's main attraction was understood to be its widescreen "travelogue" treatment of San Francisco. Thus, the restoration's major visual revelation is the additional weight given the prolonged, gliding, all but wordless automotive chase that made the *New Yorker*'s critic complain that he was carsick: Stewart's Scottie pursuing the ghostly jade green Jaguar driven by Novak's Madeleine through SF's hilly streets.

Vertigo bogs down more than once in tedious exposition. But although literal-minded critics continue to knock Hitchcock's implausible narrative, this seems a bit like complaining that *Un Chien Andalou* is too discontinuous or the myth of Orpheus and Eurydice lacks the necessary verisimilitude. *Vertigo*'s evocatively imminent, emptied-out world has the melancholy solitude of a de Chirico city, just as Madeleine's uncanny movements in and out of frame suggest Maya Deren's montage.

There is a sense in which *Vertigo* sums up thirty years of Surrealist (and Surrealist-into-advertising) imagery. With its long late-afternoon shadows, pervasive anxiety, terrifying intimations of the void, frozen immobility, feeling of elastic time, charged symbols, uncanny portraits, and general sense of weirdness in broad daylight, *Vertigo* could have been subtitled after de Chirico (*Nostalgia of the Infinite*) or Deren (*Meshes of the Afternoon*). Taking the term that Joseph Cornell applied to the somnambulant star Hedy Lamarr, Madeleine describes herself as a "wanderer." Like the Surrealist heroine Nadja, Madeleine lives out her dreams—or are they Scottie's?

Vertigo is not without its dark humor, but it is an intensely, almost shockingly, romantic movie: like bereft Heathcliff in the second half of

Wuthering Heights, shell-shocked Scottie pleads with his lost love to haunt him. And once she does return from the dead—her kiss obliterating time and space as Herrmann works variations on Wagner's *Tristan und Isolde*—the movie's own current resurrection becomes secondary.

There'll never be a better opportunity to see *Vertigo*. Still, when its drama is distilled to overwhelming desire (and the desire to be desired), when its narrative is vaporized by the force of mutual (and mutually exclusive) longings, this movie could cast its spell from a nine-inch black-and-white TV set. [J. Hoberman, 10/15/96]

Videodrome (1983)

Dir./Scr. David Cronenberg

89 min.

Videodrome is the slickest, most entertaining and ambitious David Cronenberg film I've seen—a Boschian brew of lurid S and M, hallucinogenic TV transmissions, and biomorphism run amok. The movie is conceptual gibberish, but its malignant seediness stays with you like a dream.

Cronenberg's scummy hero (James Woods), a Canadian cable entrepreneur who breakfasts on cold pizza and has a complexion to match, falls under the simultaneous spell of two media emanations. The first is Debbie Harry, the shrink star of a call-in radio program; the second is a sinister transmission intercepted by Woods's resident video pirate that features heavy-duty bondage and torture. Harry and Woods meet cute on a TV talk show. She turns out to be a jaded masochist—give the girl a postcoital cigarette and she'll stub it out on her thorax—and she inflames his professional interest in the pirated snuff telecast. Unfortunately for him, the show is merely the come-on for a new video signal that not only produces mindbending bummers but effects physical transformations on the body as well.

With its druggy, convoluted plot, not to mention touches like the Cathode Ray Mission where derelicts are "saved" through intensive exposure to television ("watching TV patches them back into the world's mixing board," the proprietress explains) or even the characters'

Videodrome, 1983; written and directed by David Cronenberg

names (Brian O'Blivion, Barry Convex), *Videodrome* bears a marked resemblance to the social science fiction of the late Philip K. Dick. Cronenberg, however, is a good deal less coherent; his yarn unravels as fast as he can spin it. *Videodrome*'s metaphysical assumptions, such as they are, marry Marshall McLuhan to Bishop Berkeley. "There is nothing real beyond our conception of reality," pontificates TV sage O'Blivion. Television is posited as part of the brain, "the retina of the mind's eye," which explains, I suppose, why Woods's hallucinations can be played back on videotape.

Still, long before Woods becomes "the video word turned flesh" and *Videodrome* grinds to an abruptly unsatisfying halt, you've come to grok that Cronenberg's narrative is merely the pretense for his imagery. An adolescent prankster like Brian De Palma, Cronenberg envisions life as some sort of disease, and he has no difficulty understanding media as "the extensions of man." Videocassettes writhe and sweat, TV consoles buckle, Harry's celebrated lips swell through the cathode ray tube in a parody of rampant concupiscence. If you shoot one of these Sonys, believe me, it bleeds. (The effects, by Rick "*An American Werewolf in*

London" Baker, are exceedingly polished; Cronenberg's least successful bit of camera magic is his attempt to make Toronto look decrepit.)

Cronenberg carries his literal-mindedness into the realm of social satire. So the medium fucks us, doesn't it? Under the baleful influence of the "videodrome signal," Woods grows a giant orifice in his stomach and gets programmed by neo-Nazi heavies through the insertion of organic videocassettes. A corollary to the lethal, retractable penis Marilyn Chambers sprouted under her arm in *Rabid*, Woods's "vagina" comes complete with teeth and, at one point, devours a bad guy's arm. [J. Hoberman, 2/15/83]

Wanda (1971)

Dir./Scr. Barbara Loden
102 min.

That Barbara Loden, a woman, happens to be the director of *Wanda* invites the contemporary reviewer to all sorts of speculations about a distinctly female point of view on film. The trouble is that there have been relatively few woman directors in the history of the medium, and of these, even fewer have been more than marginally prominent. Women-written films are something else again. Anita Loos alone could keep (and has kept) MOMA hopping for months on end, and Betty Comden, Frances Goodrich, Ruth Gordon, Sonya Levien, Frances Marion, Jane Murfin, and Bella Spewack were no slouches either, not to mention Mae West and Ayn ("*Love Letters*") Rand.

But what does one say about a woman qua woman directors that is not condescendingly sexist? I cannot think of any pejoratively "feminine" quality that is not found in a vast number of male artists. Indeed, the fluttery, excessively lyrical, unduly intuitive characteristics commonly labeled feminine are often precisely the qualities superior women tend to discard in order to be taken seriously by the male establishment. And it is certainly not in these obvious ways that I take *Wanda* to be a movie by a woman. Quite the contrary. Barbara Loden comes on stylistically hard rather than soft, analytical rather than rhapsodic, harsh and awkward rather than smooth and graceful.

Up to the time Wanda encounters Mr. Dennis (Michael Higgins), the unromantically criminal Clyde to her Bonnie, the film is constructed as a series of alienating friezes of man (and woman) submerged in the mineral kingdom of coal, rock, steel, glass, asphalt. Miss Loden's style alternates between Antonioni on the hillsides (two-dimensional pointillism) and Fellini on the horizon lines (de Chirico in Disneyland). But once Miss Loden stops sketching her environment and begins inhabiting it, her characterization comes to life. The museum shots of the milieu are superseded by intensive cross-cutting between two loners groping for each other across the infinite distances in the front seat of a moving car. There are none of Godard's lyrical windshield two-shots filmed from outside the car alongside Coutard. Barbara Loden is inside the car, body and soul, and she keeps looking at the man to whom she has entrusted her life, and sometimes he is in profile looking ahead at the road, and sometimes he is in full shot looking sidewise from the road at her.

And always he is gruff in his groping way. He gives her money to buy a hat so as to discard the hair curlers that make her a caricature of lower-middle-class America. He wants her to have class. He buys her a dress and throws her slacks out on the turnpike. An unconscious touch of American affluence is in that gesture when compared to a similar situation in François Truffaut's *The Soft Skin*, in which Jean Desailly induces Françoise Dorléac to change from slacks to a dress so that he can look lecherously at her legs while he is driving. But there is no question of throwing away the slacks in the land of de Maupassant. And more important, Truffaut cannot resist showing the audience the lecherous spectacle of Dorléac's legs. Barbara Loden, by contrast, withholds the sensual spectacle of her own legs until they are about to be used and abused by the man in her life. No anticipatory glances at the legs. Only eyeball-to-eyeball confrontations via head shots.

And when her man has been killed, and she allows herself to be picked up by a soldier in a brown uniform and he tries to impose his chromatic bulk over her body on the front seat of his car, she breaks away and runs into the forest and breaks down in tears that inform her tired flesh that she had been emotionally alive for so short a time and we don't really need the spider web to round out the sequence but somehow I didn't mind it and the movie seems at an end but keeps starting up again and again until it is mercifully extinguished in a freeze frame and all in all it is the extraordinary good fortune of Barbara Loden the director to have had Barbara Loden the actress to manipulate with such impulsive immediacy. [Andrew Sarris, 3/18/71]

Weekend (1967)

Dir./Scr. Jean-Luc Godard
105 min.

Weekend consolidates Jean-Luc Godard's position as the most disconcerting of all contemporary directors, a veritable paragon of paradoxes, violent and yet vulnerable, the most elegant stylist and the most vulgar polemicist, the most remorseful classicist and the most relentless modernist, the man of the moment and the artist for the ages. When I bore witness to *Weekend* at the Berlin Film Festival back in June, Godard seemed to be tuned in to the youthful frequency of the future. He lost me somewhere between the garbage truck of the Third World and the slaughtered pig of the new breed, but I did feel the film unwinding with all the clattering contemporaneity of a tickertape, and the reading for Western Civilization was down, down, and out.

Seeing *Weekend* again on a chill Nixonish November in New York, I am struck more by Godard's melancholy than by his message. As much as Godard indulges in the rhetoric of rebellion, his deepest feelings seem to be situated before the revolution. He was born, he implies, too soon and too late, too soon to forget the sweetness of the past and too late to perpetuate that same sweetness, particularly in the remembered realm of movies with subjects not yet swallowed up by the subjective. Godard seems to want it both ways as the prime prophet of the first-person film and the lead mourner of the third-person movie. Indeed, Godard has been bemoaning the death of movies ever since *Breathless*, a period of almost a full decade, long enough to turn the tears of a meaningful prophet into the tears of a professional mourner.

Godard's strengths and weaknesses are immediately apparent in the opening shots of *Weekend*. Husband, wife, and wife's lover-analyst sit on a leafy terrace. Phone rings, and intrigues commence. Wife is cheating on husband and husband on wife, talk of poisons and inheritances, lust and avarice on the Jeeter Lester level of characterization, barnyard animal dramaturgy out of the nastiest comic strip capitalism imaginable. But Raoul Coutard's fully textured, subtly shadowed color cinematography undercuts the calculating crudity of the dialogue. Within the same sequence, Godard demonstrates his formal mastery. The three bourgeois characters look down from their balcony at a street accident culminating in a violent brawl between the two drivers. Godard stages the brawl from such an insistently overhead viewpoint that he creates a metaphor for bourgeois detachment from social turmoil. The verticality of the viewpoint is sustained long enough to remind the educated moviegoer of a similar metaphor in Luis Buñuel and Salvador Dalí's more overtly surrealist classic, *Un Chien Andalou*. Whereas Buñuel and Dalí treated apparent moral indifference as actual metaphysical liberation, Godard treats idle curiosity as immoral complicity. The difference between Buñuel-Dalí and Godard is therefore the difference between irony and allegory. Furthermore, Godard's brawl is staged so elaborately that its violence is more rhetorical than real, more for the sake of a voyeuristic spectacle than for the release of psychic tensions. Hence, and this is true throughout *Weekend*, Godard's violence is more cerebral than visceral.

The bourgeois couple impersonated by Mireille Darc and Jean Yanne are less the involved subjects of *Weekend* than its detached objects. Never before has Godard been so far outside a pair of protagonists. Never before has he shown so little concern for their fate and so few close-ups of their features. Far from being treated as the victims of bourgeois society, they emerge as its arch villains. Symptomatic of Godard's intransigent indifference toward this despised duo is that the death of the husband and the desecration of the wife transpire offscreen with the most callous casualness.

Weekend is most likely to be remembered for the sustained tracking shot of a traffic tie-up extending for miles across the dull French landscape. The first time I saw *Weekend*, I was struck by Godard's lack of comic inventiveness in the description of the delay. I wasn't impressed even when Godard sought to implicate the audience in the discovery of the bloody bodies that enabled our stalled motorists to speed away with a lyrical vavoom to liberty and grace. Still, I recognized that old familiar feeling of survival of the fittest (or the luckiest) on the open road. I just happened to be one or two beats ahead of Godard in anticipating his moralistic tag shot, and so I wrote off the scene as a failed shaggy-dog story. This time around in New York, I was struck more by the insanely insistent honking of horns for minutes upon minutes until the bloody bodies became a blessed relief even to this forewarned spectator. Again, the morbid beauty of the camera movement convinced me that this was indeed no time for comedy or even satire. There was something too deterministic about that inexorably moving camera across the intransigently neutral landscape. Mere litterateurs can never appreciate the intoxicating quality of a meaningful camera movement as it obliterates the formal boundaries of the picture frame.

The high point of *Weekend* is the culmination of the second circular camera movement around a pastoral, even rural, agricultural, performance of Mozart's Piano Sonata, K. 576, by Paul Gégauff, one of Chabrol's wilder scriptwriters. Gégauff's argument, perhaps Godard's also, is that so-called serious modern music has less to offer the modern listener than do such genuinely Mozartian descendants as the Beatles and the Rolling Stones. Godard would seem to be establishing a different critical line for music (his avocation) than for cinema (his vocation). It doesn't matter. Godard is interesting less for his attitude toward ideas than for his aptness for images together with the feelings these images express. Godard's concert is the most beautiful expression of the rapport between art and nature I have even seen on the screen. The beauty may be attributable to the fact that Godard is somewhat ill at ease with both nature and art, and thus emotionally responsive to both. [Andrew Sarris, 11/21/68]

White Dog (1982)

Dir. Samuel Fuller; Scr. Samuel Fuller and Curtis Hanson
84 min.

The most sought-after and elusive of shelved studio releases, Samuel Fuller's *White Dog* has finally been unleashed. The movie gets its theatrical premiere this Friday, nine years after Paramount decided it was too troublesome to open and sent it to the pound.

Adapted from Romain Gary's 1970 nonfiction novel, *White Dog* is an unusually blunt and suggestively metaphoric account of American racism. In the original story, Gary and his then wife Jean Seberg find a stray German shepherd who, as they soon discover, has been raised to attack blacks on sight. Although told that the dog is too old to be deconditioned, they ultimately turn him over to a black animal trainer who vengefully reprograms the creature to maul whites (including, at the book's climax, Gary himself).

It's possible that Fuller was the only American filmmaker who could successfully short-circuit Gary's "civilized" irony and present *White Dog* head-on, treating the yarn with the sort of absurdist humor and unabashed didacticism the material warranted. Indeed, intuiting his potential audience, Fuller reconceptualized the movie to put the conflict inside the dog's brain. "You're going to see a dog slowly go insane and then come back to sanity in front of you," he promised *Variety*.

Fuller altered Gary's ending (making it more pessimistic and irrational), modified the character of the black trainer (Paul Winfield), and changed the protagonist from an activist movie star into an aspiring actress (childlike Kristy McNichol in her first "adult" role), whom the dog initially saves from a white rapist. In Fuller's world, unlike Gary's, racial paranoia doesn't drop from the sky but is associated from the onset with the paternal protection of the Law.

That, in homage to Seberg and Gary, Fuller maintains the initials J.S. for McNichol's character and R.G. for her writer-boyfriend is suggestive of his film's boldly abstract tabloid stylistics. Filmed in headlines, framed as allegory, *White Dog* combines hardboiled sentimentality and hysterical violence, sometimes in the same take.

White Dog's iconic visuals and cartoon dialogue ("Your dog is a four-legged time bomb!") are given unexpected dignity by the somber piano doodlings and tense, moody strings of Ennio Morricone's brilliant score. Still, this is an animal film—replete with dog-level tracking shots and frequent close-ups of the dog's eyes. Given the surplus violence of the animal's savage, not always predictable, attacks—their locations ranging from McNichol's living room (TV blasting) to a movie set (a process shot of Venice flickering in the background) to a church (St. Francis of Assisi looking on)—and Fuller's regard for the dog as an alien intelligence, *White Dog* infuses a politically conscious variant of *Jaws* with intimations of Bresson's sublime *Au Hasard Balthazar*, not to mention the director's own unclassifiable nuttiness.

Where else but in a Fuller film would a purveyor of trained animals (Burl Ives) hurl darts at a poster of R2D2 ("That's the enemy!") or, having doubled for John Wayne in *True Grit* by reaching into a nest of rattlesnakes, proffer his paw with the invitation to shake "the hand that helped Duke win the Oscar!" Of course, the choice contradictions are reserved for Fuller's hero. "To me, this is a laboratory that Darwin himself would go ape over!" Winfield exclaims of the animal farm where he works. "How I wanted to kill that son of a bitch!" he describes his response on discovering the white dog trotting away from his latest victim. "But you can't experiment on a dead dog!" By the time Winfield swears that if he fails to cure this animal, he'll find another and another until he does, he has come to seem like a black Captain Ahab.

Fuller—who strongly criticized American racial attitudes in a number of his 1950s action flicks (and made them the subject of *The Crimson Kimono*)—is responsible for some of the toughest social-problem films ever made in the U.S.A. It's understandable that the NAACP would have taken an interest in *White Dog*'s production; it's unfortunate that, by warning Paramount that the film might give racists ideas and encourage the production of actual white dogs, the NAACP provided the studio—and later NBC—with an excuse to suppress what seems to me one of the most unflinching statements to ever come out of Hollywood—something like *Rin Tin Tin Joins the Ku Klux Klan*.

White Dog "naturalizes" racism in a strikingly unnatural way. While the movie's white characters are invariably amazed by the whole idea of the "white dog," most of the black characters treat his existence as a brute fact of life. Unlike in Gary's novel, the dog here doesn't seem to have a name—he's referred to once as "Mr. Hyde," leaving us to consider just who his "Dr. Jekyll" might be. Late in the day, we discover that his creator is a kindly old codger, with two little granddaughters and a box of candy for the lady who sheltered his pet.

What's stunning about *White Dog* is how it gives race hatred both a human *and* a subhuman face. Which is the mask? Conditioned as it is to fear Willie Horton, white America might well ponder the bloody image of that snarling canine. [J. Hoberman, 7/16/91]

The Wind Will Carry Us (1999)

Dir./Scr. Abbas Kiarostami
118 min.

"We're heading nowhere," a disembodied voice complains as a battered jeep crawls up a winding road through harsh, scrubby terrain. So begins *The Wind Will Carry Us*—the latest and, to my mind, the greatest film by Iranian master Abbas Kiarostami.

An engineer and his two never-seen assistants are traveling from Tehran to the remote Kurdish village of Siah Dareh. If the directions they attempt to follow are puzzling, so, too, are their intentions. These outsiders won't say what brings them to Siah Dareh, although they jokingly tell the village boy who has been appointed to guide them into town that they are looking for "treasure." It's soon clear that this treasure has something to do with a sick old woman (also never seen), but it's never directly revealed what that something is.

The Wind Will Carry Us is a marvelously assured film—at once straightforward and tricksy. It's also bracingly modest. For all the self-important claims certain experts have made on Kiarostami's behalf, his films are anything but pompous. Typically understated, *The Wind Will Carry Us* is less amusing than bemusing. Kiarostami's sense of humor feels as dry as the countryside he depicts; the film is in many regards a comedy. The timing is impeccable, the dialogue borderline absurd. The gags, if that's the word, are predicated on formal elements—including the filmmaker's rigorous, somewhat ironic use of point of view and voice-over. The same routines are repeated throughout, often punctuated by amplified animal sounds, to establish a musical structure. (Shots often end with a herd of goats crossing the screen.) In this sense, *The Wind Will Carry Us* resembles the films of Jacques Tati.

The city folks' obscure mission to Kurdistan is but one of the movie's modernist tropes. The villagers call the protagonist the Engineer in somewhat the same spirit that the outsider antihero of Kafka's *Castle* is known as the Land Surveyor. Indeed, having switched from cosmic long shot to more humanizing medium shot once the Engineer (Behzad Dourani) arrives in Siah Dareh, Kiarostami spends considerable time establishing the village's baffling geography—the steep, whitewashed maze of alleys and courtyards that are terraced into the hillside.

Taken as a documentary, which it is in part, *The Wind Will Carry Us* largely concerns the town's daily life—its laconic customs and puzzling arguments. But Kiarostami's method points toward something more. This is a movie of disembodied voices and offscreen presences, including half the characters and a newborn baby. Like the Engineer's two-man crew, who are always indoors and supposedly eating strawberries, Kiarostami is forever drawing attention to that which cannot be seen—or shown.

In one (literally) running gag, the Engineer is required to scramble to the village's highest point so that his cell phone can receive an incoming signal from Tehran. (When he finally gets the connection, he discovers that he doesn't want the call.) The village graveyard is also located atop the hill—a coincidence that allows for another sort of dematerialized conversation. While catching his breath, the Engineer has a series of conversations with an unseen ditchdigger who is excavating the cemetery to facilitate some mysterious form of "telecommunications." (The Engineer is mildly interested, and in a blithely metaphoric move, the ditchdigger throws him a bone.)

In what may be the strangest scene in this extraordinarily subtle and nuanced film, the Engineer uses an excursion to buy fresh milk as a pretext to drop in on the ditchdigger's girlfriend. She, too, he discovers, lives in darkness. He finds her in one of the village's subterranean caverns, milking a goat, and is moved to recite the Forugh Farrokhzad poem about loneliness that provides the movie's title.

At last, the Engineer has put something in words. Skinny and balding, peering at the village through steel-rimmed glasses, this dungaree-wearing character is an example of what used to be called the intelligentsia. He is also a parody director who makes a few lame attempts to photograph the villagers, while more than once employing the actual camera as a mirror, peering directly into it as he shaves. The Engineer is interested in life. At one point, he idly flips a tortoise on its back—perhaps to see how it will squirm. But at another, more crucial moment, he demonstrates that he cannot take action himself but can only direct others to do so.

It's part of the movie's formal brilliance that, suddenly, during its final ten minutes, too much seems to be happening. *The Wind Will Carry Us* is a film about nothing and everything—life, death, the quality of light on dusty hills. Effortlessly incorporating aspects of documentary and confessional filmmaking into an unforced, open-ended parable, *The Wind Will Carry Us* transforms barely anecdotal material into a mysteriously metaphysical vision.

For all its glorious time-wasting, *The Wind Will Carry Us* is essentially a deathwatch. Late in the movie, it's casually revealed that the Engineer has been hanging out in Siah Dareh for two weeks. When night finally falls, however, it's as though the time he's spent there has been a single golden, purposeless, perpetual afternoon. [J. Hoberman, 8/1/00]

Winter Soldier (1972)

Dir. Winterfilm Collective
96 min.

Winter Soldier—a straight recording of the confessions of war crimes given by American veterans in Detroit 1971—had an explosive impact on the international press at Cannes 1972. But the horror of what these ordinary, likeable veterans recount and the courage they show by admitting to the blood on their hands is an experience every American owes himself, no matter how sick he is of hearing about the war. If these are the acts we are committing, we should at least take the responsibility of knowing about them.

As a significant example of how far we are from knowing, consider the reaction of Thomas Quinn Curtiss in the *International Herald Tribune*: "The witnesses disqualify themselves to some extent by their appearances . . . seeming on sight to be members of fanciful Bohemia. But if there is truth in their testimony, all reputable people will be deeply disturbed." Reputable people are presumably those who wear ties, shave, go to film festivals, and are thus eminently qualified to comment on the crimes of Vietnam, unlike the badly groomed slobs who committed, witnessed, suffered, and confessed them.

If there is truth of a representative kind in this reaction, then perhaps it is too late for this film—or film festivals—to have much meaning. But if any nerves or morals are left to be educated, *Winter Soldier* demands to be seen. [Jonathan Rosenbaum, 6/29/72]

Winter Soldier is a rarely glimpsed document, shot and assembled by an anonymous filmmaking collective, of the 1971 "Winter Soldier Investigation." A month after the news of My Lai shook Americans rigid, more than a hundred returned vets testified in a Detroit Howard Johnson conference room that My Lai was no aberration, but a paradigm of U.S. activity in Vietnam. The resulting first-person-witness assault demonstrates, in the fashion of *Shoah*, that being told can be more lacerating than being shown; we experience not only the atrocities but the shock waves felt by the witnesses and the emotional venom that still necrotized their lives. Not that the sympathies lie only with the terrifyingly calm and earnest speakers; every story is a story about farmers butchered as a kind of sickened imperial bloodsport, and the bootprint the movie leaves might be the deepest of any 'Nam doc.

It's difficult to stomach "Proud Vietnam Vet" bumper stickers after *Winter Soldier* or even to endure American cinema's self-pitying bankload of fiction movies about the war. (No less unchewable is the subsequent career of John Kerry, a peripheral presence in the movie, in light of his role in the hearings.) Of course, no news outlet would cover the event, and no distributor or broadcaster would touch the film record. Whoever saw it in 1972 saw it at the Whitney; after that, only WNET threw it on once unannounced as a replacement program. Otherwise, the fifteen filmmakers—including Barbara Kopple and David Grubin—have had to host private screenings themselves. So, what was intended to be a public turning point in our knowledge of the war's true nature was effectively run underground—which makes the film imperative viewing. The afterlife of the Vietnam home front experience indicates that we saw it all in our living rooms, or in *Hearts and Minds*—but, no, we didn't. A *Winter Soldier* screening should be a voter registration requirement. [Michael Atkinson, 8/9/05]

The World of Apu (1959)

See The Apu Trilogy

Written on the Wind (1956)

Dir. Douglas Sirk; Scr. George Zuckerman
99 min.

The most violent and hyperbolic of family melodramas, Douglas Sirk's *Written on the Wind* may be the quintessential American movie of the 1950s. The film turns a cold eye to the antics of the desperate super-rich, with Robert Stack and Dorothy Malone as two overaged juvenile delinquents, one a lush, the other a nympho, the wayward offspring of a Texas oil billionaire. Trash on an epic scale, it's a vision as luridly color-coordinated, relentlessly high-octane, and as flamboyantly petit-bourgeois as a two-toned T-bird with ultrachrome trim.

Written on the Wind has risen steadily in critical esteem since the Sirk revival of the early 1970s. The film is not only the ancestor of *Dallas*, *Dynasty*, and the other imperial soaps that ruled prime time during Reagan's first term, but, in its delirious pessimism, it's the Hollywood corollary to Allen Ginsberg's "Howl." But then who in America would have been sufficiently alienated to appreciate Sirk's brilliance at the time of the movie's original release?

To watch *Written on the Wind* is to enter a semiotic jungle and encounter a ferocious irony. Sirk, who achieved his greatest success directing glossy soap operas for Universal, was one of the century's more displaced persons. In his youth, he studied with the great art historian Erwin Panofsky and translated Shakespearean sonnets. Sirk was a European intellectual, and, if not exactly Adorno in Hollywood, he was nevertheless temperamentally suited to appreciate the exuberant one-dimensionality, the fantastic *Ersatzkeit* of his adopted culture. Long after he returned to Europe, Sirk maintained that he would have made his Hollywood swansong, the monstrous *Imitation of Life*, for the title alone.

Written on the Wind is not simply kitsch—it has a lurid classical grandeur that suggests Norman Rockwell redecorating Versailles (or Jacques-Louis David painting Vegas). Sirk dots the screen with stylized patches of hot canary and flaming turquoise, doubles the image with reflections, skews it with shock tilts, slashes it with flagrantly unmotivated shadows. *Written on the Wind* is the original Technicolor noir. It's fabulously ill, it reeks of autumnal rot. "It is like the Oktoberfest," Sirk's admirer Rainer Werner Fassbinder once wrote. "Everything is colourful and in motion, and you feel alone as everyone [else]." And, as with the Oktoberfest, a good many of the characters are stumbling around sloshed.

The movie is at once overexcited and detached, embodying a distinctively contemporary attitude that some have associated with the postmodern. Although Sirk keeps things hyper with much brisk cutting on movement, his camera consistently dollies back, transforming point-of-view shots into two-shots, to emphasize relationships and prevent easy identification with his characters. Throughout, Sirk deploys mirrors and rear-screen projection in the service of a distanced antinaturalism. Nature is even phonier than the barren forest of oil rigs that signifies the Hadley wealth; it's like a museum diorama in which everything has its didactic place. A tree only exists to show the initials that were romantically carved there fifteen years earlier and have been perfectly preserved ever since.

There's a monumental Edward Hopper quality to the town pharmacy—the emptiness, the stylized light pattern, the thicket of banners emblazoned "Buy Quality Drugs Here"—that epitomizes the film's frantic affect and seductive flatness. It is in that drugstore that *Written on the Wind* has its natural home. The images are as flashy and iconic as the cover design of a paperback novel. Everything in the film is exaggerated, heightened, concentrated—and theoretical. The lizardlike, liver-spotted patriarch of the Hadley clan (Robert Keith) sits beneath his painted image; his daughter (Malone) makes love to a photo of the film's star and universal object of desire (Rock Hudson), a Hadley serf who spurns her advances because he's in love with her sister-in-law (Lauren Bacall).

A genius at juggling volumes, doling out light, positioning the camera, Sirk is also supremely tactile, with a sculptor's flair for juxtaposing unexpected textures. Everything in *Written on the Wind* feels sealed in plastic, airbrushed to the point of reflection. The sets are a hermetic succession of furniture showrooms. Like Frank Tashlin, Sirk anticipates the commodity artists of the 1980s. No director has ever made more expressive use of decor or the objective correlative. *Written on the Wind* creates a shorthand lingo of fast cars, cigarettes, and booze. This

Written on the Wind, 1956; directed by Douglas Sirk; written by George Zuckerman

is a universe where people dress like mood rings and surround themselves with totemic fetishes: the model oil-rig phallus that dominates the patriarch's desk, the silver poodles that guard Bacall's calendar, the crimson anthuriums and étagère of perfume bottles that decorate Malone's boudoir. Nothing is funnier than the little bits of world culture, ancient statues, and abstract paintings Sirk scatters as tchotchkes throughout the Hadley mansion.

The Hadleys are Sirk's embodiment of America, a small-town family grown rich beyond measure. But rather than staid burghers, these yokels are laughably (and magnificently) petit bourgeois—the emotionally deprived rich kids acting out their domineering father's rapacious desires, one craving sex, the other seeking oblivion.

Written on the Wind is not simply epic trash but meta-trash. As the pulp poetry of the title suggests, it's about the vanity of trash, set in a world Sirk finds poignantly innocent. This is the land of simulacrum, a hall of mirrors in which the reflection of an image substitutes for the image itself. The last shot is of a black servant closing the gate; you expect him to roll up the lawn and strike the set. [J. Hoberman, 10/27/87]

Yeelen (1987)

Dir./Scr. Souleymane Cissé
105 min.

The stereotyped image of African Cinema is one of films about poverty—a bit boring, but sincere—whose technical clumsiness should be overlooked in deference to the nobility of their sentiments. The clichés don't apply to *Yeelen*, an astonishing work of great virtuosity, arguably the most beautiful African film ever made. Its director, Souleymane Cissé, born 1940 in Mali's capital, Bamako, spent five years at film school in Moscow, where he studied with Eisenstein's ex-pupil Mark Donskoi. *Yeelen* is his fourth feature.

The film is set in a remote era, among the Bambara, before the coming of Europeans to Africa. It follows the trajectory of a long initiation rite: Nianankoro, the young hero, must learn the science of the gods, knowledge that will help him make his way in the world. Soma, his father, does not want to be supplanted and refuses to pass along his knowledge—he's preparing to immolate an albino human in order to

Yeelen, 1987; written and directed by Souleymane Cissé

destroy Nianankoro. "My son, your father is a terror," the youth's mother warns. He flees his father's wrath and goes on a journey to meet his uncle, acquiring a wife and fathering a son of his own along the way. The uncle presents him with a magical wooden "wing" so that he can do battle with Soma's mystical pestle. At their final encounter, both son and father are destroyed by the "brightness" (*yeelen*) generated by their magical machines. When the light dies down, Nianankoro's naked child unearths two giant eggs in the sand—sharing of knowledge and the regeneration of the world will proceed from them.

A plot summary can do little justice to the sumptuousness of this enchanting and fluidly directed road movie, which is full of broad, sweeping landscapes of swamp and plain. Jean-Noël Ferragut's breathtaking cinematography bathes the film in an uncanny soft golden light. Cissé's uncluttered directorial style is a model of visual shorthand—in brief shots, objects somehow seem to evoke states of grace. Since there are no stage companies in Mali, Cissé simply found his performers by wandering through towns and villages. Most of the actors are nonprofessionals who cannot read; all are remarkable. The young hero is played by Issiaka Kane, bright of eye and long of limb, discovered by the director at a Bamako neighborhood dance contest. His graceful force impresses during physical and verbal duels, when the curtly percussive Bambaran language rings out as the characters "sing like the divine hyenas."

There are moments in *Yeelen* that suggest the Oedipus story, the son-father struggles of Cronus and Zeus, and, closer to home, *2001* and *Star Wars*. These are first thoughts, a tentative gloss on an extraordinary closed world that seems to embody universal passions and myths of creation. [Elliott Stein, 4/18/89]

Zero for Conduct (1933)

Dir./Scr. Jean Vigo
41 min.

Today I will praise Jean Vigo, the great poet of the screen, the author of *Zero for Conduct*. Here is a man whose each frame was inspired, each scene, each idea. Every image of *Zero for Conduct* bears the imprint of an inspired imagination and the temperament of a genius.

What can I say to you about this film? Tell you that it is a masterpiece? Or that Vigo sings as no one else has ever sung about childhood and school days? *Zero for Conduct* is an autobiographical poem, a pedagogical satire, a psychological tract, a memory of childhood, and an act of rebellion.

And why is it that all great art is so simple, so direct, so unmistakably true, so unmistakably great, without any complicated plots, meanings? One thing about the *Zero for Conduct* plot: instead of adhering to a surface scheme, it follows an unpredictable inner logic. Vigo reaches straight into the most personal experiences, memories, images. Vigo shoots straight into the bullseye, as only a great artist—a genius—can. He sings with images that are so simple but that tremble nevertheless with a tremendous inner force and are open to as many interpretations as there are human memories, childhoods.

Those faces of children in *Zero for Conduct*! In no other film have I seen faces like these. Those eyes, those motions, those smiles, those countenances, always ready for mischief. None of the sweet faces that we usually see in films about children. Even the boy in *L'Atalante*—how alive he is, his characterizations, his sitting, his standing. Vigo's children are young animals. The children of *Shoeshine* or even *The 400 Blows* are sweet little puppies compared with the children of Vigo. I grew up with the children of Vigo; I recognize every one of them.

Just imagine: the New York State Education Department wanted to cut out chunks of *Zero for Conduct*, afraid of the naked behinds of little children. Only the persistence of the Bleecker Street people saved Vigo's film from those mad scissors. What ignorance! What confounded arrogance! Okay, we don't give a damn about our living artists, but hell, shouldn't we pay some respect to our dead artists? If chopping Vigo is education, then our state education is run by morons and schlemiels. [Jonas Mekas, 3/29/62]

PHOTO CREDITS

Page 13, courtesy of Wellspring.

Pages 16, 84, 106, 163, and 308, courtesy of Kino.

Pages 26, 78, 100, 110, 121, 178, 225, 249, 260, 274, 293, and 307, courtesy of Criterion Collection.

Pages 50 and 175, courtesy of Universal.

Page 128 courtesy, of Guy Maddin.

Pages 129 and 207, courtesy of New Line.

Page 200, courtesy of *The New Yorker*.

Page 272, courtesy of Strand Releasing.

INDEX OF DIRECTORS AND ACTORS

Page numbers in **bold** appear with directors' names and indicate the pages on which reviews of the directors' films begin.

6/10 (1) 4/10

3/13 (3) 4/12

3/17 (6) 5/15